Emplotting Virtue

SUNY series in Environmental Philosophy and Ethics

J. Baird Callicott and John van Buren, editors

Emplotting Virtue

A Narrative Approach to Environmental Virtue Ethics

Brian Treanor

SUNY
PRESS

Published by State University of New York Press, Albany

© 2014 State University of New York

For information, contact State University of New York Press, Albany, NY
www.sunypress.edu

Production by Eileen Nizer
Marketing by Michael Campochiaro

Library of Congress Cataloging-in-Publication Data

Treanor, Brian.
  Emplotting virtue : a narrative approach to environmental virtue ethics /
Brian Treanor.
      pages cm. — (SUNY series in environmental philosophy and ethics)
  Includes bibliographical references and index.
  ISBN 978-1-4384-5117-6 (hardcover : alk. paper)
  ISBN 978-1-4384-5118-3 (pbk. : alk. paper)
  1. Virtue.   2. Ethics.   3. Environmental ethics.   4. Narration (Rhetoric)   I. Title.

BJ1531.T74 2014
179'.1—dc23   2013021456

10 9 8 7 6 5 4 3 2 1

For my parents, Richard Treanor and Margaret Treanor,
and my siblings, Erin, Adam, and Michael, with love

❧

Contents

Acknowledgments

Given that this is, in part, a book on narrative, I am acutely aware of the diverse cast of characters who contributed, each in his or her own way, to this project. The story of writing this book intersected a variety of other stories at various points in its development.

I am fortunate to have a very fine group of friends and associates who helped me in one way or another during the process of writing. My colleagues at Loyola Marymount University are, to a person, supportive and encouraging; many of them provided feedback on early attempts to grapple with some of the main themes of this book. Jason Baehr was a source of much useful discussion on virtue theory and Scott Cameron has been a sympathetic ear and ally on issues hermeneutic and environmental. Chris Kaczor, my regular lunch partner, not only encouraged me in my work, but also provided so many helpful suggestions related to my scholarly habits that I've turned over a new leaf as a writer in the process of finishing this project. In the field of environmental philosophy, I've been fortunate to receive helpful feedback at various times from Phil Cafaro and Ron Sandler—both advocates of a virtue ethics approach to environmental ethics—and, more recently, from Katie McShane, whose thinking on narrative pushed me to clarify my position in helpful ways. Forrest Clingerman, David Utsler, and Martin Drenthen have been both collaborators (on other projects) and commentators on my work; their friendship and collegiality is much appreciated.

In addition to these colleagues, I have been blessed with a number of truly remarkable students during the past few years, several of whom worked through the ideas presented here in classes on either environmental virtue ethics or narrative and virtue: Greer Gosnell, Kim Tomicich, Annie Daly, Dan Gray, and Bianca Darby-Matteoda deserve special recognition for their active and enthusiastic engagement with the ideas developed in this book. My graduate assistant, Donald Boyce, was a great help in preparing the final manuscript. In addition to saving me from myriad slips and typos with a keen editorial eye, his philosophically astute comments and questions aided me in clarifying the argument.

The work of finalizing this project was done under the auspices of a College Fellowship provided by the Bellarmine College of Liberal Arts at Loyola Marymount University. I very much appreciate this institutional support for my work. Thanks are also owed Dean Rosnau, of June Lake, and his family, whose remarkable hospitality enriched the summer of 2011 for me and for my family while I worked on an early draft of the book.

I am indebted to John Van Buren and Baird Callicott, as well as Andrew Kenyon at SUNY Press, for their confidence in me and in this project, their support during its development, and their patience during the process. Thanks as well to production editor Eileen Nizer and copyeditor Sharon Green, who helped in the final preparation of the manuscript for publication. I also must thank the anonymous readers who reviewed the manuscript for SUNY. I have had numerous other projects reviewed in the course of publication, and served as a reviewer myself on many occasions. I can honestly say that the readers for this project went far beyond the call of duty in their careful reading of the manuscript and in their many helpful comments, questions, and objections. Although I imagine that they will still find arguments and stylistic choices with which they disagree, and raise concerns I was unable to take up in the pages of this book, the project was certainly improved by responding to their questions and criticisms. I owe them a deep debt of gratitude.

Finally, none of my work, here or elsewhere, would be possible without the love and affection I have for and receive from my family. My wife Gitty has long been an intellectual friend and partner, in addition to all the other ways in which she supports my endeavors. She reads drafts of much of my work, and listened indulgently as I wrestled out loud with many of these subjects over the past few years. My daughters, Darya and Ciara, regularly (and thankfully) pulled me away from writing and were always quick to remind me that we should be climbing, camping, skiing, biking, and swimming more often—which given our regular and passionate pursuit of such activities is, I'm proud to point out, saying something.

As I've indicated, the ideas in this book have developed over time and germinated in other works. Various publishers have graciously allowed me to reproduce work that has appeared elsewhere. The following essays have appeared in print previously and contributed in ways direct and indirect to the argument in this book.

Chapter 4 draws heavily on "The Virtue of Simplicity," which first appeared in *The Concord Saunterer*, vol. 15, 2007. This essay also contributes to Chapter 2. Elements of Chapter 5 come from "Blessed are Those Who Have Not Seen and Yet Believe," *Analecta Hermeneutica*, vol. 2, 2010, as well as "Judging the Other: Beyond Toleration" in *Interpretando la experiencia de la tolerancia* (Interpreting the Experience of Tolerance), ed. Rosemary Rizo-Patrón de Lerner (Lima, Peru: Pontificia Universidad Católica del Perú/Fondo Editorial, 2006) and "Constellations: Gabriel Marcel's Philosophy of Relative Otherness," *American Catholic Philosophical Quarterly*, vol. 80, no. 3, 2006. Parts of Chapter 6 first appeared as: "Narrative and Nature: Appreciating and Understanding the Non-Human World" in *Interpreting Nature: The Emerging Field of Environmental Hermeneutics*, eds. Forrest Clingerman, Brian Treanor, Martin Drenthen, and David Utsler (Fordham University Press, 2012); "*Phronesis* without a *Phronimos*: Narrative Environmental Virtue Ethics" in *Environmental Ethics*, vol. 30, no. 4, 2008; and "Emplotting Virtue" in *A Passion for the Possible: Thinking with Paul Ricoeur*, eds. Brian Treanor and Henry Isaac Venema (Fordham University Press, 2010). "Turn Around and Step Forward: Ideology and Utopia in the Environmental Movement," which contributed to aspects of Chapters 4 and 6, first appeared in *Environmental Philosophy* vol. 7 (2010): 27–46.

I would also like to thank Counterpoint Press and the estate of Wallace Stegner for permission to use the excerpt from Stegner's "Wilderness Letter" with which this work opens (Copyright © 2007 by Page Stegner from *The Selected Letters of Wallace Stegner* by Wallace Stegner. Reprinted by permission of Counterpoint).

Just What Sort of Person Would Do That?

It really is of importance, not only what men do, but also what manner of men they are that do it.

—John Stuart Mill, *On Liberty*

Now I see the secret of making the best persons, / it is to grow in the open air and to eat and sleep with the earth.

—Walt Whitman, *Leaves of Grass*

One of life's quiet excitements is to stand somewhat apart from yourself and watch yourself softly becoming the author of something beautiful. . . .

—Norman Maclean, *A River Runs Through It*

Introduction

Few environmentalists in the United States are unfamiliar with Wallace Stegner's famous "Wilderness Letter," written in 1960 to David Pesonen of the Outdoor Recreation Resources Review Commission. The letter is an eloquent and heartfelt paean to the importance of wilderness and wildness—not as a source of raw material for production, or a pool of biodiversity, or even as an arena in which people can pursue certain activities they are unable to pursue elsewhere. Rather, Stegner seeks to draw our attention to wildness as a "spiritual" resource, one that has "formed our character" and "shaped our history"[1]:

Something will have gone out of us as a people if we ever let the remaining wilderness be destroyed; if we permit the last virgin forests to be turned into comic books and plastic cigarette cases; if we drive the few remaining members of the wild species into zoos or to extinction; if we pollute the last clear air and dirty the last clean streams and push our paved roads through the last of the silence, so that never again will Americans be free in their own country from the noise, the exhausts, the stinks of human and automotive waste. And so that never again can we have the chance to see ourselves single, separate, vertical and individual in the world, part of the environment of trees and rocks and soil, brother to the other animals, part of the natural world and competent to belong in it. Without any remaining wilderness we are committed wholly, without chance for even momentary reflection and rest, to a headlong drive into our technological termite-life, the Brave New World of a completely man-controlled environment. We need wilderness preserved—as much of it as is still left, and as many kinds—because it was the challenge against which our character as a people was formed. The reminder and the reassurance that it is still there is good for our spiritual health even if we never once in ten years set foot in it. It is good for us when we are young, because of the incomparable sanity it can bring briefly, as vacation and rest, into our insane lives. It is important to us when we are old simply because it is there—important, that is, simply as an idea.

We are a wild species, as Darwin pointed out. Nobody ever tamed or domesticated or scientifically bred us. But for at least three millennia we have been engaged in a cumulative and ambitious race to modify and gain control of our environment, and in the process we have come close to domesticating ourselves. Not many people are likely, any more, to look upon what we call "progress" as an unmixed blessing. Just as surely as it has brought us increased comfort and more material goods, it has brought us spiritual losses, and it threatens now to become the Frankenstein that will destroy us. One means of sanity is to retain a hold on the natural world, to remain, insofar as we can, good animals. Americans still have that chance, more than many peoples; for while we were demonstrating ourselves the most efficient and ruthless environment-busters in history, and slashing and burning and cutting our way through a wilderness continent, the wilderness was working on us. It remains in us as surely as Indian names remain on the land. If the abstract dream of human liberty and human dignity became, in America, something more than an abstract dream, mark it down at least partially to the fact that we were in subdued ways subdued by what we conquered. . . .

. . . As a novelist, I may perhaps be forgiven for taking literature as a reflection, indirect but profoundly true, of our national consciousness. And our literature, as perhaps you are aware, is sick, embittered, losing its mind, losing its faith. Our novelists are the declared enemies of their society. There has hardly been a serious or important novel in this century that did not repudiate in part or in whole American technological culture for its commercialism, its vulgarity, and the way in which it has dirtied a clean continent and a clean dream. I do not expect that the preservation of our remaining wilderness is going to cure this condition. But the mere example that we can as a nation apply some other criteria than commercial and exploitative considerations would be heartening to many Americans, novelists or otherwise. We need to demonstrate our acceptance of the natural world, including ourselves; we need the spiritual refreshment that being natural can produce. And one of the best places for us to get that is in the wilderness where the fun houses, the bulldozers, and the pavement of our civilization are shut out.[2]

The "wilderness debate" is long and complex, and it remains lively to this day.[3] However, for the moment I want to draw our attention not to the wilderness debate itself—whether it is an idea or a thing out there, how much is left and what to do about it, and so on—but rather to Stegner's account of wilderness's effects, and to the language he uses in evoking what he calls the "geography of hope."

First, Stegner's focus here is on the effects wilderness has on us—both as individuals and as a nation. The wilderness has "formed our character" and "shaped our history." Wilderness "worked on us" even as we "worked on it." The changes the wilderness works on us do not build us in the manner of assembling pieces of a machine or puzzle; rather they help us to grow and develop in the manner of an unfolding narrative. This view of wilderness takes it to be a "spiritual resource" intimately linked with our identity, and if we lose it, "something will have gone out of us." Elsewhere in the letter—perhaps recalling John Muir: "I only went out for a walk, and finally concluded to stay out till sundown, for going out, I found, was really going in"[4]—Stegner tells us that in looking into wilderness, we look into ourselves. The recurring theme is that there is an intimate relationship between the environment, in this case the wilderness, and the kinds of people we become. If we have been shaped by the wilderness, in losing the wilderness we will become different sorts of people.

Second, Stegner's letter connects these effects to language and literature. The various ways in which we express ourselves are intimately and inextricably tied to who we are (identity, character); but our identities (social and individual) are inseparable from our environment and how we live as part of it. Thus our language and literature reflect a constellation or network of relationships where individual identity, social identity, world, and environment intersect and are entangled. Stegner argues that the ailing, embittered, and faithless aspects of our literature are manifestations of a broader illness and malaise stemming from a distorted relationship with the environment. The stories we tell bear witness to our ongoing struggle between health and illness, hope and despair, refinement and barbarism, wildness and domestication, naturalness and counterfeits, genuineness and insincerity—they testify to our nature, to our way of being in the world, and to our limitations and our possibilities. Art imitates life, not as a carbon-copy to be sure; but we narrate from the situation in which we find ourselves, and our imaginative engagement with the past, present, and future all take shape from our own lived experience.

Finally, it's worth noting that Stegner uses poetic language in making his own plea. He does not refer to research or to data, nor does he argue by syllogism; rather he uses personal and anecdotal narrative to make his case. Later in the letter he cites Sherwood Anderson:

> Is it not likely that when the country was new and men were often alone in the fields and the forest they got a sense of bigness outside themselves that has now in some way been lost . . . [?] Mystery whispered in the grass, played in the branches of trees overhead, was caught up and blown across the American line in clouds of dust at evening on the prairies. . . .[5]

Stegner himself speaks of wilderness not only in the abstract, but also in particular manifestations, specific places that mark significant episodes in the narrative of his life: Robber's Roost, Capitol Reef, San Rafael Swell, the Aquarius Plateau, and so on. He recalls his boyhood on the Saskatchewan prairie, full of animals he came to see as brothers, where the sky "came clear down to the ground on every side, and it was full of great weathers, and clouds, and winds, and hawks," and in which he learned something from "looking a long way, from looking up, from being much alone."[6] Such language is not accidental, nor is it irrational or ineffective. We will come to see that imaginative, metaphorical, narrative expression, far from misrepresenting, distorting, or otherwise removing us from reality, actually more fully and more deeply connects us with it. Stegner's decision to frame his paean to wilderness in such language represents not only an honest and personal plea, but also one of the most effective ways of communicating value. If art imitates life, life, Stegner hopes, can also imitate art.

Bracketing for a moment Stegner's specific concern with wilderness, these three aspects of his approach in the letter suggest a certain conception of ethics, one quite unlike mainstream philosophical discourse. He addresses the plasticity of identity, the building of character, the importance of certain vanishing virtues, and the relationship of these three with literature and art. Within the field of environmental literature, his treatment of these themes is far from unique: Ralph Waldo Emerson, Henry David Thoreau, John Muir, David Brower, Ed Abbey, Doug Peacock, Black Elk, Gary Snyder, Annie Dillard, Jane Goodall, Walt Whitman, Mary Oliver, Jack Turner, and many, many others testify, explicitly or implicitly, to the connections between nature, virtue, and narrative. This approach—embracing a broad ethical view rather than a narrow moral one, attuned to the significance of non-human nature, and sensitive to the power of narrative—challenges the dominant frameworks with which we make our private choices and in which we conduct our public discourse, including that of environmental acts and omissions, rights and wrongs, goods and ills.[7]

Moral Reasoning in Contemporary Ethics

The various frameworks with which we commonly address moral life in general and environmental ethics in particular are the result of the historical circumstances in which environmental concerns came to light. While it has arguably been anticipated in the worldviews of various indigenous peoples, Romanticism, American transcendentalist thought, and numerous other myths and stories, the environmental movement as we currently understand it is a modern phenomenon. Whether one marks the beginning of contemporary environmentalism by preservation of Yosemite in 1864 and the creation of Yellowstone National Park in 1872, by the publication of Rachel Carson's *Silent Spring* in 1962, or by the celebration of the first Earth Day in 1970, environmentalism as we know it is distinctively modern. This is particularly true with respect to the ethical framework used to ground environmental arguments, a framework that was shaped by philosophies forged during the dawn of the modern period in the Enlightenment.

Until fairly recently, virtually all modern interest in philosophical ethics followed in the wake of one of two major theories born in the late eighteenth and early nineteenth centuries: utilitarianism (from the work of Jeremy Bentham and John Stuart Mill) and deontology (originating with Immanuel Kant).[8] With certain notable exceptions, alternative approaches such as virtue ethics were of mostly historical interest, if they were engaged at all. And while theoretical, academic ethics promulgated this binary view of ethics, a similar orientation was even more glaring in the various fields of applied ethics, including environmental ethics. If academic ethics tended to focus narrowly on utilitarianism and deontology, applied ethics was virtually blind to any alternatives.

Immanuel Kant argued that the foundation of morality rests on a priori concepts of reason, concepts that we can know with certainty abstracted from any particular context or experience. Such a foundation means that morality will make sense for, and apply to, all rational beings regardless of their particular situations. These moral rules have the same authority and apply in the same way to men and women, to people in ancient Greece and contemporary America, and, assuming they are in fact rational beings, to dolphins, extraterrestrials. Moral actions, argued Kant, are those that conform to a universal law of reason. Because morality is grounded in rationality, it is ultimately the motive or maxim for the action, rather than the consequences of the action, that determines its moral worth. Thus, acts are good insofar as the maxims on which they are based are good, that is, rational. Since the motive is the determining factor, morally good actions are those that not only conform to the moral law, but which are also done for the sake of the moral law.[9] A person who is honest because "honesty is the best policy" is not really acting morally; she may be prudent, calculating, or a clever businessperson, but she is not moral. The moral person must be honest *because* honesty conforms to the moral law.

How can we determine which actions conform to the moral law? Kant argues that moral actions are those which have motives that we can turn into universally applicable maxims. This claim is most clear in Kant's famous "categorical imperative," the "supreme principle of morality."[10] The categorical imperative is actually expressed in a number of different formulations in *The Groundwork of the Metaphysics of Morals*; however, the first and most oft-cited formulation is: "I ought never to act except in such a way that I could also will that my maxim should become a universal law."[11] What this boils down to, in ordinary language, is that an action is moral if we can will that everyone else act in the same way. For example, is it morally permissible to lie? Kant argues that it is not.

> Truthfulness in statements that one cannot avoid is a human being's duty to everyone, however great the disadvantage to him or to another that may result from it; and although I indeed do no wrong to him who unjustly compels me to make the statement if I falsify it . . . I bring it about, as far as I can, that statements (declarations) in general are not believed, and so to that all rights which are based on contracts come to nothing and lose their force; and this is a wrong inflicted upon humanity in general.[12]

Because the duty to tell the truth is absolute, Kant maintains that we are required to tell the truth even *in extremis,* as when a murderer asks for the location of his intended victim.[13]

However, the categorical imperative has several other formulations. One very important formulation for the way in which deontology has been received by contemporary environmental ethics is the formula of "humanity as an end in itself": "So act that you use humanity, whether in you own person or in the person of any other, always at the same time as an end, never merely as a means."[14] Kant argues here that any human being, indeed any rational being, exists as an end in itself, not merely as a means to be used for other ends.[15] Things have conditioned worth, they are good *for* something else; rational beings have unconditioned worth. Rational beings, in other words, have "intrinsic" value, not merely extrinsic value. Consequently, if we want to be moral we cannot use people as if they were mere things. Things are valuable because they are useful for something; rational beings have a worth independent of any usefulness they might have.

Utilitarianism gives us a very different answer to the question "what should I do," and the sharp contrast between utilitarianism and deontology is one reason that the two theories are so often juxtaposed when analyzing ethical issues. Although utilitarianism proper began with Jeremy Bentham, its most popular and well-known exponent is John Stuart Mill. In *Utilitarianism* Mill argues, contra Kant, that there is no objective and a priori basis for morality. Nevertheless, because there is a rather broad agreement on many moral questions, there must be some underlying, if unrecognized, principle at work. This principle, Mill claims, is the principle of utility or the "greatest happiness principle," which states that "actions are right in proportion as they tend to promote happiness, wrong as they tend to produce the reverse of happiness."[16] "Happiness" here means pleasure and the absence of pain, and it is the only thing inherently good and desirable as an end in itself.

Put simply, moral actions produce the greatest happiness for the greatest possible number of people, while minimizing any necessary suffering and confining it to the smallest possible number. In contrast to Kant's abstract rationality, Mill claims that one argument in favor of maximizing utility is that it underlies the way in which most people actually do make moral decisions—we are motivated by pleasure and pain. Given the emphasis on promoting happiness, it should be clear that Mill believes that the morality of an action is determined by the consequences it brings about rather than by the motive or maxim on which the action is based.

Mill is quick to point out, however, that the greatest happiness principle will not lead us to an animal life of base hedonism. There are a number of things that bring us pleasure, and while "sex, drugs, and rock 'n' roll" will indeed bring a person pleasure, so will education, friendship, contemplation, and political engagement. Indeed, Mill goes so far as to argue that these "higher" pleasures are superior to, and therefore more worthy and greater contributors to total happiness than, "lower" pleasures. He famously claims, "it is better to be a human being dissatisfied than a pig satisfied; better to be Socrates dissatisfied than a fool satisfied. And if the fool, or the pig, are of a different opinion, it is because they only know their side of the question."[17]

Nevertheless, all pleasures, the base and the refined, must be taken into account. In doing so we attempt to account for both quantity (the number of people affected) and quality (the relative worth of the given pleasures). Each person, including the person acting, counts as one and only one. That is, the happiness of each affected person is taken into account and weighted equally. While the pleasure of education is superior to the pleasure of alcohol, the pleasure that the agent gets from the last Guinness in the refrigerator is counted alongside the pleasure her roommate would have received from it, and therefore to the pain she suffers in foregoing it.

These two approaches, the utilitarian and the deontological, dominated ethical discourse for more than two hundred years and our contemporary ethical discourse, including most environmental ethics, still draws heavily on these traditions. The utilitarian impulse can be seen in various stripes of consequentialism, and Kant's influence is evident in various contemporary deontologies, and especially in theories of intrinsic value. The influence of these two approaches is evident, for example, in arguments about animal welfare, as the two major arguments in favor of extending ethical consideration to non-human animals draw directly on utilitarianism and deontology.

Peter Singer's ethical reasoning follows Jeremy Bentham, arguing that we should maximize aggregate happiness and that doing so requires that we take into account, equally, all relevant interests: "each to count for one and none for more than one."[18] However, Singer is quick to point out that in determining which interests are relevant, we cannot look to characteristics like reason, or language, or risibility, or tool-making, or membership in the species *homo sapiens*, without falling into unjustifiable speciesism. Rather, the morally significant characteristic is "having interests," the hallmark of which is the suffering endured when those interests are frustrated: "If a being can suffer, there can be no moral justification for refusing to take that suffering into consideration."[19] Thus, for example, since the trivial enjoyment derived from eating a hamburger cannot compare to the fundamental suffering of the death of the cow in order to do so, people should not eat hamburgers, or *mutatis mutandis*, any other meat. Tom Regan, however, rejects utilitarian arguments for many of the traditional reasons associated with its focus on aggregate happiness to the (potential) detriment of individual well-being. Adapting Kant as Singer adapts Bentham and Mill, Regan insists that every *"experiencing subject of a life"* possesses inherent worth, and that all that possess inherent worth "possess it *equally, and all have an equal right to be treated with respect,* to be treated in ways that do not reduce them to the status of things, as if they exist as resources for others."[20] The upshot of this argument is the total abolition of animal experimentation, harvesting animals for food, hunting and trapping for sport, and so on.

Although there are arguments for animal welfare from other ethical perspectives, they get relatively little attention, in part because of the general focus on utilitarian and deontological arguments. Singer's and Regan's arguments for animal rights appear in almost every anthology of environmental ethics, but a virtue ethics argument for vegetarianism is almost nowhere to be seen.[21] The debate about animal welfare is only one instance of a very common predisposition to limit ethical accounts to consequentialist or deontological arguments. This tendency—dominant in academic discourse and ubiquitous in applied ethics—seems for all intents and purposes universal in popular discourse. Outside the rarified air of academia, utilitarianism and deontology have a virtual duopoly on the ethical imagination of the average person. If you look at everyday conversations, public discourse on topics of moral and ethical significance, or economic and political arguments you will find that people most often assert that something is wrong either (1) because it brings about undesirable consequences, generally by producing more misery than happiness, or (2) because it is "just wrong" or violates a moral law that we are duty bound to obey. Conversely, things are good either because they produce more happiness than misery or because they "just are" things we ought to do or value.

However, while utilitarianism and deontology enjoy pride of place in contemporary ethical debates, they are not without problems. Certain criticisms of deontology and utilitarianism are fairly well-rehearsed, as they crop up each time one side weighs in on contemporary ethical issues, at least in academic papers. Probably the most commonly raised objection to deontology is the fact that its dogmatic insistence on absolutes can lead to disastrous consequences, in part because it is tone-deaf to potentially relevant aspects of context. This is true not only in far-fetched philosophical examples, but in other more common circumstances. In addition, various forms of deontology are criticized for their inability to establish a non-controversial source of moral duty; as a consequence, the foundations of deontological duties are, it is suggested, wanting. Moreover, deontology is complicated by the extreme difficulty of forming consistent universalizable maxims. That is to say, different people will form different maxims or principles of action. Almost any maxim can be universalized as long as one formulates it creatively. As Kant says, formulating the correct maxim requires "judgment sharpened by experience," a turn of phrase that both undermines the rigor to which deontology aspires and seems like a nod toward practical wisdom and virtue ethics.[22] Finally, deontology is criticized for insufficient recognition of the various ways in which legitimate duties may conflict with each other. Kant goes so far as to insist that a "conflict of duties is inconceivable," a claim that beggars belief.[23]

Turning to utilitarianism, it is often objected that it is difficult to determine an accurate method for valuing happiness or pleasure, that utilitarianism reduces people to mere containers of satisfactions and ignores or denies any inherent worth in individuals, and that utilitarianism can lead to conclusions that fly in the face of widely accepted moral and ethical intuitions. However, Martha Nussbaum raises some additional objections that will prove highly significant in what follows.[24] Utilitarianism, especially as expressed in various versions of rational-choice theory, attempts to consider all valuable things commensurably in a way that makes them measurable on a common scale. Such measurement only takes into consideration differences in quantity, not quality. In addition, utilitarianism seeks to view such data in aggregate, rather than individual, terms. Focusing on the aggregate total of some commensurable good, utilitarianism seeks only to maximize that good. Finally, the utilitarian approach assumes people's preferences are easily identifiable, as when classical economists suggest that we can discern what contributes to people's happiness by looking at how they spend their money—as if people were infallible in determining what best contributes to their happiness and as if preferences were not malleable, social, and cultural in nature.

However, while Kant construed morality as a function of the *motive* or *intent* of the agent and Mill argued that the morality of an action was a function of the *consequences* it brought about, these apparently antagonistic approaches have a number of underlying similarities that give rise to additional problems common to both approaches.[25] First, the way in which these two approaches strive to generate clear rules for action is problematic. It's not that rules or guidelines for action are inherently bad. Far from it. We naturally seek to form rules and use them as cognitive shortcuts to avoid having to think every ethical situation anew.[26] However, both utilitarianism and deontology tend to lead us into an overly-legalistic view of ethics by attempting to develop a single universal rule that, if followed, will serve as a litmus test for and accurate guide to moral action. Articulate the right rule, and good conduct follows from that. This is not to say that it always *will*, but that it *can*: if you have the right rule—whether the utilitarian "greatest happiness principle" or the "categorical imperative" of deontology—you just need to apply it.

But while universal rules tend to work well in relatively clear-cut situations, they often fail us in confusing, ambiguous, or novel situations, which are precisely the sorts of situations in which we most need ethical guidance. Take a simple and apparently clear rule like "thou shall not kill." It's pretty easy to follow this rule in everyday life, but for most people it's also not very helpful. Few of us wake up each morning with the uncontrollable desire to kill in cold blood. When we really need ethical guidance is in those situations where we are tempted to kill; but it is often precisely these situations in which "thou shall not kill" is not as useful. Simple rules like "thou shall not kill" seem straightforward until we begin to consider just war, self-defense, killing to prevent greater evils, passive euthanasia, active euthanasia, assisted suicide, and abortion, to say nothing of whether or not this prohibition applies to any forms of non-human life (a thrice-daily decision for most of us). In these situations, precisely those situations in which a person might want a bit of ethical guidance, the Fifth Commandment begins to seem much less helpful, much more complicated, and much more difficult to apply. Similarly, it is fairly easy to conform to apparently clear environmental rules like "don't pollute" in the case of egregious littering and the like. Although exceptions remain, relatively few people today will thoughtlessly dump used motor oil into the street or burn plastic trash to dispose of it. However, "don't pollute" runs into trouble with more difficult cases. Can I drive my car to the local market rather than walk, bike, or use public transportation? If the market is several miles away? What if I'm tired or ill? What if it is raining? The devil, as they say, is in the details, and while universal rules operate quite well in the rarified air of theory, they are considerably less serviceable in the muddy world of particulars in which we live and act.

I should hasten to reiterate that, as we will see below, these criti-cisms of ethical legalism are not meant to be an indictment of rules per se. Rules for action are both useful and necessary. Rather, it is a question of where one places the emphasis: on the articulation of the rule or on the subtlety of its application, on the act or the agent? Both utilitarianism and deontology are at odds with the deep and nuanced appreciation of the ethical and moral significance of particularity that is evident in the best narratives.[27] The "judgment sharpened by experience" required to correctly apply ethical rules complicates any easy application of such imperatives in difficult or novel circumstances.[28] And, critically, any contemporary ethic that takes seriously environmental issues is forced to concede that complex, difficult, and novel ethical dilemmas are precisely the sorts of situations with which we will be increasingly confronted as phenomena like climate change and peak oil play out.

The second commonality between utilitarianism and deontology is that both approaches have a tendency to narrowly focus moral and ethical debate on intersubjective, and specifically *human*, issues—giving preference to questions of, for example, justice between persons—and, when they do address the environment, they only take up issues congenial to a deonto-logical or consequentialist response (for example, whether animals have intrinsic or extrinsic value). It's tempting to frame this objection in terms of anthropocentrism, the belief that humans hold a unique value that makes them the center, or even the sole resident, of the world of moral and ethical concern. Like most ethical theories, utilitarianism and deontology can be and often are articulated in anthropocentric terms—indeed human inter-ests and perspectives are so unreflectively central to much of our thinking that they completely occlude any alternative—and many ethicists ignore animals and the environment completely.

However, if this is the objection, it must be acknowledged that virtue ethics—the approach that this inquiry will investigate—is itself suscep-tible to claims of anthropocentrism. Moreover, there is no obvious reason that utilitarianism and deontology must be anthropocentric. Peter Singer's utilitarianism and Tom Regan's theory of intrinsic value, for example, both embrace a broad ethical field—broader, at least, than is common in other modern moralities. Therefore, one might argue that anthropocentrism is more of a general tendency in our thinking rather than a theoretical defi-ciency of either utilitarianism or deontology.

Perhaps, then, we should frame the distinction not in terms of anthro-pocentrism but in terms of scope. Utilitarianism and deontology have a rather narrow scope; they seem to constrain ethical discourse through their reluctance, even inability, to address certain issues. Ronald Sandler draws our attention to a useful distinction between first-, second-, and third-generation environmentalism.[29] The first generation focused on problems that were "over there," including wilderness preservation in remote locations. The second focused on problems "here" such as pollution, urban sprawl, and environmental justice. The third-generation-addressed problems that are "everywhere," including climate change and resource depletion. Finally, Sandler suggests that we may be on the verge of seeing "fourth-generation" problems, wherein the global and distant "everywhere" of third-generation problems takes a disturbing turn toward a very personal and intimate "everywhere" with genetic engineering and nanotechnology. One front of fourth-generation environmentalism is located, I would argue, in the mysterious loci and interstices of human identity and character—not in *what we do* but in *who we are*, though the former is certainly a manifestation of the latter. Utilitarianism and deontology, however, seem to come up short with respect to some of these third- and fourth-generation issues, and this is especially the case with respect to character. It's hard to see, to make use of a non-environmental example, what deontology or utilitarianism might say about pushing past one's perceived limits in a sporting event. Take, for example, a marathon. It's difficult to see what duty might be involved in finishing the race without projecting all sorts of hypothetical fantasies onto the question. Likewise, there is, or need be, no real net happiness at stake: giving up and ending the suffering might well counterbalance the happiness associated with enduring and finishing. Nevertheless, we rightly think that there is something worthwhile, something both laudable and proper, in trying one's best and striving to push past one's limits.

Third, utilitarianism and deontology tend to speak in terms of prohibition, as opposed to, for example, aspiration. They express themselves in the imperative mood, rather than the optative mood. Although there are exceptions, traditional modern approaches to ethics tend to focus on what is morally prohibited, and tend to express themselves in various forms of "thou shall not." Although Kant does address "meritorious duties," the application of the categorical imperative does not naturally lend itself toward ascertaining what is praiseworthy, commendable, or good. Rather, the application of the categorical imperative naturally leads us to apply ethics in terms of what is prohibited. If the maxim in question is universalizable, the action is permitted; if it is not, it is prohibited. This differentiation—the permissible and the prohibited—suggests that categorical imperative is not that useful for determining what is ethically excellent or superior. Another way of thinking about this problem is to point out, as does Phil Cafaro, that judgments based on duty and obligation "often uphold *minimal* standards of conduct and (partly for that reason) assert or imply a moral 'ought.'"[30]

Like all legalism, ethical legalism is effective for establishing a minimal common standard to which everyone will be held accountable. But legalism falters when it attempts to account for superior conduct, conduct that is laudable and admirable. You can't legislate excellence. Of course, determining what is prohibited is not wrong. Indeed, it is very helpful. However, simply determining what is wrong, even when coupled with determining what is compulsory, encompasses only part of what a full-fledged ethics should accomplish.[31]

Utilitarianism fares slightly better here. Because it seeks not just happiness but the greatest happiness, one could argue that utilitarianism is inherently exhortative and aspirational—it demands our best. However, while utilitarianism does sometimes enjoin us to do something positive—as when Peter Singer argues that we should give a substantial percentage of our wealth to those in absolute poverty—in practice, utilitarianism tends to prohibit unkind or unfair actions as often as it advocates for kind or just ones. It rarely explicitly exhorts us to excellence, precisely because it doesn't care if we are excellent; it only cares about the maximization of a single good. Maximizing that single good requires that, as Martha Nussbaum points out, utilitarianism view all goods as commensurable so that it can measure them in terms of a single standard of value, such as happiness or pleasure.[32] Such measurement recognizes only differences in quantity, ignoring or denying qualitative differences. Because of this leveling demand for commensurability, utilitarian calculations tend, in practice, to be fairly simplistic, glossing over the substantial difficulties associated with measuring and comparing happinesses. Such simple calculations push toward a minimal, or at least merely moderate, standard. The broad generality of utilitarian accounts of happiness and the single standard by which they are measured—which Nussbaum points out completely misses the variety and complexity of goods—means that in order to make its calculations utilitarianism either measures only fairly gross and simple kinds of happiness or grossly simplifies more subtle sorts of happiness. Concerned only with quantity, utilitarian models end up focusing on the total aggregate amount of the good measured, without regard to the differences that were ignored by imposing a commensurable standard of measurement. Commensurability and aggregation, in turn, ensure that the goal of utilitarian thinking is always maximization of the good in question. Finally, in measuring goods like happiness, pleasure, interests, and so on, utilitarianism assumes that "people's preferences are *exogenous*." That is to say "they can be taken as given" without regard to the fact that preferences are malleable, strongly shaped by cultural norms and narratives, and that people can be—and, we will see, frequently are—wrong about what will make them happy or what will contribute to their flourishing.[33]

Virtue Ethics

In 1983, Thomas Hill raised a novel question for environmental ethics.[34] Beginning with the story of a man who, not being fond of flora, razed the trees, plants, and flowers on his beautiful property and paved over the yard with asphalt, Hill developed an example that called into question common ways of discussing ethical praise and blame. He developed the example so that one might plausibly conclude that there is no difference in utility between paving the land and preserving it, and in which the evaluation of all pertinent rights weighs equally for both options. However, despite the apparent equivalence of the options from utilitarian and deontological perspectives, Hill suggests that we might well conclude that there is some cause for concern. That is to say, he attempted to draw our attention to the fact that there are ethically significant choices that have nothing to do with maximizing utility, discharging duties, or respecting rights. What Hill did was to apply an ancient way of thinking (virtue ethics) in a distinctively contemporary context (environmental destruction). In situations such as the one on which Hill focuses, questions like "how shall I maximize utility" or "where does my duty lie" or "which rights must be protected" fail to adequately or fully capture what is at stake. In such situations we need to fall back on an alternative question: "What sort of a person would do a thing like that?"[35] Answering this kind of question requires a different language, one that speaks of virtues and vices, human excellences, beauty, nobility, ways of being in the world, and what it means to live well.

These days, talk of virtue and vice sounds "old-fashioned and hardly relevant" outside of fairly narrow academic or religious discourse.[36] We don't commonly speak of virtuous people or of deadly sins in the way that the Greeks, the Romans, or the Church once did. Over time virtue and vice staged a slow retreat, fading from common use and public language, to the more narrow and more or less private sphere of sexual or religious morality, and eventually to near extinction outside of a few specialized disciplines. Nevertheless, something like virtue-talk crops up with surprising regularity when we find our familiar, ready-to-hand ethical language unsuited to the task of praising or blaming someone: when we find ourselves at a loss regarding how to condemn someone who has done something bad, even though she has done nothing illegal, immoral, or evil, or when we want to praise someone for exhibiting certain character traits that we find meritorious but not mandatory. In cases like these, we often find ourselves at a loss for words, and as we search for the language we need we often reach back to something like virtue-talk.

Even in the relatively unsophisticated domain of the nightly news, we can see something like virtue ethics crop up. This usually happens in the wake of a major crisis in which the failure of ethical legalism becomes apparent—think of the Enron disaster, the sub-prime mortgage collapse, innumerable political scandals, the Deepwater Horizon blowout, or the decades-long misinformation campaigns to obscure the science linking cigarette smoke to mortality, chlorofluorocarbons to the ozone hole, and fossil fuels to greenhouse gasses and climate change. In many of these situations, it is quite clear that people knew that what they were doing was wrong but did it nevertheless. In the wake of such crises, we inevitably ask questions about the character, rather than the intellect, of the wrongdoers. The issue is not discovering whether the people in question *knew* that what they were doing was wrong—in many situations it is obvious they did—but rather ascertaining *what kind of person* would act in the way that they did.

In the United States, a 2010 Gallup Poll suggests that Americans are increasingly concerned about the decline in public morality: only 15 percent of respondents felt that the state of morals in the country was excellent or good while 45 percent rated them poor, with fully 76 percent believing that the United States is on a downward trajectory in this regard.[37] More broadly, a poll for the World Economic Forum found that "two thirds of the people across ten G20 countries believed that the economic recession had been caused by a crisis of ethics and values."[38] This sense of moral and ethical decay is no doubt connected with cases of behavior that are neither illegal nor immoral (in the sense that it violates some abstract moral law), but which are nevertheless blameworthy.

One of the recent crises in which we found ourselves less-than-articulate in condemning poor conduct was the "sub-prime" mortgage crisis in the U.S. economy that came to a head in 2007–2008, as well as similar and related conduct in other economies. The causes of this crisis are complex and include among them a number of virtue-relevant issues. Imprudent homebuyers borrowed well in excess of their means in order to jump into the housing market, and unwise homeowners refinanced, borrowing against their homes, in a similarly injudicious manner. By the time the bubble burst U.S. household debt was in excess of 125 percent of disposable income. Such leveraging was often done with adjustable-rate mortgages in the unwarranted belief that skyrocketing housing prices were a "sure thing" on which one could never lose, leading to widespread housing speculation. Imprudent borrowing and speculation were exacerbated, and in certain cases caused, by predatory lending practices—some illegal and others "merely" unethical—and by the entrance of banks into the highly speculative mortgage bond market. When President Obama explained why his Attorney General failed to prosecute Wall Street malfeasance such as the Lehman Brothers actions related to the sub-prime crisis, he said, "one of the biggest problems about the collapse of Lehman's and the subsequent financial crisis and the whole subprime lending fiasco is that a lot of that stuff wasn't necessarily illegal, it was just immoral or inappropriate or reckless."[39] So, on all sides—homebuyers, homeowners, lenders, bankers, and politicians—there seems to be grounds for quite serious chastisement; but outside of a few specific cases this behavior was not a matter of illegal activity. Rather the sub-prime crisis came about because people were "immoral," and that immorality itself is not unpacked in terms of evil or duty or utility, but in terms of virtue: individuals acted "inappropriately," they were "imprudent," or "reckless," or "greedy," or "unwise."

Similar post hoc reliance on virtue-laden language has occurred in other cases. In the case of the Enron accounting scandal, while charges were brought against Ken Lay, Andrew Fastow, and Jeff Skilling, there were scores, perhaps hundreds, of other people who knew that something was amiss and did nothing. Kurt Eichenwald's *Conspiracy of Fools* tells the story of an out-of-control corporate environment—one which lacked sound basic principles to guide the judgments and actions of its members—which allowed the greed of powerful individuals to run rampant, undoing the company and devastating thousands of employees whose retirements were heavily invested in company stock.[40] Lay, Fastow, Skilling, and others acted in ways that were both illegal and immoral. But what of the others who, while not actively participating as "pigs at the trough," allowed things to proceed unchecked? Here, as in other business and accounting scandals, there was surely un-virtuous behavior that contributed to the damage caused by immoral and illegal behavior.

Or again, think of the decades-long denial that cigarette smoking caused cancer. While many cigarette company executives lied and perjured themselves in court and before Congress, what of the others who knew of the truth and the program of disinformation and, without telling overt lies, did and said nothing? Here, as elsewhere, individuals lacked the integrity and the courage to do the right thing; they lacked the virtues that would have allowed them to act as they should have. It's worth noting, given my focus on environmental virtue, that the very same strategies used to obfuscate the truth about cigarettes are being used to obfuscate and obstruct the truth about climate change. Not only is the pattern the same, but a number of the lobbyists and consultants orchestrating climate change denial are, quite literally, the exact same individuals who coordinated the attempt to deny and discredit the effects of cigarettes.[41]

We've lost or abandoned the language to talk clearly and compellingly about ethical shortcomings when they don't fall into the categories of illegal or immoral, the latter either overlapping the former or reducible to a fairly narrow band of behaviors related to serious breaches of traditional religious morality—the seven deadly sins, mortal sin, and so on—although for the most part now divorced from religion. Having rejected or abandoned many of the traditional institutions in which it was natural to talk about good and evil, right and wrong, virtue and vice, we've lost the language to take up these critically important issues and, so, we rarely have significant public discussions about them. We've ceded the sphere of discourse about right conduct to the social sciences or, most troublingly, to economics and the market.[42] We no longer know how to talk comfortably about ethics. In terms of wrongdoing, it is easy to distinguish between the illegal and the legal, and there is a wide cultural agreement on judgments about gross moral violations. But we no longer regularly speak of actions or character traits as disgraceful, shameful, ignominious, low, mean, or unworthy. Without this language, we miss the opportunity to engage a large segment of ethically significant behavior. Though we fair slightly better with respect to virtue than vice, we rarely make subtle distinctions between the upstanding, decent, honorable, estimable, virtuous, noble, and heroic, and consequently find ourselves unable to differentiate between minor ethical achievements and genuine ethical excellence. Think here of the rampant abuse of the word "hero" to apply to anyone who has committed an admirable act, however small. Today someone is a "hero" for simply holding a certain job: nurse, teacher, social worker, police officer, firefighter, or soldier. Many people in those professions are no doubt admirable for devoting themselves to the common good, but if every soldier is a "hero" we lose the ability to speak adequately about the soldier who wins Grass Crown, the Victoria Cross, or the Congressional Medal of Honor.

The result of this linguistic impotence is that we become accustomed to thinking of ethics in terms of minimal standards regarding what is prohibited, and this way of thinking about ethics is transmitted to the environmental movement, which for a long time tended to express itself in terms of a list of "thou shalt nots" and sacrifices we must shoulder to avoid greater catastrophes.

But despite this lapse, virtue talk has not entirely disappeared from public discourse. Organizations like the Boy Scouts and Outward Bound were explicitly founded to cultivate virtues. Robert Baden-Powell founded the scouting movement because he found the young people of Britain without strength of character, resourcefulness, initiative, or guts for adventure—certainly virtue-laden language. Outward Bound, the well-known outdoor education program, has a similar origin and mission. Founded by Lawrence Holt and Kurt Hahn, Outward Bound began training young men to survive at sea (the organization being named for ships "outward bound" into the hostile seas of WWII). When ships were torpedoed, among those who went into the water the older often survived better than the younger. The conclusion was that the younger generation lacked the tenacity, confidence, and perseverance born of challenge and struggle, and the school would help to develop these characteristics. Similar sentiments can be found in William James's celebrated essay "The Moral Equivalent of War," which Hahn referenced with some regularity.[43] James believed that there are virtues cultivated by war which are difficult to cultivate in the security, affluence, and comfort that characterizes the daily life of many Americans. The solution? A "moral equivalent" to war that would allow people, especially young people, to cultivate and exercise these dispositions without the carnage and depravity that so often accompanies actual armed conflict. "The Moral Equivalent of War" can be seen as a philosophical foundation for not only Outward Bound, but for the Peace Corps, Civilian Conservation Corps, AmeriCorps, and the like.

But virtue-talk also crops up beyond the efforts of groups focused on specialized forms of education. In 2010 journalist Madeline Bunting helped to found the Citizens Ethics Network, an organization that asks pointed, virtue-relevant questions about value, economics, politics, and social life. The Network published an impressive collection of essays, *Citizen Ethics in a Time of Crisis*, which included contributions from a broad range of intellectuals and evinced a deep appreciation for something like virtue ethics.[44] Rowan Williams, former Archbishop of Canterbury and contributor to *Citizen Ethics*, writes that we have no other way to adequately talk about the qualities that make us fully human other than talking about virtues: qualities like "courage, intelligent and generous foresight, self-critical awareness . . . fortitude, prudence, temperance, and justice . . . faith, hope, and love."[45] Williams believes that we must think about virtue and value not merely because we face urgent social, economic, and environmental challenges, but rather, or in addition, because they are questions about "how we live humanly, how we live in such a way as to show that we understand and respect that we are only one species within creation."[46] Our various environmental crises are material and ecological, and they are economic and political, but they are also existential and ethical. They are about what it means to live as a human—understanding our place, possibilities, and limitations—in the world we've been given, along with all the other beings that inhabit it. Journalist, author, and environmentalist Bill McKibben is another source of explicit virtue-talk in popular discourse. Although most well known for his work to focus attention on the chemical and physical certainties of climate change, as well as the political and economic uncertainties, he has written eloquently and at length on topics than resonate with concern for virtue. In *Deep Economy*, McKibben argues that we need new "virtues" and "values" that encourage self-restraint, an appreciation for place, community connections, and local creativity.[47]

In fact, something like a concern for virtue has always remained dormant in the cultural imagination. It manifests itself each time we talk about a person's character, even if we often confuse character with "personality," or when we consider who is or is not a good role model, or when we wonder what it means to lead a good life. A number of our traditions—social, cultural, religious—exhort us to develop certain virtues or to mold certain character traits. Think here of Aesop's fables, or the Boy Scouts, or the volunteer activities of many religious congregations, or family traditions that honor and pass down habits of character like frugality or industry. Although most people think and argue in terms that are either utilitarian or deontological, many of us have practices or participate in traditions that acknowledge in some way the importance of virtue and character.

The problem is that we talk about virtue relatively rarely, and when we do it is almost always in terms that suggest virtues are a strictly private matter that, like religion, has no business in the sphere of public concern.[48] Thanks to utilitarian and deontological logic, "public discourse regarding the environment is framed almost exclusively in legislative and regulatory terms" making it all too easy to reduce the field of environmental ethics to a fixation "on what activities ought to be allowed or prohibited."[49] Broader and subtler concerns about what it means to flourish as a human being, what characteristics contribute to that flourishing, and how those characteristics impact other people and the wider world of non-human nature are ignored. But relegating such concerns to the private sphere has real impacts on the well-being of individuals, groups, and places.

There is a tendency to think of virtue, especially environmental virtue, in terms of an optional and personal choice. Vice President Dick Cheney gave voice to this perspective when he famously quipped that environmentalism is merely a "personal virtue,"[50] implying such dispositions are something that might contribute to the personal happiness of those so inclined, precisely and only because they are so inclined, but which are neither essential for flourishing nor social in scope. The suggestion seemed to be that environmental virtues are something like upper-class social graces or exceptional penmanship—valuable to those for whom they matter, and only to those for whom they matter, but ultimately nothing more than a certain sort of fussiness. We might dismiss Cheney's comment as the opinion of an individual known for his anti-environmental views; however, even among those who embrace environmentalism, there is a tendency to think in terms of personal choices and to focus on acts rather than agents. This is perhaps why so much environmentalism is focused on lifestyle choices—with the emphasis on *style*—having to do with "green" consumption. Even for those who have made a connection between virtue, in whatever terms they speak of it, and the environment, it is all too easy to fall into thinking of virtue as a merely personal goal, a sort of self-help program detached from the wider world of society and nature.[51]

Taken together, our various environmental crises—anthropogenic climate change, over population, over consumption, poor land use, soil erosion, loss of biodiversity, and the like—are arguably the single greatest ethical and existential challenge confronting us in the twenty-first century. At stake is nothing less than a choice about what kind of persons we should be and what kind of world we want to live in. Who are we? Who ought we to be? What is our relationship with the wider world? What ought it to be? It is, therefore, one of the major tasks of philosophy to address these challenges in a manner that is both convincing and practical. I contend that virtue ethics is an essential component of any complete ethical response to our contemporary environmental crises, and this book is an attempt to further develop virtue theory and its application to environmental ethics.

Throughout this work, I generally prefer to speak in terms of "emphasis," "tendency," or "foci" rather than in terms of "essence" or "absolutes." This is because there are often—although not always—exceptions to rules. Aristotle points out that when addressing ethics we are "speaking about things that are only for the most part true."[52] Properly understood, this is not an excuse for sloppy thinking or lack of rigor—we should certainly aim for the rigor and precision appropriate to any field of inquiry—but rather an acknowledgement of a fact. Therefore, when I claim that virtue ethics emphasizes the agent over the act, this does not mean that virtue ethics ignores the action; it means just what it says: that virtue ethics *emphasizes* the character of the agent in its analysis. Likewise, I claim that deontology and utilitarianism emphasize developing rules for guiding action rather than developing the character of the agent, despite the fact that certain deontologists and utilitarians do speak of virtue. However, to say that virtue ethics does not stress the rule-based components of action guidance does not mean that virtue ethics has no room for such rules. Indeed, action-guiding rules are an important part of a fully elaborated virtue ethics.

Two substantive claims guide this work: first, that environmental ethics is incomplete without a robust virtue ethics component and, second, that a complete virtue ethics must take into account the important role of narrative in the understanding and the transmission of the virtues.

Virtue ethics is necessary for environmental ethics, first because we need an ethical schema that is broad enough to capture a variety of behaviors that are not commonly thought of as morally, ethically, or environmentally relevant, and which are not captured by utilitarianism and deontology. In addition, virtue ethics works especially well with the place-based and context-sensitive concerns central to many issues in environmental ethics. Finally, with respect to practical efficacy, virtue ethics frames environmentalism in terms of flourishing rather than sacrifice and in so doing makes many of the necessary behavioral changes attractive rather than onerous.

Narrative, we will see, is an essential component of any virtue ethics—and, therefore, of any environmental virtue ethics—because is it an essential component of ethical formation, whether that means the formation of children or the reformation of adults. Narrative proves helpful for solving several of the problems that beset virtue ethics absent a narrative component, including the challenge of relativism, problems associated with the cultivation and transmission of the virtues, and issues associated with *phronesis*, or practical wisdom. Thus, "emplotting virtue" takes on a double meaning with respect to environmental virtue ethics: "plot" as *mythos*, the sequence of events that make up a story, and "plot" as a piece of ground, a *place* or environment in which the story unfolds.[53]

My aim here is not to identify the proper environmental narrative for the twenty-first century. Indeed, I don't think there is a single, all-purpose narrative that captures every element of a good life or which applies universally and without modification to all the diverse people, cultures, ecosystems, and bioregions of the world. Nor do I intend to offer a list, exhaustive or otherwise, of virtuous environmental narratives. My aim is rather to argue for the importance of virtue ethics for environmental ethics, and the necessity of narrative for the full and complete articulation of virtue. Narrative plays a crucial role in ethical formation and transformation, what the Greeks called *metanoia*; it is something that influences both our willingness and our ability to change our lives. Although in the course of making these arguments I will refer to many narratives I think worthy of consideration, I'll also leave out a great many of those I esteem, and identifying the best narratives for the twenty-first century will have to await another work.

Although this is an academic book, my project here has something in common with the ancient philosophical traditions and motivations, something that is noticeably absent in a great deal of contemporary academic philosophy. The issues addressed in this book will, I hope, actually help people to live better lives by focusing on the virtues, and help them to pass on this concern to live well to others by reminding them—for as children most of us recognized it, if only dimly—of the importance of stories for their lives. How and why contemporary academic philosophy has lost sight of this important practical goal is no doubt a complicated tale having to do with the professionalization of philosophy, the fragmentation of knowledge into relatively insular disciplines, and historical chance that has led a great many philosophers to focus on minute and esoteric details of interest only to other specialists, or to write in a manner so plodding and obscure as to make their work inaccessible to a general educated audience. Overcoming these challenges does not require that philosophy get "dumbed down" or express itself only in monosyllabic language; it does mean that we should take seriously general questions related to living well alongside our specialized debates, and that we should be able to express ourselves, when appropriate, in a manner that allows us to communicate with non-specialists. As Aristotle reminds us in one of the founding texts of virtue ethics: "We are inquiring not in order to know what virtue is, *but in order to become good.*"[54]

2

Virtue Ethics and Environmental Virtue Ethics

I believe that what we become depends on what our fathers teach us at odd moments, when they aren't trying to teach us.

—Umberto Eco, *Foucault's Pendulum*

Education worthy of the name is essentially education in character.

—Martin Buber, *Between Man and Man*

Sow an act, and you reap a habit. Sow a habit, and you reap a character. Sow a character, and you reap a destiny.

—attributed, and misattributed, to many

It makes sense to begin with Aristotle, not because his is the final word on virtue ethics, but because his was one of the first and because his influence will be felt throughout my own account.[1] The broad outline of his ethical work—indeed many of its details—rings true even today. It is difficult to read the *Nicomachean Ethics* without feeling that Aristotle is explaining something quite common sense; but its commonsense appeal belies its wisdom and the clarity with which it is communicated. J. O. Urmson points out, in a wonderfully pithy witticism, that "Aristotle's works are full of platitudes in much the same way as Shakespeare's *Hamlet* is full of quotations."[2] What is actually wise and insightful appears, retrospectively, to be platitudinous precisely because Aristotle communicates something that is true and, in some sense, universal about ethics and morality. Nevertheless, there are important instances in which Aristotle is clearly in error. Commonly cited examples include his relatively static view of culture, the very unfair treatment of women in his work, and his belief in the "unity" of the virtues—the idea that genuinely possessing one virtue entails possessing

25

all the virtues. Therefore, I won't claim to be faithful to every letter of Aristotle's work in what follows, but rather to the spirit that animates it.

In the *Nicomachean Ethics*, Aristotle offers us an ethical treatise quite different from the utilitarian and deontological examples to which we are accustomed. Although I touched on some of these differences in the first chapter, a more thorough account of virtue ethics is necessary before we proceed. However, it's not possible to provide a full and detailed account of Aristotle's ethics in part of a single chapter. Therefore, in what follows I'll focus on painting, in fairly broad strokes, a picture of his ethical project that will be useful for those unfamiliar with that work and, in addition, pointing out some of its most salient features from the perspective of environmental virtue ethics.

Virtue and Flourishing

Aristotle begins his inquiry, not by asking what actions are right or wrong, but by asking after the characteristic "good of man," that is to say, the *telos*, or goal, of a good human life. This teleological approach is, as Alasdair MacIntyre points out, something central to virtue ethics and, significantly, something foreign to the utilitarian and deontological approaches.[3] A human flourishes—that is to say she is good—to the extent that she achieves this distinctively human goal.

Although we don't always consider the *telos* of human being in our everyday activity, all human activity aims at something.[4] For example, a person takes the bar exam in order to practice law. If she did not want to practice law, she would not take the bar exam. Likewise, when a person eats food it is, generally, in order to satisfy hunger; if she were not hungry, she would not eat. The activity of eating aims at satiating hunger.[5] However, Aristotle isn't so interested in these contingent goods, which are only desired in order to get some other good or achieve some other goal. He is concerned with the "highest" or "final" good for humans, the goal at which human life taken as a whole aims. Or, put another way, the point is to identify a final or ultimate good that is desirable in itself rather than for the sake of something else, and which is the goal that the merely contingent goods serve.

Aristotle claims that this ultimate good is *eudaimonia*, a term that is often translated as "happiness" but which is better rendered as "well-being" or "flourishing." That's because happiness sounds like something that is transitory and has to do with merriment or delight, and a life spent maximizing this narrow sort of pleasure, a life of hedonism, even enlightened hedonism, is a lesser life than that to which we should aspire. Flourishing captures more clearly Aristotle's meaning. A being is flourishing when it is thriving in all the ways it should. For example, a plant is flourishing when it has access to all the proper nutrients it needs, sufficient water and sunlight, an ample number of the right kind of pollinators to facilitate reproduction, adequate defenses against pests and disease, and so on. The plant flourishes when it exhibits well all the characteristics proper to the sort of plant that it is. Likewise, a human flourishes when she exhibits the excellences characteristic of human beings. Such flourishing is the goal of all human activity; we all want to thrive, to "live and fare well."

So far so good; but the crux of the matter, as Aristotle clearly saw, was determining how to achieve *eudaimonia*. Everyone wants to be "happy" in this way, but some people seek happiness in wealth, others in fame, and others in power; our various attempts to flourish are as diverse as our constitutions, dispositions, and worldviews. This diversity will prove to be a significant problem for virtue ethics, one to which I will return at length in later chapters. For now, let's consider that many of the most common strategies for achieving happiness fail to do so. The blind pursuit of material wealth is perhaps the most common life goal in industrialized Western nations, though it is fast gaining traction elsewhere as well. However, a mountain of research illustrates that this goal and materialist orientation that accompanies it do *not* tend to bring about deep or lasting happiness. In the United States, people are no happier than they were in the 1950s even though living standards have more than doubled.[6] It's true that when raising oneself out of abject poverty material wealth will increase one's happiness and well-being, but only up to a point. We have been taught over the course of history that we get better when we get more; the problem is, as Bill McKibben points out, that we continue to purse this strategy when conditions have changed and it is no longer appropriate.[7] Today we find ourselves caught on a "hedonic treadmill" on which we work harder and harder without really getting anywhere.

While an exhaustive list of the components of flourishing may not be possible, we can nevertheless describe some of its most salient features. Aristotle tells us that such a life must be active, that flourishing does not come about as the result of some passive disposition. He also argues that human flourishing must revolve around some distinctively human activity, which he identifies as reason, and that it has to do with excellence or virtue. Ideally, flourishing takes place over one's entire life, for just as a promising book can be ruined by terrible final chapters, a good life can be seriously harmed by disasters—ethical or otherwise—later in one's life. Aristotle does admit that a person needs a number of things in order to

flourish, including things we have by luck of birth, like a properly functioning body, and external goods we can secure as we journey through life,
like some measure of material wealth. Many of us focus on this final point
and spend our lives obsessively chasing and accumulating these external
goods, which, unfortunately, are only a small part of the larger picture of
flourishing. This is a case of misplaced priorities. While things like an
adequate—rather than exorbitant—amount of money are indeed necessary to flourish, Aristotle believes that they play a relatively minor role in
determining our well-being. The key determinant of flourishing is virtue,
and it is for this reason that Aristotle's approach is called "virtue ethics."

As *eudaimonia* suffers from the commonplace translation as "happiness," "virtue" is a potentially misleading translation of the Greek *arete*.
When we hear the word virtue, we are more apt to think of a certain Vic-
torian prudishness or fastidious piety than we are to think of the essential
characteristics and dispositions of a good person. However, for the Greeks
arete carried connotations of both virtue and excellence; it includes aspects
of behavior that would fall under the moral domain most commonly associated with the modern use of "virtue," but is much more expansive than
that narrow use, encompassing intellectual, moral, and physical excellences.
When Aristotle says that someone possesses the virtue of courage he means
that that person has cultivated a certain human excellence, in this case
courage, to a sufficient degree that it contributes to her flourishing. Thus,
for Aristotle, the goal of life is to flourish (*eudaimonia*) and cultivating
the virtues (*arete* or human excellences) is, in large part, the path to such
well-being.

Acquiring Virtue

Now, while Aristotle does argue that certain external goods are a kind of
prerequisites for flourishing and that some of these goods seem dependent
on one's fate—according to him we need to be born into circumstances
that will at least allow for the possibility of flourishing, and it seems difficult
to see how a person can truly flourish if she is born into truly desperate
poverty or with a profoundly crippling disease—he nevertheless makes clear
that no one is born virtuous. Virtue is not simply a matter of luck related
to one's birth: "Neither by nature . . . nor contrary to nature do the virtues
arise in us; rather we are adapted by nature to receive them, and are made
perfect by habit."[8]

Moral virtues like courage, temperance, and generosity are developed
by a process of habituation (*hexis*) through which we develop the proper
disposition and accustom ourselves to acting in a certain way.[9] No one is

born courageous or temperate. We become courageous by practicing courage and temperate by practicing temperance. Likewise, a person becomes cowardly by repeating cowardly acts and self-indulgent through repeated acts of self-indulgence. The same holds true for many virtues associated with environmentally beneficial behavior: simplicity, care, emplacement, and the like. Although developing certain virtues (or vices) might be somewhat easier for one person as opposed to another, virtues, in a manner analogous to physical strength, must be exercised if they are to be developed and maintained.

Because virtue is a matter of habituation, chief among the prerequisites associated with the luck of one's birth is having the right "breeding," so to speak. This has little to do with one's bloodline, but everything to do with how one is brought up. Given the necessity of habituation, it is easy to see the significance of how one is raised by one's parents. Indeed, whenever I teach Aristotle the full weight of the responsibility of parenthood presses down on me. Childhood habituation is not only about developing or laying the groundwork for certain virtues, like courage. Even more important is instilling the desire to be virtuous, the desire to be an *excellent* person, to be *good*. A person must be brought up in such a way that being good matters to her, for if she is not it seems highly unlikely that she will concern herself with it as she continues to develop.[10]

Aristotle never attempts to offer us an exhaustive list of the virtues. Given the nature of the topic it's not entirely clear that such a list would be either possible or desirable. This is true both because the "science" of virtue is inexact and because virtues are tied to a particular view of the good life. That is to say, different visions of the good life will have different lists of virtues or different accounts of familiar virtues. According to Aristotle, humility is a vice associated with insufficient pride; however, for a Christian philosopher like Thomas Aquinas, humility is a virtue.[11] Similarly, what counted as courage in feudal Japan differs from what counts as courage in contemporary Denmark. The diverse accounts of flourishing, as well as the virtues that contribute to it, raises problems that we will have to address as we proceed. For now, suffice it to say that a virtue is a characteristic or disposition that is conducive to flourishing, and that while the system of such characteristics or dispositions will certainly vary over the course of history and from culture to culture, there will nevertheless be some agreement as to the identity of the virtues. Although people will certainly argue about which virtues are most important to our well-being and how those virtues express themselves in action, we can nevertheless name a number of these traits that would prove relatively unobjectionable to people in diverse times, places, and cultures, including courage, truthfulness, friendliness, temperance, and so on.

Once we have named a given virtue, we have to ask of what it consists. What, for example, is courage? Aristotle cautions us that we cannot
precisely define the virtues, but assures us that this is not a fatal problem. A discussion of virtue is "adequate if it has as much clearness as the
subject-matter admits of, for precision is not to be sought for alike in all
discussions. . . ."[12] Indeed, he tells us that, in the field of ethics, "we must
be content . . . in speaking of such subjects and with such premises to
indicate the truth roughly and in outline, and in speaking about things
that are only for the most part true, and with premises of the same kind,
to reach conclusions that are no better."[13] This is *not* an excuse for a lack
of rigor, but an honest recognition of the *type* of rigor that is possible and
an acknowledgement that different disciplines demand different degrees of
exactitude. Not all things that are true are true in the same way. It is as
foolish to expect mathematical precision in a poetic description of love as
it is to accept poetic approximations in attempting to prove a mathematical conjecture. Moreover, less precision does not necessarily mean a less
worthwhile or useful discipline. Hence the humorous distinction between
a mathematician and an engineer: the engineer rounds off π to three.[14]

Although virtue cannot be exactly prescribed, we can say that it
is "destroyed by excess or defect, and preserved by the mean."[15] We can
describe most moral virtues as a mean, or point of balance, between two
extremes or vices. Take the virtue of courage for example. Clearly a person
can fail to be virtuous by being insufficiently courageous; such a person
would be a coward and have the vice of cowardice. However, it is also possible to be excessive in confronting danger. In this case the person would
actually be rash rather than courageous, which is just as much a vice as
cowardice. Fools rush in where angels fear to tread. We can say the same
thing of most moral virtues; one can fail either by going too far or by not
going far enough, and therefore virtue occupies a position between excess
and deficiency.

Because moral virtues are the result of habituation, virtues and their
corresponding vices are acquired in very similar ways. A person becomes
a good builder of homes by actually building; no one can do it naturally
and no amount of reading about it will allow you to square the frame of
a house. You need to practice. At first, no doubt, you will frequently fail.
Nevertheless, with diligence, a person can develop the ability to build
houses very well. Crucially, however, the same sorts of acts by which a
person becomes an excellent builder of houses can make her a terrible
builder. If you practice doing things the right way, the right way becomes
a habit; if you practice things inattentively, or poorly, or sloppily, those
ways will also become habits. As a coach from my youth used to remind

me—inevitably delivered via a booming shout during the most difficult and exhausting drills, when we were most tempted to slack off—"Dammit boys! Practice doesn't make perfect; *perfect* practice makes perfect!"

What is true for building houses or training for athletic competition is, says Aristotle, true for virtue. No one is born courageous, and no amount of reading about courage will suffice to make a person courageous (though I will return to this issue below). Rather, a person becomes courageous through habituation. She practices courage by doing courageous acts until being courageous becomes part of who she is; that is, until it is an entrenched habit. Likewise, if a person repeatedly does things that are cowardly or rash, she will, over time, develop an entrenched habit of either cowardice or rashness.

The Middle Way

According to Aristotle, virtue is a disposition to choose the mean.[16] Being virtuous means choosing the middle path between two vicious extremes, which are themselves characterized by having too little or too much of a good thing. Courage, we said, is a virtuous point of balance between the imbalanced extremes of cowardice and rashness. I often point out to undergraduate students that they are already familiar with this point of view. Moral virtue operates on a sort of "Goldilocks Principle." How does Goldilocks evaluate things? She avoids extremes. Too big; too small; just right. Too hot; too cold; just right. The Goldilocks Principle works well for illustrating some of Aristotle's other claims about virtue as well. Goldilocks not only avoids extremes, she looks for what "fits" her. A bed too big for Goldilocks might be just right for me, and porridge just right for Goldilocks might be too hot for me. Aristotle is well aware of this variability, pointing out "the master of any art [including a given virtue] avoids excess and defect, but seeks the intermediate and chooses this—the intermediate *not in the object, but relative to us.*"[17]

Of course, not all virtues are balanced in the manner like the midpoint on a number line or the centroid of a triangle. In fact, few virtues are. Courage, which is about facing danger and fear, is closer to rashness than it is to cowardice, and so while it is intermediate between rashness and cowardice, it is not midway between them. Remember the Goldilocks Principle. If one bowl of porridge is too cold at 0°C and another is too hot at 100°C, it does not follow that porridge is just right at 50°C. Most folks like porridge hot, perhaps 60°C or hotter. Virtues are a point of balance between excess and defect, but just as with physical objects this point may not be at the center of the continuum. So, Aristotle's "Doctrine of the Mean" is not necessarily a recipe for moderation. Sometimes, as Oscar Wilde's Lord Illingworth quipped, "nothing succeeds like excess."[18] Not only are some virtues, like courage, much closer to one of their two contrary extreme vices, some virtues and vices are extreme by their very nature. Adultery, theft, and murder are bad per se; it is impossible to do too few of these actions.[19]

At this point, a fairly obvious objection should come up. These characteristics—virtue as a somewhat vague mean between extremes, which we can only circumscribe roughly, and is relative to each individual—inevitably raise the specter of relativism.[20] If there is no universal or objective criterion to which virtuous actions must conform, can any decision, act, or lifestyle "count" as appropriately virtuous merely because the agent in question feels she is acting virtuously? It is not too difficult to imagine a spendthrift exerting a very minor degree of restraint and claiming that she is acting with virtuous economy simply because she genuinely feels like she is hitting the mean between profligacy and miserliness. Can each of us assert, like Goldilocks, that a given action or emotion fits us "just right"?

Aristotle is well aware of this problem. He does not mean to make each of us an unimpeachable judge of our own virtue—which would be a bit like having the fox guard the henhouse—but instead qualifies all the individual variability that characterizes the virtuous mean by asserting that the mean must be one that is reasonably determined: "Virtue, then, is a state of character concerned with choice, lying in a mean, i.e., a mean relative to us, this being determined by a rational principle, and by that principle by which the man of practical wisdom would determine it."[21] All virtue must conform to a rational principle, and in the particularly hard cases we should take special note of the rational principle as determined by the *phronimos*, the man or woman of practical wisdom.

The *phronimos* is a person who has fully developed practical wisdom (*phronesis*), a person whose character is disposed to choose the virtuous mean. A person with fully developed practical wisdom can be thought of, loosely, as an expert in and model of virtue. *Phronesis* is a critical intellectual virtue. Unlike the moral virtues we have been discussing, intellectual virtues can be taught; *phronesis* in particular depends on both instruction and sufficient life experience.[22] It is the ability to "deliberate well about what is good and expedient . . . [the] sorts of things that conduce to the good life in general," a "true and reasoned state of capacity to act with regard to the things that are good or bad for man."[23] Thus, *phronesis* allows a person to make good judgments with respect to human conduct. As I noted above, anyone can follow a rule in situations that are, at least relatively, clear-cut.

A child, who is morally and ethically immature, or a computer, which is not even sentient, can follow clear rules in situations where the application of those rules is unambiguous. *Phronesis* comes into its own in the messy situations of ethical ambiguity. The person with practical wisdom is able to judge well with respect to choices in particular circumstances that do *not* fall neatly under general rules for conduct, either when the particular situation seems to merit an exception to the universal rule or when two ethical guidelines or rules come into conflict. In such circumstances it is the person of practical wisdom who will be able to choose well. Classic examples of conflict between universal rules are evident when Antigone must decide whether or not to bury Polynices in Sophocles's *Antigone,* and when Orestes must decide whether or not to kill his mother—his wretched, "What shall I do?"—in *The Libation Bearers.* However, the infamous HAL 9000 computer from the novels of Arthur C. Clarke offers an alternative and particularly illuminating example of the relationship between experience and *phronesis.*[24] HAL's malfunction, which led him to kill the astronauts onboard the spaceship *Discovery,* came about as a result of its inability to negotiate the conflict between two of its programmed directives or rules: (1) to accurately process information without distortion or concealment (that is, to be honest) and (2) to keep the nature of the mission secret from the astronauts until directed by mission control to reveal it. Although HAL is described as conscious, aware, and intelligent it is, presumably, lacking *phronesis*—if for no other reason than it was only operational for four years prior to its malfunction, leaving it without the necessary experience to develop the sort of sensitivity to context required by *phronesis.*

Individual idiosyncrasies ensure that each person is unique in ethically significant ways, which means that each person exhibits or manifests the virtue of courage differently. Moreover, contexts often differ in ethically relevant ways. This means that there is often not a single "right thing to do" in a situation; indeed, we generally cannot even say "what the virtuous person would do," because people are virtuous in different ways and, therefore, there are multiple different possible virtuous responses to any situation.[25] While it is certainly true that a physically frail person in her eighties and a healthy and active person in her twenties would exhibit courage differently in a given situation—say, when confronted by an assailant—it is not the case any action by any agent would qualify as courageous. The 80-year-old would be justified in being, and indeed should be, courageous in a different manner than the 20-year-old. As long as each person hits the mean relative to him- or herself both are courageous, even though their actions and emotions will be very different. However, no one could flee from harmless insects, or be reduced to incapacity by the dark, and justifiably claim to be courageous. Thus, while a person might feel comfortable fleeing from insignificant threats, and may even feel that her conduct is rational, appropriate, and reflective of a virtuous character that strikes the mean between cowardice and rashness, her peers in society, and especially the *phronimos*, are justified in condemning such behavior as a vicious extreme (cowardice) rather than a virtuous mean (courage).

Emotion and Action

In order to be virtuous, however, it is not enough to do the right thing; one must do the right thing in the right way. If you are coerced into doing the right thing, or if you do it to avoid social reprobation, or if you do the right thing accidentally, you have not acted virtuously. It is true that doing the right thing is essential; however, if you hope to be virtuous you must do the sorts of acts that a virtuous person would do, and do them as a virtuous person would do them. You must do the right action in the right way, at the right time, for the right reason, with reference to the right objects, and so on.[26]

One of the criteria that must be satisfied for an act to be genuinely virtuous is that it must be done with the "right emotion," which is also often a midpoint between extremes. Because virtue is a mean of both action and emotion, it is difficult, if not impossible, to determine with certainty whether or not another person has acted virtuously. Indeed, because we are not always transparent to ourselves, we can doubt whether we acted with the proper emotion or whether we took pleasure in the virtuous act. Given these challenges, even if we are attentive to the specificity of the situation and the unique character of the agent, talk about virtue will tend to be general rather than specific. One gets the feeling that accounts of virtue will look more like an heirloom cooking recipe given a personal flourish—a dash more garlic, a splash more wine—and less like the precise, standardized, and impersonal formula of a nutritionist or pharmacist. A bit more of the art of the cook, and a bit less of the science of the chemist, so to speak.

A person may commit a courageous act without yet being courageous, as when a cowardly person dares to fight because she has been backed into a corner. But, in order to qualify as virtuous, one must, among other things, also feel the right emotion while doing the right thing. Thus, courage is a mean between cowardice and rashness, and the courageous person is distinguished by feeling the proper balance of fear and confidence. On Aristotle's account, if a person feels too much fear, she is merely a coward doing a "courageous" act; if a person feels too much confidence, she is a rash person committing a "courageous" act. Although this distinction may not be in full accord with modern conceptions of a given virtue, it is essential to Aristotle's position because it helps to distinguish virtuous acts committed by virtuous persons from virtuous acts committed by normal, or even vicious, persons. It may help to differentiate between admiring someone for doing something virtuous when it is difficult for her, and admiring someone in the sense of wanting to be like her.[27] While we may admire the pluck of a timorous person who nevertheless stands her ground in a desperate situation, we would, on reflection, all prefer to *be* the person who, in the same desperate circumstances, courageously makes a stand.

The distinction between a virtuous act committed by a virtuous person and virtuous act committed by another person is evident in whether or not the agent enjoys doing the action, in the sense that one enjoys doing the right thing.

> We must take as a sign of states of character the pleasure or pain that supervenes on the acts; for the man who abstains from bodily pleasure and delights in this very fact is temperate, while the man who is annoyed at it is self-indulgent, and he who stands his ground against things that are terrible and delights in this or at least is not pained is brave, while the man who is pained is a coward.[28]

So, the pleasure or pain accompanying an action helps to indicate the character of the actor. A virtuous person takes pleasure in virtuous acts and is pained by vicious acts. Conversely, a vicious person takes pleasure in vicious acts and is pained by virtuous acts. Because of this, becoming virtuous is likely to be a very difficult process. This is both daunting and heartening. It is daunting because if one allows oneself to develop bad habits that become genuinely entrenched, it is very, very difficult to break those habits and commit or recommit oneself to virtue. But it is, or should be, heartening because we can consciously and actively work on becoming better people and, with enough diligence, actually accomplish it. Moreover, once we deeply entrench virtuous habits they, just like deeply entrenched vicious habits, are unlikely to change.[29]

Imagine, by way of analogy, trying to become physically fit—not an Olympic athlete but simply a person who engages in the sort of regular, strenuous physical activity that is associated with good health. If a person is not yet fit, her initial efforts are likely to prove uncomfortable. It will not feel good to wake up an hour earlier to run, bike, or row before getting ready for the day. The soreness and the sweat will be off-putting. If a person who is not yet physically fit uses pleasure as her guide—"I'll only run as much as feels good"—she is very likely not to become fit at all. Her habitual preferences make inactivity comfortable and activity uncomfortable. Similarly, when a person resolves to become courageous, temperate, generous, or simple she will find the behaviors associated with these virtues unnatural, burdensome, and uncomfortable, and will only perform them with difficulty. She takes no pleasure in the virtuous action, though she may take some pleasure in the fact that she is working at becoming virtuous. During this process, she may, it is true, perform virtuous actions, but not in the way in which a virtuous person would perform those actions, that is to say, with pleasure. When a person takes pleasure in doing virtuous acts, it shows that the virtue in question has become her habitual disposition and that she is, in fact, virtuous. If our hypothetical aspirant perseveres and eventually achieves a moderate level of fitness, she will begin to take pleasure in her daily exercises and, indeed, feel out of sorts on days when she is unable to work out.

However, the practical and normative difficulties of this position, which asks us to aim for the middle path while insisting that the middle path cannot be precisely defined, are substantial. It is difficult indeed to hit a specific target when its location is only known generally—"we must be content [in speaking of virtue] to indicate the truth roughly and in outline . . . speaking about things that are only for the most part true, and with premises of the same kind, to reach conclusions that are no better."[30] What is the likelihood of throwing a bull's-eye on a dartboard in a dark room, after being spun around with your eyes closed? Aristotle, of course, is well aware of the difficulties associated with becoming virtuous.

> . . . [I]t is no easy task to be good. For in everything it is no easy task to find the middle . . . so, too, anyone can get angry—that is easy—or give and spend money; but to do this to the right person, to the right extent, at the right time, with the right motive, and in the right way, that is not for everyone, nor is it easy; wherefore goodness is both rare and laudable and noble.[31]

We will return to the difficulties associated with cultivating virtue in due course. Fortunately, however, Aristotle himself supplies us with several useful "aiming instructions" for trying to hit the virtuous mean. First, in aiming for the mean one should avoid the more contrary extreme. For example, courage is about confronting dangers and so is closer to rashness than to cowardice. When in doubt, steer a bit closer to the Scylla of rashness than to the Charybdis of cowardice. Second, in aiming for the mean one should take into account one's own tendencies or inclinations. If one tends to be timorous, one should move a bit closer to rashness; if one is inclined to reckless actions, one should move a bit closer to cowardice. Finally, in seeking to hit the virtuous mean, one should be wary of pleasure. Why? Because if we are seeking to habituate ourselves to the virtuous mean we, presumably, are not yet virtuous. While it is true that a virtuous person takes pleasure in virtuous acts, the vicious person takes pleasure in vicious acts. If the vicious person does what feels good, she will only further habituate herself to vice.

Virtue and the Environment

The Resurgence of Interest in Virtue Ethics

In 1958 Elizabeth Anscombe published an essay entitled "Modern Moral Philosophy," which is often credited with beginning the contemporary resurgence of interest in virtue ethics.[32] Over the past 50 years, interest in virtue ethics has continued to grow, fueled by work done by a number of philosophers either following Anscombe's lead or working from their own philosophical interests. Among the more notable contributions are works by Philippa Foot, Rosalind Hursthouse, Peter Geach, Martha Nussbaum, Alasdair MacIntyre, and Paul Ricoeur. We can't, given the limited the space available, adequately address all these philosophers, or indeed address any one of them exhaustively. However, it is worth noting two underlying themes that will have significance for later chapters: first, the naturalistic approach of Foot and Hursthouse and, second, the attention to narrative found in varying degrees in MacIntyre, Nussbaum, and Ricoeur.

The naturalistic approach to virtue taken by Foot and Hursthouse influences, directly or indirectly, a number of environmental virtue ethicists, including the work done in Ronald Sandler's comprehensive book-length treatment, *Character and Environment*. Briefly, for we will have more to say in the next chapter, the naturalistic approach claims that virtues should be evaluated in the ethological context of the type of biological being a living thing is. When we call a living thing "good," we do so in the context of the type of being that it is and the characteristic functions of its type.[33] Moving from naturalism to narrative, we should take note of the work done by MacIntyre, Nussbaum, and Ricoeur to address the important role that narrative plays in virtue ethics. They take up topics as varied as the role of narrative in cultivating both the emotions and reason, the necessity of a narrative context for framing ideas about flourishing and the virtues that constitute it, and the role of narrative in self-understanding and in the formation of identity; but they are unified in their respect for the power of narrative. Chapters 6 and 7 will argue at length for a very robust account of the role of narrative in environmental virtue ethics. For now, suffice it to say that this approach has been anticipated by a number of prominent philosophers.

Environmental Virtue Ethics

Despite the contemporary revival of interest in virtue theory, the approach has remained the province of a relatively small number of academics. Utilitarianism and deontology have remained the preferred tools for scholars, especially when dealing with contemporary ethical problems. Certainly outside of the academy, the popular imagination remains fully captive by the utilitarian-deontological duopoly on ethical debate. Nevertheless, the revival of virtue ethics has begun to chip away at the modern ethical "duo-lith."

Louke van Wensveen's *Dirty Virtues* marked an important turning point in the development of environmental virtue ethics, being among the first to identify it as a distinct field of study (although this was anticipated by shorter works like Geoffrey Franz's "Environmental Virtue Ethics: A New Direction for Environmental Ethics" and Thomas Hill's "Ideals of Human Excellence and Preserving Natural Environments").[34] It's not that other thinkers had failed to use virtue language to address environmental issues. Indeed, the opposite is true. Wensveen argues that the vast majority of environmental and ecological writing has, for a long time, *already* been employing "virtue language": "I have yet to come across a piece of ecologically sensitive philosophy, theology, or ethics that does not in some way incorporate virtue language."[35] Though this seems obvious in retrospect—think of Thoreau, Muir, Brower, Leopold, Abbey, Foreman, Dillard, Carson, and Goodall, to say nothing of popular contemporary writers like McKibben and Pollan—raising awareness about the use of virtue language and focusing on the apparent underlying concern with character inspired a small group of scholars to adopt a virtue theory approach, and "environmental virtue ethics" took off as an explicit field of study. Wensveen catalogues in great detail examples of virtue language culled from social ecology, deep ecology, bioregionalism, animal rights, creation theology, environmental philosophy, ecofeminism, and more.[36] Though such language is pervasive—even popping up in works with a high degree of technical focus attempting "objective" treatment of the issues—it is most evident "when authors assume a hortatory, personal, reflection-filled mode of writing."[37] That is, when they engage in what I will broadly refer to as the narrative mode.

There is no one way to "do" environmental virtue ethics, but there are a number of common strategies that seem to crop up again and again. Ronald Sandler suggests that there are at least four approaches that appear regularly in discussions of virtue and the environment.[38] One common approach is to address environmental virtue by "arguing by extension from standard interpersonal virtues, that is, from virtues that are typically applied to relationships among humans."[39] Such an approach simply extends traditional virtues like temperance and generosity to cover explicitly environmental concerns. A second method, based on the role played by flourishing (*eudaimonia*) in virtue ethics, is to focus on the benefit that environmental virtues have for the agent, how such habits and dispositions will directly contribute to the flourishing of the individual in question. Another tactic, often part of the naturalistic approach to virtue spearheaded by Foot and Hursthouse, is to argue that environmental virtues are among the traits constitutive of human excellence, the characteristics that make their possessor a good human being.[40] Finally, some people adopt the "environmental exemplar" approach, in which one argues that traits are virtues because they were possessed, and often exemplified, by people we admire and hold up as models: Thoreau, Muir, Leopold, Carson, Brower, and so on.[41] However, while it is useful to isolate these general strategies, certain themes and thinkers seem to crop up again and again in the literature, and combinations of these approaches are frequently found together in accounts of environmental virtue ethics. Thus, one might begin with the model of environmental exemplars and, simultaneously, argue that the traits they exemplify are constitutive of human flourishing.

The Advantages of Virtue Ethics

Increasingly, philosophers have come to appreciate the potential contributions of virtue ethics to questions and issues of environmental concern. Although this approach is not without problems, addressing environmental issues under the rubric of virtue ethics does offer a perspective that integrates environmental beliefs, dispositions, and character traits into a larger picture of human flourishing. One of the great benefits of this approach is the possibility of framing environmental virtues as essential to the good life, rather than merely a burden we must shoulder out of necessity. Such an approach is essential if there is to be any hope of widespread development of environmental virtues prior to environmental collapse.[42]

When we look at our heroes, environmental or otherwise, what is it that we admire? It is true that we admire their actions, the things that they *do* or *did*; however, it is also true that we often admire their characters, the persons that they *are* or *were*. This does not mean that we have to view such people through the rose-colored lens of hagiography, ignoring their personal flaws and peccadilloes. It does mean that in looking to such examples we can learn not only from the dramatic and overt actions of an admirable person, but also from her general comportment, her "way of being in the world" and the less-dramatic actions and traits that circumscribe it. The latter is a necessary condition for the former. This broader sort of assessment and appreciation encourages us to take seriously the need to address our own characters as part of a holistic approach to ethics.

Sandler opens *Character and Environment* with a wonderfully apt epigraph from C. S. Lewis's *Mere Christianity*.

> What is the good of drawing up, on paper, rules for social behavior, if we know that, in fact, our greed, cowardice, ill temper, and self conceit are going to prevent us from keeping them? I do not mean for a moment that we ought not to think, and think hard, about improvements in our social and economic system. What I do mean is that all that thinking will be mere moonshine unless we realize that nothing but the courage and unselfishness of individuals is ever going to make any system work properly . . . You cannot make men good by law: and without good men you cannot have a good society. That is why we must go on to think of the . . . morality inside the individual.[43]

Lewis's critique anticipates Anscombe's: a legalistic conception of morality fails to capture something foundational about ethics and morality. Without accounting for the virtues and character traits that make a person good, all the moral rules in the world are so much moonshine. Any comprehensive ethics must address this fundamental truth.

So there are important reasons to think that any ethics lacking an account of character and virtue is incomplete. And we will see as we proceed that there are some distinct advantages to bringing a virtue theory perspective to environmental ethics. However, for the moment, it's worth returning to the three criticisms of utilitarianism and deontology that were raised in the previous chapter. In Chapter 1, I noted that deontology and utilitarianism are hamstrung by an over-emphasis on rules for conduct, by a relatively narrow conception of the sorts of issues that are addressed by moral philosophy, and by rhetorical problems associated with a tendency to express themselves in terms of prohibition. Although virtue ethics is not without its own difficulties, some of which will be addressed in what follows, it does have advantages with respect to these problems.

First, although virtue ethics is not opposed to rules, it dispenses with the impossible task of coming up with a *single* rule or litmus test—like the categorical imperative or the greatest happiness principle—that would provide sufficient guidance for ethical living. It is a common error to move from the conclusion that something is true or right in this situation to the claim that it is true or right full stop. Virtue ethics recognizes that ethical rules are only "for the most part true," that is, they may have to be bent or broken in specific, uncommon situations; therefore, it relies instead on the idea that cultivating a virtuous character will enable one to take into account any relevant rule or guideline and make the best choice in fluid and complex real-world situations. It's useful to have rules as a kind of shorthand for ethical deliberation, especially if those rules have been well thought out and tested by experience over the course of history in one cultural tradition or another. However, in the lonely emergencies of life, confronted by really difficult dilemmas or genuinely novel circumstances, we fall back on character.[44] This would be true even if one were trying to be a strict deontologist or utilitarian, because a good person and a bad person will formulate and apply the categorical imperative and the principle of greatest happiness differently. Rules are useful, but in real crises it is character that counts.

Second, virtue ethics suggests that the field of ethical relevance is much, much wider than is generally the case under a traditional deontological or utilitarian approach. The latter approaches tend to focus on relationships between rational beings or, if undertaken with an environmental consciousness, on questions that lend themselves to deontological or utilitarian analysis. Because of this they are well-suited to addressing certain sorts of questions, such as those having to do with justice (e.g., the equitable distribution of resources), honesty (e.g., whether or not a person should tell the truth), or value (e.g., whether ecosystems have extrinsic or intrinsic value).

However, when we focus on what it means to be a good person— that is, when we focus on the agent rather than the action—a number of things come to light that never appear when we merely ask what makes a particular action moral or right. While questions of justice and honesty are important, the virtue ethicist is also concerned with temperance, self-cultivation, courage, humility, simplicity, and similar dispositions, always with a view toward how virtues contribute to individual, social, or environmental flourishing. This wider ethical scope is welcome both because it paints a more accurate and more complete picture *and* because it naturally lends itself to encompassing heretofore hidden areas of ethical relevance, including the environment. The relative lack of emphasis on rules in virtue ethics stems, in part, from its keen sensitivity to context and attention to relevant details. This goes well beyond an appreciation of the differences between different agents. Sensitivity to context and attention to detail will also include an appreciation of the time, place, and history relevant to the ethical choice in question. That kind of sensitivity and attention to detail leads quite naturally to an appreciation of the environment and its role as the background context in which all action and all flourishing take place.

Third, and perhaps most importantly, environmental virtue ethics shifts the focus of environmental thinking away from a discourse of prohibition and sacrifice toward a discourse of flourishing. Consider here the problem of the broad-but-shallow support for the environment among Americans: a large percentage of Americans claim to be concerned about environmental issues, but most of them are unwilling to make changes in their lifestyles, "sacrifices," in order to do anything about it.[45] If the academic (and activist) expression of environmental ethics has been formed by post-Enlightenment ethical thought, the practical consequence of this is that the public hears the imperatives of environmental ethics in terms of a list of rules—"thou shalt nots" that, collectively, represent a series of *sacrifices* we are duty bound to make in order to forestall an even greater catastrophe. A sacrifice is generally seen as burden or an evil to be avoided. As such, it is usually only undertaken in order to avoid an even greater evil. For example, a person might sacrifice eating rich foods in order to avoid the greater evil of a second heart attack. However, as long as environmentalism is seen as a sacrifice—a cross we must bear or an albatross hung on our collective neck by the previous generation—people are unlikely to enthusiastically embrace environmentalism or any of the changes it suggests to our current lifestyle. Most people will put off making a sacrifice until it is absolutely necessary and, unfortunately, all current models suggest that such a delay is likely to have disastrous consequences.

A virtue-oriented approach, however, is capable of framing responses to environmental crises in terms of flourishing and living well rather than, or in addition to, sacrifice. It speaks in the optative mood as well as the imperative and prohibitive moods. And framing makes all the difference in terms of rhetorical efficacy. Nobody wants to *sacrifice*, but everyone wants to *flourish*. Reframing the problems in these terms reveals environmental virtues such as simplicity, sustainability, localism, and restraint to be desirable traits rather than sacrifices or impositions. It does this by considering what it means to flourish or live well and by figuring out which things (dispositions, behaviors, goods, and so forth) genuinely serve this goal and which do not. In contemporary America, many of the things that we pursue as goods are not only environmentally destructive but also work at cross-purposes to our own flourishing. Once we realize this, giving up these things is no longer seen as a sacrifice, because the things in question are no longer seen as goods. Imagine the power of a discourse that argues simple living would be desirable even if we lived in a world of infinite resources. Environmental virtue ethics makes, to use a well-known aphorism, a virtue of a necessity.

Of course, this is not to say that achieving environmental ends will be as simple as changing the way that we make our point, nor to say that there is not a role for rules, prohibitions, and imperatives. Things are much more complex—psychologically, politically, and socially—than that. Nevertheless, at the very least environmental philosophers and activists should couple the "doom-and-gloom" approach—often perceived as alarmist, even if true—with an approach that addresses the innate desire of most people to live well. In advocating for environmental causes we should address people's *hopes* as well as their *fears*, and virtue ethics—especially, as we will see, when articulated through narrative—seems to offer one of the very best ways to combine these tactics.

3

Virtue

A Constellation of Concerns

It is no easy task to be good. For in everything it is no easy task to find the middle . . . anyone can get angry—that is easy—or give and spend money; but to do this to the right person, to the right extent, at the right time, with the right motive, and in the right way, *that* is not for everyone, nor is it easy; wherefore goodness is both rare and laudable and noble.

—Aristotle, *Nicomachean Ethics*, II.9

One ought to be brave . . . because it is noble [*kalon*] to be so.

—Aristotle, *Nicomachean Ethics*, III.8

Moral education is impossible apart from the habitual vision of greatness.

—Alfred North Whitehead, *The Place of Classics in Education*

Virtue and Living Well

What Is Virtue?

In the next chapter, I'll discuss simplicity as an archetypal virtue. However, before doing so, some preliminaries need to be addressed. Chief among these issues is the nature of virtue itself. What does it mean to say something is a virtue?

Here we can be led astray either by the unreflective contemporary use of the term, which is largely ignorant of its philosophical meaning and history, or by overly theoretical academic accounts that sever the intimate link between virtue ethics and life. The former is hopelessly removed from the traditional meanings of virtue and unaware of its philosophical use, while the latter can be dangerously abstract and, consequently, ignored by the very people to whom it should be addressed. As Aristotle admonishes us, the point is not to determine the *eidos* of ethical desiderata in some Platonic fashion, but rather to actually become good ourselves.[1] What we need is a reasonably philosophically sophisticated account of virtue that also speaks to the common person. Such an account would be difficult at any time; however, as Alasdair MacIntyre and others have made clear, contemporary society is almost irredeemably detached from the history of ethical reflection, even from understanding the words used in talking about these subjects. Our terminology reflects a storied—but misunderstood or, more frequently, unknown—history drawing on Greek philosophy, Judaism, Christianity, Enlightenment philosophy, Freemasonry, and so on. The result? "We possess indeed simulacra of morality, we continue to use many of the key expressions. But we have—very largely, if not entirely—lost our comprehension, both theoretical and practical, of morality."[2] Consequently, speaking coherently about virtue will require the adoption of, or at the very least familiarity with, an archaic idiom and, simultaneously, a keen attention to our current social context.

Following Aristotle, I'll maintain that: virtues are character traits that dispose us to act in certain ways; virtues are something that we acquire—primarily through habituation but sometimes through more traditional teaching and learning—rather than something innate; the "habit" of virtue must be a deeply ingrained and complex disposition rather than simply a quirk or routine; genuine virtue means not only doing the right thing, but doing so with the right emotion, in the right way, at the right time, for the right reasons, toward the right objects, and so forth; and possessing virtues makes one a better person such that one is more likely to flourish. In other words I will use the term "virtue" in a manner that is broadly Aristotelian, inspired by and faithful to the spirit of his work without, however, engaging in hagiographic fidelity to the letter of his account. As fine as it is, Aristotle's account of virtue is incomplete and in need of supplementation. This is likely true in a number of ways, but none more important for the current inquiry than the fact that Aristotle does not address "environmental" virtues or the environmental manifestations of traditional virtues, nor does he fully appreciate the role of the environment in human flourishing. How, then, shall we supplement Aristotle's account?

I'll begin my own account by following certain thinkers who have laid the groundwork for a sound environmental virtue ethics. Phil Cafaro and Joshua Gambrel outline a good working definition of virtue for environmental virtue ethics by drawing on a number of prominent virtue ethicists.[3] Beginning with Aristotle and working forward to contemporary environmental philosopher Ronald Sandler, Cafaro and Gambrel circumscribe virtue in a progressively more detailed account, each layer of which expands the sphere of ethically significant dispositions and gives additional content to the account of what it means to flourish as a human being. My own account of virtue will follow theirs, with some modification, before adding a final point related to the role of narrative in virtue ethics.

Generally speaking, virtues are the traits, characteristics, or dispositions that we believe make a person a good person—"good" here taken in the broad, classical sense of excellence rather than the narrower, modern sense of virtue as law-abiding, pious, or chaste. Thus, a virtuous person is a person who is well equipped to succeed in certain distinctively human endeavors.[4] Just what these distinctively human endeavors are, and in what hierarchy they might be arranged, is the subject of much debate, and a subject to which we will return in later chapters. For now it is enough to acknowledge that the idea of virtue is inseparable from a conception of a *telos*, or goal, that orients and frames "the good life."[5] Characteristics that contribute to a worthwhile and excellent life only make sense in the context of some view of the purpose of human life. Different conceptions of the good life will necessarily entail different catalogues of the virtues.

As Cafaro and Gambrel point out, we can begin by following Aristotle, who tells us that virtues are traits that promote human flourishing, that is *eudaimonia*. That the virtues contribute to *eudaimonia*—"happiness" or "flourishing"—does not mean that being virtuous constitutes an impervious shield against the "slings and arrows of fate." Nor does it mean that a virtuous life will necessarily be full of the sort of merriment and delight we commonly think of as "happiness." Bad things can, and do, happen to good people. Good people can, and do, suffer, and sometimes they suffer precisely because they are good.[6] Nevertheless, a virtuous person is the sort of person who possesses the characteristics that are conducive to the well-being characteristic of human beings and who is, therefore, most likely to succeed in these endeavors and to flourish. Flourishing here must be viewed expansively, conceived in (at least) both individual and social terms. Friendship, for example, receives greater attention in Aristotle's main ethical work than any other subject, occupying two of the ten books of the *Nicomachean Ethics*. Moreover, for Aristotle, ethics itself is in some sense merely a propaedeutic work to politics.[7]

However, while Aristotle gives us a remarkably rich account of the virtues, environmental virtue ethicists have pointed out that an account of a successful, worthwhile, or excellent human life cannot be divorced from an account of the environment in which that life is lived. Therefore, developing the work of thinkers like Henry David Thoreau, John Muir, and Aldo Leopold, and following various contemporary environmental virtue ethicists, we must expand our account of virtue to include those traits that promote certain sorts of non-human flourishing including, potentially, that of plants, animals, ecosystems, and so forth. This is true *both* because the environment is essential to human flourishing (a degraded environment impairs our ability to flourish, and the more degraded the environment the greater the impairment) *and* because the environment and the things in it are valuable in themselves. People need "beauty as well as bread, places to play in and pray in, where Nature may heal and cheer and give strength to body and soul alike"[8]; but nature also has value of its own: "none of Nature's landscapes are ugly so long as they are wild."[9] So it seems that virtues are dispositions that support either human flourishing, whether individual or social, or non-human flourishing, or both.

Cafaro and Gambrel continue by adopting a naturalistic view of virtue—following Rosalind Hursthouse and Philippa Foot—that takes human beings as "one more natural kind that has evolved on earth."[10] As such, they assert that the model of ethological judgment used in biology proves useful for virtue ethics. Evaluating humans in the context of the "type of biological being" that they are reveals certain criteria by which we may judge an individual's flourishing or lack thereof. Philippa Foot argues that when we are speaking of the goodness of living things we are speaking of a special sort of goodness, a goodness that is different from, and which requires a different grammar than that used when we speak of, the "secondary" goodness of non-living things.[11] "Natural goodness," which is only attributable to living things, is intrinsic goodness that depends upon the relation of the individual in question to the "life form" of its species.[12] A person is, or is not, good (a good example of a person) in a manner analogous to the way in which a cactus is, or is not, good (a good example of a cactus). Of course, because cacti and people are different, they have different goods; however, in both cases the goodness of an individual member of the species is judged in reference to the goodness of the type of species of which it is a member or the type of being it is. Unpacking this naturalistic perspective suggests that a minimal account of the virtues would include those characteristics that aid survival, the continuance of the species, securing pleasure and avoiding pain, and the well functioning of social groups—the first two because we are living, the third because we are sentient animals, and the last because we are social animals.[13]

However, we are not merely living, sentient, and social animals; we are also rational animals. Therefore, following Ronald Sandler's "pluralistic teleological account" of virtue, we should adopt a position that takes into account aspects of our rational nature.[14] Sandler begins by affirming the naturalistic premise that,

> human beings are essentially biological beings. Like all other living organisms, we are composed of matter, live and die, depend upon our environment for survival, are subject to the laws of nature, and have our "nature" in our genes. We are, like them, the product of evolutionary processes that have no goal, no teleology.[15]

Questions about how we ought to live must take this naturalistic assumption into account; such ethical questions are questions about the kind of "biological beings that we are, given the particular world we are in."[16] Thus, Sandler begins by endorsing the "Natural Goodness Account" of Philippa Foot and Rosalind Hursthouse and the four criteria for identifying virtues described above.

However, Sandler also points out that these basic naturalistic claims don't get us too far beyond the sorts of claims made by botanists and zoologists. These are useful claims to be sure and they cannot be ignored; but while they are all very well and good for botany and zoology, virtue ethics is complicated by the rational aspects of a human being and must say more. Scientific naturalism is incomplete.[17] Sandler's approach favors instead "ethical naturalism," which is less reductionist and evaluates human flourishing in terms of physical, emotional, environmental, and psychological criteria, not all of which are captured by scientific naturalism. Sandler begins with the naturalistic ends justified by scientific naturalism and the natural goodness approach to ethics, but he does not end there because there are other aspects of flourishing opened up by our rationality and its expression in culture, social practice, technology, and common beliefs about human flourishing.[18] Thus, to the four eudaimonistic ends identified by the natural goodness approach—(1) survival, (2) continuance of the species, (3) freedom from pain and securing characteristic pleasures, and (4) well-functioning social groups—Sandler adds three other broadly eudaimonistic ends: (5) autonomy; (6) the acquisition of knowledge; and (7) a meaningful life. Lastly, in a key move for *environmental* virtue ethics, Sandler includes (8) the realization of any non-eudaimonistic ends that make claims upon us.[19] The final account is naturalistic insofar as it is consistent with and motivated by scientific naturalism, teleological because traits are evaluated according to the conduciveness to achieving certain ends, and pluralistic because those ends are both eudaimonistic and non-eudaimonistic.[20]

In what follows we'll have occasion to return to the nature of pluralism, teleology, and naturalism; but for now we've summed up a functional
framework for addressing environmental virtue by drawing on thinkers
from Aristotle through Sandler. However, anticipating subsequent chapters, I would add here—following in various degrees thinkers like Ricoeur,
Kearney, MacIntyre, and Nussbaum—that our ideas about flourishing—
happiness, success, excellence, what constitutes a worthwhile life, and so
forth—are *primarily grasped and articulated in narratives*.[21]

Aristotle himself recognized the inescapable aesthetic component of
ethics when he described virtues as *kalon*, a term that is variously rendered
as "fine," "beautiful," "noble," or "good."[22] He goes so far as to claim that
the virtuous person chooses virtuous actions because they are *kalon*. Virtuous acts are praised precisely because, "as a result of virtue men tend to
do *kalon* deeds."[23] Indeed, it is the hallmark of virtuous people that they
take pleasure in *kalon* acts.[24] While this may initially sound odd to our
ears, accustomed as they are to thinking of good people being concerned
primarily with duty or consequences or the like, on reflection a significant
part of our conception of a good character trait or of a good life is the
sense that it is one that produces or can be recounted in a good story, both
well-formed and ethically admirable. Or again, when we think of the lives
we would want to lead, or celebrate the lives of those who have lived well,
there is an undeniable aesthetic element at work. When we live well, our
lives are beautiful, fine, and noble, even if we no longer commonly employ
adjectives like fine or noble either to the idea of a life story or to much else
in life. The fact is that we are as much narrative animals (*zoon poetikon*,
homo narrans) as we are rational animals (*zoon logon echon, homo sapiens*).
Or, put another way, aspects of our rationality are inherently, essentially,
inescapably narrative. Indeed, many of the aims of virtue enumerated in
the previous paragraphs are inextricably caught up in narrative structures,
and this is especially true of the more distinctively human aims developed
in Sandler's account. Therefore, by way of anticipation or foreshadowing,
I'll add a final point to the description of virtue: (9) that virtues are traits
that have a *kalon* aspect to them and which we understand narratively;
and, therefore, a fully articulated virtue ethics must include a robust narrative component.

Teleology

But in defining virtues in terms of "the good life," we have implicitly
raised the issue of a *telos*, the goal at which life aims and, if it is a good
life, the achievement of which makes it good. This is not accidental, for

any coherent account of virtue presupposes an account of the aim or goal of the virtues.[25]

> Within [the] teleological scheme [of the *Nicomachean Ethics*] there is a fundamental contrast between man-as-he-happens-to-be and man-as-he-could-be-if-he-realized-his-essential-nature. Ethics is the science which is to enable men to understand how they make the transition from the former state to the latter. Ethics therefore in this view presupposes some account of potentiality and act, some account of the essence of man as a rational animal and above all some account of the human *telos*.[26]

However, the discussion of a human *telos* or humans-as-they-ought-to-be (putting aside for the moment the notion of an "essential" nature) strikes many secular intellectuals and environmentalists as appealing to either religious faith or outdated metaphysical biology. There is, some argue, no human *telos*, no way that persons ought to be. The Enlightenment freed us from such notions and twentieth-century existentialism put the final nail in the coffin with Sartre's insistence that "existence precedes essence."[27]

The problem, MacIntyre points out, is that we began with a schema that assumed a difference between people-as-they-are and people-as-they-ought-to-be, and from there developed a theoretical and practical discipline called ethics to help people move from the former state to the latter. However, in our post-Enlightenment, post-existentialist world we are left with only people-as-they-are and with the ethical schema designed to achieve a *telos* we have abandoned or rejected. The ethical schema was developed with the *telos* in mind, but we have removed the *telos* and kept the ethical schema it oriented. "Since . . . moral injunctions were originally at home in a scheme in which their purpose was to correct, improve and educate . . . human nature, they are clearly not going to be such as could be deduced from true statements about human nature or justified in some other way by appealing to its characteristics."[28]

In certain circles it is fashionable to maintain, following Hume, that one cannot derive an "ought" from an "is." That is to say, beginning only with a-person-as-she-is we cannot legitimately derive a statement about a-person-as-she-ought-to-be. However, MacIntyre points out that this view is very obviously false in the case of "functional concepts" like "watch" or "farmer."[29] We define watches and farmers in terms of the purposes they are expected to serve—telling time and growing food, respectively. If a watch does not tell time, or is too cumbersome to be portable, it is a *bad* watch. If a farmer regularly harvests impressive yields of produce, and does so without harming her land and soil, she is a *good* farmer. So, at least in some cases, it clearly is possible to derive an ought from an is.

Moreover, while the Enlightenment and various subsequent philosophical traditions have sought to efface it, there is reason to think that we can, and sometimes still do, use "human" as a functional concept. Charles Taylor argues that personhood is closely tied to the question of who I ought to be. A person, on his account, is someone who can raise the question "Do I really want to be what I now am?," a subject "who can pose the *de jure* question: Is this the kind of being I ought to be, or really want to be?"[30] The view that humans have a characteristic function was certainly the norm for the classical Aristotelian tradition that gave us virtue ethics.

> But the use of 'man' as a functional concept is far older than Aristotle and it does not initially derive from Aristotle's metaphysical biology [or from Judeo-Christian theology]. It is rooted in the forms of social life to which the theorists of the classical tradition give expression. For according to that tradition to be a man is to fill a set of roles each of which has its own point and purpose: member of a family, citizen, soldier, philosopher, servant of God. It is only when a man is thought of as an individual prior to and apart from all roles that 'man' ceases to be a functional concept.[31]

It is the solipsism of Descartes, and the philosophical and intellectual traditions that followed from it, that has lead us to believe that there exists an independent, individual, monad-self prior to relationships with others and the world. While thinkers like Emmanuel Levinas and Paul Ricoeur were at pains to point this out, many people continue to believe and act as if the self is primordial and sociality is nothing but a secondary phenomenon added on, as it were, after the fact.

Virtue, then, does not spring fully formed from the void; it is related to social groups, traditions, and cultures. Cultivating virtues has to do with, among other things, what we do with what we inherit (our tradition, culture, language, but also our material circumstances, environment, and bodies), and this inheritance must always be taken up in light of our *telos*, itself circumscribed by the general human *telos*, by any other ends appropriate to our various roles, and by an ideal represented by a "fully" virtuous person. There are a variety of ways to think of the function of humans and of the human *telos*: based on a metaphysical biology (Aristotle); based on human capabilities (Nussbaum, Sen, Ricoeur); based on a transcendent or eschatological goal (various religious worldviews); based on the strivings of individual organisms or types of organisms (Sandler); and so on.

All this talk of *teloi* and of humans-as-they-ought-to-be might seem to suggest a transcendent or eschatological ideal. However, the bare notion that humans ought to live or be in some characteristic way neither requires nor rejects a transcendent aim, the existence of which would be beyond the scope of this inquiry. But, in any case, whether or not we include some transcendent element in our understanding of the human *telos*, our sense of a humans-as-they-ought-to-be should not fly in the face of biology, ecology, and other scientific modes of inquiry. Indeed, MacIntyre later acknowledged that, in his early work, he "was in error in supposing an ethics independent of biology to be possible."[32] The question isn't whether science and biology are necessary to understand human flourishing. They are. The question is whether science and biology are sufficient to understand human flourishing. They are not.

On my account the goal or intention of the virtues, the *telos* at which they aim, is broadly eudaimonistic, encompassing both nature and culture, both biology and narratology. Ignoring either side leaves us with an incomplete account of virtue and flourishing. Certain aspects of our flourishing are clearly grounded in a biological ethology of our nature. This is perhaps most clear in assessing the biological components of our well-being suggested by the natural goodness approach: survival; the continuance of the species; and securing the pleasures appropriate to our kind and enjoying freedom from pain. However, as Sandler rightly points out, a purely scientific or biological ethology cannot account for, much less exhaust, all the various components of our flourishing, especially those stemming from our rational nature. To say that ethics is not independent of biology need not, and should not, mean that ethics is reducible to biology, even very sophisticated biology.

A purely biological ethology does not capture the whole picture, and if we retain ethology as a model it must be in line with the etymology of the term. Ethology is "the study of" (*logia*) "character" (*ethos*). And while there are certainly very important biological aspects to character, biology does not exhaust the full range of what we mean when we speak of a person's character. Character is a product of both nature and nurture, biology and culture—of genes, experience, reflection, tradition, and habit. The naturalistic premise that we should make ethical evaluations in light of the "type of biological being a given being is" is exactly right, so long as it is not taken to mean that such evaluation should be made *only* in terms of the type of *biological* being a given being is. For example, it is culture, not nature, that suggests that our own flourishing includes paying attention to certain non-eudaimonistic values (although, again, we must be careful with too-easy nature/culture distinctions). Or, put another way, our "nature" includes not only our biological makeup but also the fact that we are rational animals, political or social animals, narrative animals, cultural animals, aesthetic animals, and so forth.[33]

A Typology of Virtue: Individual, Social, and Environmental

The differentiation between Aristotelian eudaimonistic virtue and the expanded catalogue of virtues implied by the progression through the successive stages outlined above seems to suggest that there are "non-environmental" virtues, dividing virtues into two types: (a) those that might fit in Aristotle's catalogue of virtues, and perhaps Hursthouse's and Foot's, and (b) "environmental" virtues, those that would be recognizable to Thoreau, Muir, and Leopold, as well as Sandler. Do "environmental" virtues and "non-environmental" virtues have different aims, goals, or ends? If so, could we run into situations wherein a disposition that facilitates individual flourishing undermines some sort of environmental flourishing, or wherein a disposition that promotes environmental flourishing undermines individual or social flourishing?

Yes, and no.

Common sense suggests that there are indeed "non-environmental" virtues. Certainly there are a number of virtues that contribute to individual or social flourishing, but which have little or nothing to do with the environment and environmental flourishing. For example, courtesy is a social virtue and, while it may, perhaps, have some incidental individual benefits, there are no discernable environmental benefits. Likewise, environmental virtues like non-anthropocentrism may lead us to value non-eudaimonistic ends that have little or nothing to do with individual or social flourishing. Some of these traits, like non-anthropocentrism, are exactly what Sandler has in mind when he discusses "non-eudaimonistic" virtues. So, on one hand, it does seem as if we must speak in terms of environmental and non-environmental virtue. Indeed, the monocular focus on non-environmental dispositions, and the consequent blindness to the environment, is the cause for the development of "environmental virtue ethics" in the first place. Thus there seems to be a good *prima facie* case for distinguishing between environmental and non-environmental virtue. On the other hand, even a cursory reflection will suggest that our individual flourishing cannot be so neatly separated from social flourishing, and neither individual nor social flourishing can take place independent of environmental flourishing. Can a trait really be a "virtue" if, in securing benefits for the individual, it unjustifiably and irrevocably destroys fundamental building blocks of social or environmental flourishing?

One way to think about this is to consider three broad areas of ethical concern: the self, others, and the environment.[34] Although we can distinguish between individual virtues, social virtues, and environmental virtues—or individual flourishing, social flourishing, and environmental flourishing—doing so can only be accomplished by an abstraction that is illusory and potentially misleading. In reality—that is, in the context of actual lived human lives—all three of these areas are intimately related and intertwined to the extent that we must also say that any character trait that *by its very nature* undermines flourishing in one or more of these spheres cannot be an authentic virtue.[35] So virtues are characteristics that facilitate either individual flourishing *or* social flourishing *or* environmental flourishing, *and* which do not by their very nature undermine any one of these three goods. This is not to deny that there are instances wherein virtues come into conflict and where we may need to choose between advancing a social good at the cost of an individual good, or an individual good at the cost of an environmental good. Doing so would fly in the face of both reason and experience. Rather, it is to acknowledge that while circumstances can bring genuine virtues into conflict, genuine virtues do not, *per se*, undermine any of these sorts of flourishing.

However, in the complexity of life competing goods cannot always be reconciled, competing virtues can come into irreconcilable conflict, moral luck influences who lives the good life, and experience is littered with inescapable tragic situations. I've already mentioned the cases of Antigone and HAL 9000; however, the frequency with which virtues come into conflict or goods are irreconcilable makes examples, both actual and literary, easy to come by: Agamemnon's sacrifice of Iphigenia; Abraham's (near) sacrifice of Isaac; Eteocles before the gates of Thebes; *Sophie's Choice*; the example of the young man seeking counsel in Sartre's *L'Existentialisme est un humanisme*; Euthyphro's dilemma at the beginning of the dialogue that bears his name; Truman's decision to drop a nuclear bomb on Hiroshima; Jean Valjean's theft of bread to feed members of his family in *Les Misérables*; the philosophical thought experiment proposed by Carneades of Cyrene in which one drowning sailor saves himself by using a plank that is therefore no longer available for a second sailor, who drowns; the various tensions between friendship and higher values in Somerset Maugham's *The Razor's Edge* or between solitude and sociality in Thoreau's *Walden*; Kathy's conflict between her friendship with Ruth and her love of Tommy in Kazuo Ishiguro's *Never Let Me Go*; and many, many others. The list of literary and historical examples is for all practical purposes endless, as are the host of decisions in each of our lives in which values come into conflict.

Human consumption, to use a specifically environmental example, clearly has environmental consequences. In fact, it would be safe to say that human consumption—exacerbated by both the level of that consumption and the number of people doing the consuming—is currently *the* primary driver of environmental degradation: loss of biodiversity, disruption of eco- systems, anthropogenic climate change, and so forth. As such, one might be tempted to think of consumption as a vice. However, to do so means pitting human survival (a good—for we have to consume some resources to survive) against environmental well-being (another good), and doing so in a confused manner. Human consumption is not *malum in se* and is no more inherently environmentally destructive than ursine consumption or cetacean consumption. Consumption itself is not environmentally vicious; the well-being of ecosystems *depends* on consumption between its constitu- ent parts. If our current patterns of consumption are vicious, it is because of the unsustainable extremes to which we have let our consumption grow. It is the reasons for which we consume, the manner in which we consume, the amount that we consume, and the excessive number of human con- sumers that make our consumption vicious, not the fact that we, like all other members of the biotic community, consume resources. It is entirely possible—if, today, practically very difficult in most societies—to consume virtuously and sustainably.

Therefore, in one sense calling something an "environmental virtue" is a pleonasm, for a virtuous person will necessarily possess dispositions and act in ways that support the flourishing of the environment, and any characteristic that fundamentally and unjustifiably undermines the ability of the environment to flourish is not a genuine virtue. It is, to be sure, a pleonasm with rhetorical uses insofar as it calls attention to the general neglect of the environmental aspects of virtue and flourishing in traditional accounts; however, if "environmental virtue ethics" is a pleonasm with rhetorical uses, we should hope that they will be short-lived and that, eventually, virtue ethicists will realize that any complete account of virtue must include the attitudes and dispositions that we currently address under the rubric of environmental virtue. A non-environmental virtue ethics is simply incomplete, just as an asocial virtue ethics would be incomplete.

However, while in one sense all virtues belong to a single class of virtuous dispositions, in another sense—speaking again in terms of emphasis rather than *eidos*—it does make sense to abstract and differentiate indi- vidual virtues, social virtues, and environmental virtues from virtue *tout court*. While virtue is one when we think of its essence (*eidos*) as "those characteristics a good person possesses, which make her good," they are multiple when we consider their different emphases as focused on individual, social, or environmental flourishing. So it can in practice be useful to speak of "environmental virtues." First, because clearly articulating the aim or intention of a given virtue helps us to better understand it. Second, because different virtues will in fact sometimes come into conflict and understanding the nature of each will make adjudicating these conflicts easier. Third, because the subclass of environmental virtue is underappreciated in talk about virtue, which is itself underappreciated in talk about ethics. Let's look briefly at three different traits that typify, respectively, individual virtue, social virtue, and environmental virtue, before moving on in the next chapter to a final example of a trait that exemplifies the inner unity of these three abstract categories.

"Individual" Virtue: Temperance

Individual virtues are traits aimed at the well-being or flourishing of the individual agent; they are eudaimonistic in the narrower, classical sense.[36] Although Aristotle was keenly aware of the interdependence of the individual and the community (or *polis*), his account of *eudaimonia* focused squarely on the former. This is so much the case that he even characterizes the love of true friendship as a form of self-love. While authenticity is perhaps the archetypal individual virtue and characteristics like integrity would also make good examples, a well-documented individual virtue, one that Aristotle addresses at length, is temperance.

Temperate persons strike the virtuous mean between excessive abstinence and self-indulgence, and they are sometimes characterized as self-controlled.[37] Temperance, like many of the virtues, is not a median point; it is generally closer to abstinence than to self-indulgence. Indeed, temperance would feel like abstinence to many contemporary Americans due to their largely self-indulgent habits. For example, the Food and Agriculture Organization of the United Nations suggests that the average daily consumption of Americans may be as high at 3,700 calories per day—this when an adult needs somewhere between 1,600 and 3,000 calories per day, depending on age, activity level, and so forth.[38] Not coincidentally, one in three Americans is currently classified as obese and another third are overweight.[39] However, while many people err toward self-indulgence, it is possible to fall into the contrary extreme of vicious abstinence. Insofar as abstinence is arguably a name for a legitimate virtue—for example, in the context of alcoholism or in certain religious traditions—we ought to keep in mind that here it designates a kind of self-destructive and vicious form of denial. Think here of self-destructive dieting. And, since virtue is concerned with choice, let's confine ourselves to considering the myriad ridiculous and faddish diets freely chosen out of a desire to achieve a certain look rather than psychological diseases like anorexia nervosa, which in some way compromise free choice.

Temperance is an individual virtue because its main concern is with properly regulating one's appetites—especially those having to do with bodily pleasure associated with food, drink, sex, and so forth—so that a temperate person is moderate with respect to her desires and her indulgence of them. Although there are undeniably social and environmental benefits to temperance—or harms associated with one of its corresponding vices: self-indulgence—the most direct and immediate consequences are individual and adhere to the agent in question.[40] If one's abstinence, for example, manifested itself in extreme dieting, one would be more likely to suffer from anemia, heart arrhythmias, and osteoporosis. Likewise, if one is self-indulgent and gluttonous, one is more likely to suffer from a host of ills, including obesity, diabetes, heart disease, and certain cancers. Both emaciation and obesity have numerous other consequences for one's quality of life such as habitual lack of energy, inability to fully engage in certain activities, and social reproach or stigmatization of varying degrees. Conversely, a temperate person is likely to enjoy good health, over a longer life, with greater psychological well-being and greater opportunity to participate in certain physical and social endeavors, to say nothing of a more stable personal economy (the latter in contrast, at least, to the self-indulgent). A temperate person is still able to indulge in activities that bring about bodily pleasures—indeed, insofar as extreme abstinence is also a vice she ought to do so—but she indulges in the right amount, at the right time, in the right way, with the right persons, toward the right objects, and so on, so that indulging these appetites contributes to her well-being rather than detracting from it through direct harm or by negatively affecting other, more important ends.

"Social" Virtue: Courtesy

Social or communal virtues are those traits that aim at promoting the well-being or flourishing of a social group. Courtesy is an excellent example of a social virtue, though neighborliness or civility would also serve as good examples. In contrast to temperance, courtesy is a disposition the primary aim of which is to lubricate the interactions within a social group and ensure that the relationships function well. Courtesy helps groups of people to get along better and interact more harmoniously. Of course, neither courtesy nor any other single disposition can guarantee that a social group will operate amicably, but it's relatively easy to see how such traits contribute to easier social interactions and how their absence leads to more stressful interactions, which can escalate to discord and even violence. It's true that we could point to some personal benefits that derive from having a courteous disposition, such as being thought of as a polite and agreeable person, feeling good about oneself, or simply getting to live in a more harmonious community. However, such individual benefits seem incidental to courtesy, and it's quite difficult to imagine any environmental benefit at all. The point of courtesy, not merely its intention or goal but also its main advantage, is clearly a social one.

At its most basic level, courtesy means thinking of other people and their feelings when acting, hence its association with respect, civility, and thoughtfulness. Such fellow-feeling generally manifests itself in minor gestures—saying "please" and "thank you," holding the door for others, giving up one's seat to the elderly or infirm, and so on—which will of course vary from culture to culture. While it is true that courtesy can also manifest itself in more extravagant gestures in which it approaches chivalry or gallantry, in its most common and essential manifestations it does not require extraordinary acts of sacrifice on behalf of others. Nor should we confuse courtesy with the *kabuki* of esoteric and complex styles of formal manners. Courtesy is not a country-club or black-tie virtue; it is an everyday disposition that manifests itself in actions exhibiting simple thoughtfulness and basic attentiveness to others. The excess of courtesy can be found in either obsequiousness or, perhaps, in extreme forms of self-effacement. A deficiency of courtesy, all too common in our time, is evident in the self-centered indifference to others and their feelings that we call rudeness.

"Environmental" Virtue: Holistic Thinking

Environmental virtues are traits that aim primarily at promoting the well-being or flourishing of the environment, including plants, non-human animals, and ecosystems.[41] Thus, some virtues may qualify as environmental even if they are not traits we would associate with the stereotypical environmentalist. In her groundbreaking work *Dirty Virtues*, Louke van Wensveen lists no fewer than 189 virtues gleaned from a reading of post-1970 environmental literature.[42] Many of these traits overlap heavily with those we might classify under individual virtue or social virtue, a point to which we will return in a moment; but Wensveen also catalogs a number of specifically environmental virtues, including biocentrism, cosmocentrism, (recognition of) interdependence, holistic thinking, stewardship, and sustainability.

Holistic thinking, one of the virtues identified by Wensveen, can serve as an illustration of environmental virtue. Again, it's true that such thinking is likely to have some indirect individual and social benefits; holistic thinking is, after all, holistic. Moreover, in the long run, no individual or society can flourish in a severely degraded environment. Nevertheless, precisely because of the historical neglect of the environmental aspects of the whole, its contemporary manifestation as a virtue takes the form of a marked and strident emphasis on the environment in one's thinking. Here we might take some solace in the increasing visibility of environmental issues in the public consciousness, as well as books challenging our anthropocentric bias in philosophy and other disciplines. Consider Jacques Derrida's *The Animal That Therefore I Am*, Len Lawlor's *This is Not Sufficient*, Jean-Christophe Bailly's *The Animal Side*, Kelly Oliver's *Animal Lessons*, Donna Haraway's *When Species Meet (Posthumanities)*, and many other recent efforts to rethink anthropocentrism and human exceptionalism.[43]

Holistic thinking implies the recognition of interconnectedness and interdependence, would recommend itself to virtues like stewardship and sustainability, and is more than congenial to biocentrism and non-anthropocentrism. Too little holistic thinking manifests itself in certain forms of abstraction, about which I will have more to say later, which err in viewing parts as neatly separable from the whole. It also results in narrowness of vision or concern, blindness to connections between parts of a system, an unjustifiable care for a part of the world at the expense of the whole, losing the forest for the trees, and so forth. This deficient vice is evident in the view that the world is nothing more than a well of resources for us to use, exploit, or degrade, in whatever way best serves our short-term interests. It is the characteristic worldview of the industrial age. In contrast, an excessive commitment to holistic thinking would fall prey to a sort of ecological utilitarianism where the well-being of the whole, taken in the broadest sense, becomes the only concern and the constituent parts are only considered in terms of instrumental service to this broader goal, if at all. Such thinking leads to a detached and speculative sort of environmentalism that thinks holistically but lacks any deep connection with or concern for *particular* places and *specific* beings. That lack of concern for particulars can also result in arguments that, moving beyond legitimate and necessary critiques of population growth, view humans as a "virus" that, by its very nature, is incompatible with the flourishing of the planet.

Virtue

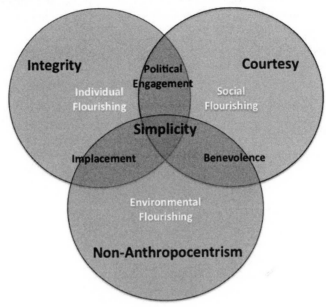

The figure above attempts to convey the way in which different virtues operate in different overlapping spheres; but, again, we must keep in mind that these are matters of emphasis rather than *eidos*. It is true that a number of virtues have more than one benefit, and in some cases it will be a matter of debate whether a given trait is more properly individual, environmental, or social in nature: non-anthropocentrism may have some individual or social benefits, courtesy may have individual benefits, temperance has social and environmental benefits, and so on. I distinguish these spheres theoretically in order to draw attention to the different aspects of flourishing—individual, social, and environmental—and the way in which different dispositions contribute to different spheres, while acknowledging that a number of virtues clearly have influence or manifestations in more than one sphere. In fact, in practice—that is to say, in life, where all this really matters—individual virtues, social virtues, and environmental virtues overlap to a surprising degree. This feature of virtue is one of the happy truths of environmentalism: the things we need to do in order to "save the planet" are very often also things that will improve our communities and our own individual lives. Simplicity, the topic of the next chapter, is an excellent example of this synergy. Nevertheless, we should be on guard against a too-rosy Pollyannaism that ignores conflict and tragedy. Individual virtues can come into conflict with social virtues or environmental virtues. And the flourishing of the society or environment might sometime require sacrifice by the individual. But these are simply particular cases of a more general ethical reality: virtues, of whatever sort, can come into conflict with other virtues. Conflicts, real or potential, between honesty and loyalty, or between simplicity and charity, are not an indication that any one of these traits is not a virtue; rather, it is an indication of the irreducible complexity of ethical life.

A Story of Simplicity

A Case Study in Virtue

A man there was, though some did count him mad / The more he cast away, the more he had.

—John Bunyan, *The Pilgrim's Progress*

A cultivated man becomes ashamed of his property, out of new respect for his nature.

—Ralph Waldo Emerson, *Self-Reliance*

In anything at all, perfection is finally attained not when there is no longer anything to add, but when there is no longer anything to take away, when a body has been stripped down to its nakedness.

—Antoine de St. Exupéry, *Wind, Sand and Stars*

Although it is useful to classify virtues as individual, social, or environmental—both in order to better understand them and in order to show that qualifying as a virtue does not require that a trait address *all* the various and sundry ills of the world—the examples used in the previous chapter should give us some indication of the extent to which the abstract categories of individual, social, and environmental virtues bleed into each other in practice and application. It's safe to say that many virtues, even when their emphasis is clearly in one area, have a scope that touches on more than one of these categories. This shouldn't be surprising; it is a natural consequence of the aforementioned intimate relationship between individual, social, and environmental flourishing. We are social beings, and any account of flourishing that fails to take into account other people and the traits that help to constitute good relationships with them fails to fully account for our flourishing. Similarly, we are fundamentally natural beings and any account of flourishing that fails to take into account the wider environment in which we have evolved and to which we are adapted, as well as the traits that help us to live in a good relationship with it, fails to fully account for our flourishing. However, while many virtues cross the boundaries between individual, social, and environmental flourishing, some virtues illustrate the intimate connections between these categories particularly well, to the extent that it would be difficult to say with certainty where their emphasis lies. Simplicity is such a virtue, and understanding it will go some way toward illustrating the extent to which individual, social, and environmental flourishing are connected.

The Scope of Simplicity: More Than Material Restraint

The virtue of simplicity is often viewed exclusively in terms of material restraint or austerity. However, while material simplicity is arguably the most significant manifestation of the virtue, or at least the most significant manifestation in a culture that is decidedly not simple with respect to materialism, it does not exhaust the scope of this disposition. Simplicity has to do with more than simply reducing consumption, though that is an integral aspect of it.[1] Instead, we should think of the virtue of simplicity in the expansive terms in which Henry David Thoreau did.[2]

Thoreau is generally not a thinker who leaps to mind when one thinks of virtue ethics. However, Phil Cafaro makes a convincing case that this is an oversight and that Thoreau can be fruitfully read as a virtue ethicist.[3] Cafaro's thesis is buttressed by a number of passages where we can find more or less explicit warrant for such a reading in *Walden* itself. For example, after devising a method for determining the depth of the local ponds through observation of the shoreline and contours of the pond in question, Thoreau claims, "what I have observed of the pond is no less true in ethics."[4]

> [D]raw lines through the length and breadth of the aggregate of a man's particular daily behaviors and waves of life into his coves and inlets, and where they intersect will be the height or depth of his character. Perhaps we need only to know how his shores trend and his adjacent country or circumstances, to infer his depth and concealed bottom. If he is surrounded by mountainous circumstances, an Achillean shore, whose peaks

overshadow and are reflected in his bosom, they suggest a corresponding depth in him. But a low and smooth shore proves
him shallow on that side.[5]

The relation between a person's "shoreline" (her patterns of behavior) and
her "depth" (her character) is "not whimsical" says Thoreau. Rather, a
person's character is shaped by her daily behaviors, and changes in the
topography of her shore (changes of behavior) will cause a corresponding
change in her depth (character). This concern with virtue and habituation
is reflected later in *Walden* in a quotation from Mencius:

> A return to goodness is produced each day in the tranquil and
> beneficent breath of the morning, causes that in respect to the
> love of virtue and the hatred of vice, one approaches a little
> the primitive nature of man, as the sprouts of the forest which
> has been felled. In like manner the evil which one does in the
> interval of a day prevents the germs of virtues which began to
> spring up again from developing themselves and destroys them.[6]

Thoreau, it turns out, is among other things a sort of idiosyncratic, poetic,
American virtue ethicist, and his reflections on simplicity paint a rich
picture of a virtue with surprising breadth and depth.

"Let us consider the way in which we *spend* our lives."[7] With this challenge, Thoreau begins *Life Without Principle*, "a brilliant summary of [his]
most fundamental and passionately held beliefs."[8] In this context, "spend" is
a well-chosen word for at least two reasons. First, it employs a fiscal analogy
that will no doubt be familiar to those most in need of hearing Thoreau's
message. Second, it reminds us of the fact that our life, like our finances,
is a finite resource. It should go without saying that the finitude of one's
life ought to give one pause not only because it is of greater value than
money, but also because, unlike one's financial books, the ledger recording
the amount of life one has left is open to God alone. Thoreau builds on
this trope by developing a sort of existential economic principle: "The cost
of a thing is the amount of what I will call life which is required to be
exchanged for it, immediately or in the long run."[9] We spend money to
get things, but spend life to get money. The underlying point, of course,
is that the lives of most people are not spent well at all:

> The better part of the man is soon ploughed into the soil for
> compost. By a seeming fate, commonly called necessity, they are
> employed, as it says in an old book, laying up treasures which

moth and rust will corrupt and thieves break through and steal.
It is a fool's life, as they will find when they get to the end of
it, if not before.[10]

In most cases, the things for which we exchange our lives are immeasurably
less valuable than the life-cost that we pay. This is the case, first, because
most people spend their lives without thought to the fact that life is a finite
resource and, second, because most people trade this most precious resource
for superfluities rather than necessities. The antidote to this murderous, or
better yet *suicidal*, economy can be summed up in one word: simplicity.

    Life Without Principle is a remarkably rich essay and, given that it
is "a brilliant summary of [Thoreau's] most fundamental and passionately
held beliefs," it is difficult to further condense his thoughts here. Thoreau
inhabits simplicity as something like a comprehensive worldview or disposition. Nevertheless, in order to frame Thoreau's call to simplicity, we can
think of his exhortation in terms of three kinds of simplicity: material,
intellectual, and vocational.

Business/Busyness

One area in which Thoreau asks us to apply simplicity is our "business."
"[T]here is nothing, not even crime, more opposed to poetry, to philosophy,
ay, to life itself, than this incessant business."[11] This simplification of business takes two forms, one specific and the other general.

    Specifically, one should "get [one's] living by loving"; that is, a person
should aim at finding a vocation rather than a career.[12] If our work is merely
a means of securing money, we have been cheated, for money—and most
of the things it buys—is not generally a commodity worth trading one's
life for. "The ways by which you may get money almost without exception
lead downward. To have done anything by which you earned money *merely*
is to have been truly idle or worse. If the laborer gets no more the wages
which his employer pays him, he is cheated, he cheats himself."[13] It is not
that work is evil per se; far from it. However, misapprehending the real
nature of flourishing can lead us to work at the wrong things, for the wrong
reasons, and in the wrong amount. Thoreau's own experiment at Walden
Pond was, in large measure, meant to help him get clear on the "chief
end of man"—that is to say the purpose or *telos* of living—so that he did
not, like so many of his contemporaries, rush to an overly hasty judgment
about it.[14] He points out that most people would be insulted if it were suggested that they be employed throwing stones over a wall and back again.
Such employment would be met with almost universal scorn because the

labor is without purpose, "but many are no more worthily employed now."[15] Such labor is Sisyphean in the true sense. Sisyphus is in Hell, not because of the weight of the rock, or the steepness of the hill, or the darkness of Hades, but because his labor has no purpose. Camus notwithstanding, the Greeks knew that Hell needed neither fire nor thumbscrews—an eternally meaningless existence is a more than adequate torture.

More generally, we ought to reduce our business qua busyness, the feeling that we need always to be doing something: "I wish to suggest that a man may be very industrious, and yet not spend his time well."[16] Most of the illnesses of the society that Thoreau critiqued are still evident today and many have worsened. However, perhaps none has become as acute as the contemporary manifestation of the drive to remain busy.[17] In the United States this busyness is evident in a manic work ethic characterized by one of the longest per-annum workloads in the industrialized world, a problem compounded by "working lunches," and "holidays" spent returning emails and cellphone calls to clients. Modern society recognizes no Sabbath, religious or secular.[18] In fact, the frenetic pace of work influences our lives more deeply than we might imagine, and even when we do take time off work, the busyness of business spills over into the busyness of leisure. "A stereotyped but unconscious despair is concealed even under what are called the games and amusements of mankind."[19] The on-the-go, 24/7 mania that characterizes much of our contemporary culture would strike Thoreau as a depressing exacerbation of the problems he observed in his own time.

Needs and Wants

The second area where Thoreau suggests we simplify our lives is closely linked to the first: he asks us to consider material simplicity and its relation to our well-being by distinguishing our needs from our wants:

> Those slight labors which afford me a livelihood, and by which it is allowed that I am to some extent serviceable to my contemporaries, are as yet commonly a pleasure to me, and I am not often reminded that they are a necessity. So far I am successful. But I foresee that if my wants should be much increased, the labor required to supply them would become a drudgery.[20]

Distinguishing needs from wants is at the root of any material simplicity seen as a virtue, but, as always, the reason or motivation matters. When we give up something we have or want in order to avoid an evil, we are not being virtuously simple. Such a sacrifice could well be a good act and a manifestation of another virtue such as self-sacrifice, compassion, care, or benevolence, but it is not a manifestation of virtuous simplicity. When motivated only by the desire to avoid a greater evil—as when we cut back on frivolous consumption to ensure there is money to pay the rent—simplicity becomes nothing more than a distasteful but necessary means to an end. However, while a virtuous person does not deny the utilitarian benefits of simplicity, she also sees simplicity as good and desirable in itself. Virtuous simplicity stems from an appreciation of the proper role of goods in human flourishing and, consequently, a desire to pursue material goods only insofar as they contribute to flourishing. Consumption is, up to a point, a necessary part of flourishing; but the opportunity cost of consuming beyond that point results in wasted effort and wasted time directed at something that is at best no longer helpful and at worst, and more commonly, actually harmful to one's well-being.

We know from *Walden* that, for Thoreau, basic physical needs are comparatively few: food, shelter, clothing, and fuel. Everything else is, strictly speaking, a want. Needs and wants are both purchased with the same finite commodity: life. We cannot forgo needs, as they are essential for the maintenance of life. However, a reduction of wants is, according to Thoreau's calculus, directly proportional to an increase in life. Having fewer wants means spending less time working to satisfy those wants. Less time working means a greater *quantity* of life, in the sense that life is spent on the "essentials" rather than on the acquisition of superfluities.[21] Because there are fewer hours that are needlessly "spent," more of one's life remains one's own. Less time working also means a greater *quality* of life: "Most men, even in this comparatively free country, through mere ignorance and mistake, are so occupied with the factitious cares and superfluously coarse labors of life that its finer fruits cannot be plucked by them."[22]

It's worth pointing out that Thoreau is not suggesting that we reject our wants and subsist by satisfying our needs alone. One want in particular will help us to see the relative value of needs and various wants: the "chief want" of all persons, which according to Thoreau is a "high and earnest purpose," that is, a meaningful existence.[23] As he put it, "[w]hen [a person] has obtained those things which are necessary to life, there is another alternative than to obtain the superfluities; and that is to adventure on life now, his vacation from humbler toil having commenced."[24] When bare existence is at stake, survival tends, rightly, to occupy one's energy. However, once a person has enough to eat, her next concern is not better food, but meaning in her life.

However, while all wants are "artificial"—because they are not needs—some wants are more artificial than others, so to speak. The chief want, a "high and earnest purpose," is important enough that it approaches the level of need. But what of other wants? How can we distinguish needs from wants, and acceptable wants from unacceptable wants? Needs are necessary for life and so can be identified though simplification. To use a somewhat absurd example, try holding your breath. Most people will find in a minute or so that, indeed, oxygen is a necessity. Anything that is not a necessity is, strictly speaking, a want. However, we can roughly distinguish between acceptable wants and unacceptable wants in the following way: acceptable wants facilitate our high and earnest purpose, unacceptable wants do not. The chief want—each person's answer to the question of life's meaning, her "high" purpose, her vocation—allows a person to place all other wants in a rough hierarchy. Why did Thoreau bring books, journals, pencils, and lamps along on his grand adventure in simplicity? Because while these things are not necessary in the strict sense, they are necessary for a man pursuing the vocation of philosopher or thinker; that is to say, these things were acceptable wants for Henry David Thoreau.[25]

Thinking

The third sort of simplicity that Thoreau asks us to consider in *Life Without Principle* is related to our thinking. Again, the point is to remove the extraneous or superficial in order to make room for the essential:

> Not without a slight shudder at the danger, I often perceive how near I had come to admitting into my mind the details of some trivial affair,—the news of the street; and I am astonished to observe how willing men are to lumber their minds with such rubbish,—to permit idle rumors and incidents of the most insignificant kind to intrude on ground which should be sacred to thought. Shall the mind be a public arena, where the affairs of the street and the gossip of the tea-table chiefly are discussed? Or shall it be a quarter of heaven itself,—a hypæthral temple, consecrated to the service of gods?[26]

As with the previous examples of simplicity, when we spend time thinking we spend life and, as in all expenditures, we may spend well or poorly. Although one might argue that we are capable of thinking while engaging in other activities, trivial thinking harbors intrinsic dangers beyond the concession to busyness that multitasking would no doubt represent for Thoreau. Trivial or superficial thinking is habit-forming: "I believe that the mind can be permanently profaned by the habit of attending to trivial things, so that all our thoughts shall be tinged with triviality."[27] Thoreau insisted that the trivial thoughts and voyeuristic gossip that masqueraded as news, culture, and intellectual exchange in his day had the effect of habituating the mind to trivial and superficial thinking—the "thoroughfare" of one's soul becoming "rutted" by the repeated movement of trivial information back and forth—leaving people incapable of inward, philosophic, or essential thinking.[28]

If the news of Thoreau's day amounted to so much gossip, inhibiting those involved from more substantial thought, what will we say of our own? Thoreau complained hyperbolically that people would, after a half hour's nap, awaken to ask "what's the news?" How much more the case is this obsessive concern with the minutia of "what's happening" in a world of Facebook and Twitter, where people check their cellphone gossip-feeds multiple times in an hour, while at dinner with friends, while on dates, while in class, in church, and at funerals? It all takes place "as if the main object were to talk [or read, or think] fast and not to talk [or read, or think] sensibly."[29] Thoreau continues, commenting on rumors of a planned trans-Atlantic telegraph cable, "we are eager to tunnel under the Atlantic and bring the old world some weeks nearer to the new; but perchance the first news that will leak through into the broad, flapping American ear will be that the Princess Adelaide has the whooping cough."[30] Looking at contemporary "news" media, his quip seems depressingly prescient.

Our society, even more than Thoreau's, presents us with substantial challenges to a simple life. In the United States, any reasonably normal person has, by the time she is old enough to come across Thoreau's work, been thoroughly conditioned by a society that ceaselessly promotes the messages that "more is better" and "too much is never enough." What, then, are we to do? "If we have thus desecrated ourselves,—and who has not?—the remedy will be by wariness and devotion to reconsecrate ourselves. . . ."[31] Such reconsecration would be equally well directed at our compulsive bus(i/y)ness, our tendency to over-indulge our wants, or our habits of trivial thinking. The remedy in each case is the same: simplicity. "The only cure . . . is a rigid economy, a stern and more than Spartan simplicity of life and elevation of purpose."[32]

So while the virtue of simplicity is indeed about the way we desire and consume material goods, it also touches on the way we earn a living, how we recreate and spend our leisure time, the sorts of relationships we have with others, and what we read, talk, and think about. Indeed, thus conceived, simplicity is a disposition or trait that speaks to an astonishingly diverse set of circumstances and issues. It is for this reason that simplicity should be considered one of the keystones of environmental virtue.

The Scope of Simplicity: A "Comprehensive" Virtue

This expansive sort of simplicity to which Thoreau exhorts us—bracketing for the moment the question of whether his own expression of this trait is appropriately virtuous—does more than touch on the three spheres of virtue—individual, social, and environmental—it is deeply involved in each one. It's true that material simplicity remains the most obvious contributor to individual, social, and environmental well-being, and the following characterizations will bear this out; however, having established that simplicity is something more than what is captured by "restrained material consumption," we are now better equipped to see clearly the ways in which simplicity supports the comprehensive sort of well-being associated with the interlocking nature of individual, social, and environmental flourishing.

Simplicity and the Individual

Thoreau's arguments in *Walden* and *Life Without Principle* paint a vivid picture of some of the individual benefits of simplicity, which we have already addressed in some detail. But not all people agree that simplicity is a virtue. Benjamin Friedman goes so far as to suggest there is a moral or ethical benefit to wealth: that a growing, more affluent economy will actually make its citizens better human beings.[33] He's not alone. George Gilder brazenly claims that entrepreneurs "embody and fulfill the sweet and mysterious consolations of the Sermon on the Mount."[34] Lloyd Blankfein, CEO of Goldman Sachs, claimed in his role as a banker he was engaged in "God's work" (this shortly after Goldman Sachs was implicated in the sub-prime mortgage crisis).[35] And former Senator Phil Gramm, an avid proponent of deregulation who lauded the benefits of high-interest, sub-prime lending, calls Wall Street "a holy place."[36]

But against these apostles of growth and consumption, contemporary scholarship—philosophical, sociological, and psychological—bears out many of Thoreau's insights, although we might quibble over details since one person's simplicity could well be too ascetic or too extravagant in the case of another person. Simplicity, he says, enables us to "pick the finer fruits of life" by protecting us from the trivial and intemperate aspects of consumption. It supports other important virtues like independence (realizing how little material goods contribute to our well-being we will be less likely to sell ourselves to jobs that are not fulfilling), self-sufficiency (because it reduces our wants, and often makes those that remain easier to achieve), and integrity (because we are less likely to compromise our conscience to save our bank account). It focuses our thinking and our purpose, enabling us to identify and pursue goals that genuinely contribute to the meaningfulness of our lives, and it strengthens our bodies.

But if simplicity is a virtue then it is possible to err in one of two ways: either by excessive simplicity (perhaps an abstinence that unnecessarily undermines other worthwhile goals or achievements) or by insufficient simplicity (wastefulness or gluttonous extravagance). While the former is not insignificant—as in cases of vicious self-denial—it is the latter with which we should be most concerned. This is because the vice of extravagance is so distressingly common. Indeed, so common that it is often overlooked as a vice, and even lauded as a virtue. To a large degree we have abandoned the notion that pride, avarice, envy, and lust are vices. Books like *Bowling Alone*, *Affluenza*, *Happiness*, *Luxury Fever*, and *The Paradox of Choice*—to say nothing of the myriad academic articles, surveys, and polls on which they are based—document in detail the disturbing and deleterious side of materialism, consumerism, and other manifestations of the vice of extravagance.[37] It boils down to this: for most citizens of the "global north" more money and increased consumption are no longer leading to increased happiness or well-being. As Bill McKibben poetically puts it, for almost all of human history the birds of More and Better sat side by side on a branch, and one could hit them both with the single stone of one's life.[38] However, in the United States and the rest of the global north, the bird of Better has flown off to a different branch. Now, if we cast the stone of our life at More, we no longer get Better as a consequence; now we must choose between More and Better.

More consumption only gets you a better life up to a certain point, and a relatively modest point at that. Different scholars may debate the details of the exact amount, which is always going to be relative to inflation, differing costs of living, diverse social contexts, and so forth. But what is fairly clear is that in absolute terms money does not contribute to happiness or well-being once one has sufficient resources to secure the basic necessities—food, shelter, clothing, reasonable security for one's family—and some modest conveniences, and that this amount is much, much lower than people generally assume in affluent societies.[39] Once we have the basics, money loses much of its usefulness. As Thoreau says, once we have secured the necessities of life, our goal should not be to secure as many of life's superfluities as possible, but to "adventure on" in life, having been freed from "humbler toil." As we'll see, beyond a modest limit, the pursuit of material gain does not contribute to our happiness and, indeed, may work at cross-purposes to it. Once we have crossed this threshold, our happiness is better served through diverse and exciting experiences, rich and rewarding relationships, and "self-actualization" or self-development.

It has been one of mankind's great accomplishments to have successfully addressed the problem of securing and consuming enough material resources to flourish; and it has been one of our greatest follies to continue to act as if we have not already successfully addressed this problem.[40]

If money does not buy happiness, why do we continue to act as if it does? There are several reasons, but surely one component is an extraordinarily successful *narrative*. One of the major reasons we continue to act as if More will get us Better is because only a few generations ago this was still the case. Even in wildly affluent nations like the United States, families are often only a few generations removed from poverty. As individuals and as a nation, we are still acting out the roles that were successful in pulling us out of the Great Depression. Or, for immigrant families, narratives rooted in *an Gorta Mór* (the Great Hunger or "Irish Potato Famine"), the economic disaster of the Soviet Bloc, famine in the Horn of Africa, or the desperate poverty of Western China. As McKibben and others point out, we act as if money will buy happiness *because it did*, and did so recently enough that we haven't noticed that, for many of us, it no longer does. We're telling the same story and playing the same roles in the context of a world that is fundamentally different from the one in which the story of More originated.

Much of classical economic orthodoxy tells us that people are rational actors and we can therefore identify what makes people happy by looking at what they in fact choose. If people choose a certain amount and certain kind of consumption it is because that amount and that kind makes them happy. We might point out that there are unfalsifiable aspects to this claim because certain choices are restricted by contemporary society; we no longer have the option of choosing a radically different way of proceeding with respect to fossil fuels, the globalized marketplace, and so on—we can no longer just "opt out" of these structures and choose a different, better reality. However, while that practical point is damning enough, the real problem with rational actor orthodoxy is that people are not simple rational actors. Far from it. People can be, and very often are, quite bad at making choices that will maximize their happiness, because they are often mistaken about what will make them happy. These errors are linked to the fact that we make choices based on a complex constellation motives having to do with reason, emotion, social pressure, interpretation of past experience, hearsay, folklore, and belief. The configuration of this constellation can be explained more accurately with the tools of narrative discernment than those of pure, rational choice. And, consequently, embracing the idea of narrative discernment in ethics will direct us to more efficacious ways of bringing about the *re*configuration of such constellations to align more truly with individual, social, and environmental flourishing.

Another reason we pursue more is the status race, the desire to "keep *ahead* of the Joneses." Research shows that a major driver in consumption is a desire to have as much as, or more than, others. Hence the old chestnut: "being rich is making more than your brother-in-law." In the late '90s students at Harvard were asked if they would prefer a world in which (a) they earned 50k and others earned an average of 25k, or (b) a world in which they earned 100k and others averaged 250k.[41] Crucially, prices remained the same in either of these imaginary worlds (that is, the same as real prices). The majority of students preferred the first world, and this response has been consistently replicated in other, similar studies. People don't care so much about money in absolute terms, but they are concerned with relative wealth, that is with making as much as or more than those in their "reference group." Problematically, however, our reference group is no longer the brother-in-law, or even our neighbors. No, today people compare themselves to the super-rich they see on television and in tabloid news.[42] The result? "We constantly distort our perception of reality by unhelpful comparisons"[43] and fundamentally misread the relationship between wealth and happiness. Celebrities are wealthy and appear happy, and we erroneously assume a casual relationship between the two. However, celebrities are not always happy, or even consistently happier than other folks; but they do have a team of PR agents at work to give just this impression, to show them only at their very best, their most beautiful and jubilant. Moreover, even if certain celebrities are very happy—happier, more content, and flourishing more than the average person—there is no reason to assume that it is their wealth that is the major factor to their happiness. Indeed, there is a mountain of research that suggests this is not the case. Nevertheless, we fixate on the wealth and this distorts our behavior: 55 percent of Americans under 30 believe they will become rich, although most models of class mobility in the United States suggest only a small fraction of them will achieve this goal.[44]

In addition to the Sisyphean nature of the status race, "adaptation" ensures that material wealth is a poor choice in the pursuit of happiness.[45] Humans can become accustomed to almost any circumstance—from severe deprivation to great abundance—and come to feel that it is "normal." Each person becomes habituated to her situation, so that living standards are to some extent like drugs—we need more and more to achieve the same effect. When someone buys a new, top-of-the-line computer, she gets a rush of excitement, perhaps reinforced by the envy of her colleagues due to the aforementioned social comparison. However, twelve months later that new, enviable computer is just run-of-the-mill. Adaptation puts us on a "hedonic treadmill," where we run faster and faster, work harder and harder for longer and longer, all to purchase newer and more numerous things; but we never really get anywhere.[46] In the United States, people spend an enormous amount of time working, on the order of 400 hours per year more than the average German.[47] This is, in large part, to fuel a level of consumption that is almost unmatched in the world. However, it is well-documented that average happiness in the United States has not increased since the 1950s, despite a level of consumption that has doubled or tripled in that time.[48] If our goal is happiness, the American experiment—unregulated capitalism, increased hours of work, expanded material extraction and consumption, and so on—has largely failed since the 1950s. As Thoreau points out, when we labor we are trading life for money, so that we may then trade money for goods. When we make this transaction we are foregoing other goods on which we might spend our lives. People, I've suggested, are meant for more than mere consumption; our flourishing requires more than simple material success. So even a very successful materialist—if materialism is her sole or main focus—has missed much of what is important about being human: an individual who wins the rat race is still a rat.

Recent studies by the Nielsen Company and Ball State University show that Americans spend between eight and nine-and-a-half "screen hours" *per day*, screen time being time spent in front of a television, laptop, smart phone, or other device.[49] This unprecedented number is due, in part, to the increasingly common practice of using two or more screens at once, as when someone surfs the Internet on a laptop while watching television. Assuming people spend about four hours per day watching television—quite conservative considering the range in the Ball State Study is from 210 to 481 minutes for people over 18 years of age—simple math suggests they will spend something close to one-sixth of their lives in front of a television. Or, if we factor in eight hours of sleep a day, about one quarter of their waking lives. It's difficult to imagine, in the twilight of one's life, not wishing to have spent those many hours on something more meaningful. Of course, television is not an unmitigated evil. It can be the source of compelling narratives, even narratives that uplift and ennoble us. Indeed, this has long been the hope of certain reformers.[50] However, the reality is that television is often less-than-noble in its intent and its effect, which is largely aimed at encouraging thoughtless consumption and pandering to our basest and most easily addressed interests in order to attract viewers-cum-customers. The list of shows pandering to sex, violence, and exploitation is extensive, so think just of the shows that celebrate extravagant consumption itself: *Lifestyles of the Rich and Famous*, *MTV Cribs*, *My Super Sweet Sixteen*, *The Shahs of Sunset*, *Keeping Up With the Kardashians*, *Real Housewives of Orange County* (and *New York*, and *Beverly Hills*), and more.[51]

Notice as well, with respect to environmental sensitivity, how the sensationalism of television can make reality, including nature, seem dull by comparison.[52] Or how, in my native California, news sources perpetuate superficial narratives about what constitutes "good" weather—"Another beautiful day: sunny and 80°, with no rain in sight! A great day to head to the beach!"—that overlook more complicated and disturbing realities: it's not supposed to be sunny and 80° in January, even in southern California; and no rain means no snow in the Sierra and more severe drought in the summer, with predictable stresses on drinking water and agriculture. The speed of television, spun to cater to short-term interests and even shorter attention spans, largely misses slowly unfolding disasters like climate change.[53] Why think about drought this summer, failing crops over the next decade, or rising sea levels by mid-century when you can lie on the beach in February?

Other studies suggest, shockingly, that Americans spend more time each week shopping (6 hours) and watching television (up to 38 hours)—the latter largely a vehicle to encourage more shopping—than they do in meaningful interaction with their children (40 minutes).[54] This proclivity for consumption as an end-in-itself is increasingly something passed on to children through "branding" and marketing. "For the first time in human history, children are getting most of their information [about what to do, who to be, what constitutes success, and the goal, purpose, or meaning of life] from entities whose goal is to sell them something, rather than from family, school, or houses of worship."[55] The result of this distortion: "ninety three percent of teenage American girls rate shopping as their favorite activity."[56] Many others refer to shopping as a "hobby" and, without irony, as "retail therapy." We've come to view shopping and consumption as *intrinsic* goods rather than *limited* and *extrinsic* goods.

While the virtue of simplicity would likely turn these priorities on their head, toward an arguably much more natural and healthy hierarchy, its absence has real consequences. On the most basic level materialism and consumerism are related to a decline in both physical and mental health.[57] In "good times" Americans regularly spend more than one hundred percent of their incomes, effectively going deeper into debt with each passing month and year, often leading to home foreclosures, bankruptcies, pervasive anxiety about money, and the like. In 1980, U.S. household debt was around 65 percent of disposable income. This grew to 125 percent by 2005.[58] In each year from 1996 to 2005, more Americans declared bankruptcy than graduated from college.[59]

Although we cannot easily opt out of using fossil fuels, or participating in an environmentally inefficient globalized economy, we have much more liberty with respect to how we spend our individual lives. One reasonable definition of "rich" is "being able to afford whatever you want." If that is the case, there are two ways to become rich: you can increase your work load, trading your life for money, so that you get enough money to satisfy your wants (though in that case you may well not have time to pursue or enjoy them); or you can reduce your wants so that your current resources can meet them. We would do well to consider carefully which wants are genuinely worth trading away, in the words of poet Mary Oliver, our "one wild and precious life."[60] Which wants contribute to our flourishing and which do not? Which wants will lose their luster through degradation or adaptation (hint: most material wants) and which wants will become richer and more rewarding with time (hint: experiences and relationships)? Simplicity is the virtue that helps us to discern the difference and focus on those wants that build us up rather than those that wear us down.

Simplicity and the Community

The virtue of simplicity also helps communities to flourish. This is most obvious because when we don't use more than we need, or more than is reasonable, there is more for others. Gandhi famously admonished, "There is enough for everybody's need, but not enough for everyone's greed." But the rising wealth and consumption in the United States is not spread evenly so that there is "more" for everyone. The United States is among the wealthiest countries in the world, but the rising tide has not, at least in the past several decades, been lifting all boats. Much of the increase in affluence has been concentrated in a very small proportion of the population, among the very wealthy. The U.S. economy is beginning to look less and less like other affluent, mixed economies, and more and more like a capitalist oligarchy such as those found in Brazil, Mexico, and Russia.[61]

Margaret Thatcher once insisted, "There is no such thing as society. There are individual men and women, and there are families."[62] This perspective has undergone a resurgence in the United States with the rise of the Tea Party and other conservative groups. One would think that tension between the hyper-individualism of Ayn Randian politics on the one hand and "family values" on the other would result in some troubling cognitive dissonance. However, disdain for communal ties is held by a large number of people one might think opposed to it on the basis of other commitments. For example, "75 percent of American Christians think the saying, 'God helps those who help themselves' can be found in the Bible . . . the Bible of course says pretty much the opposite. Every time Jesus tries to sum up his message, he falls back on the formula 'Love your God, and love your neighbor as yourself.' "[63] Edward Luttwak, author of *Turbo-Capitalism*, argues that "the contradiction between wanting rapid economic growth and dynamic economic change and at the same time wanting family values, community values, and stability is a contradiction so huge that it can only last because of an aggressive refusal to think about it."[64] And, I'd add, because of an aggressive and ongoing campaign to shape the American narrative around extravagant consumption, implying that this vice will somehow *improve* rather than *undermine* relationships and social stability. The celebrated "invisible hand" of Adam Smith's *The Wealth of Nations* is overplayed in general and outright incoherent absent the tempering ethical and philosophical foundations in Smith's regrettably less-well-referenced *The Theory of Moral Sentiments*. Though still enumerating benefits deriving from human selfishness, the latter text also emphasizes our natural sympathy for others and presupposes a natural limit on consumption.[65] Absent some moderating influence—moderate regulation, virtue, a sufficiently small society, or some similar check—the invisible hand of the free market is likely to be making a rather rude gesture behind the backs of an exploited class. This hyper-individualism, which both supports and is supported by the particular brand of unregulated and unrestrained capitalism currently dominant in the United States, "allows us to tolerate, even celebrate, inequality so gross that it is almost as much farce as tragedy."[66]

Not only has American commitment to extravagance led to broad inequalities in compensation, the work many American's undertake has increased without any real increase in well-being. The real income of 90 percent of American taxpayers actually declined between 1979 and 2005.[67] But today American workers labor 160 hours *more* than they did in 1969, a full month of extra labor, all in the service of "growth" from which they do not personally benefit, at least in terms of happiness.[68] As early as 1932 Bertrand Russell suggested the adoption of four-hour workday as a likely benefit of the increasing efficiencies in production.[69] He was not alone. "In 1965, a US Senate subcommittee heard testimony that estimated a workweek of from fourteen to twenty-two hours by 2000."[70] The increasing efficiency of modern production could have bought us more leisure, requiring us to work half as much to produce the same amount—an amount that was already adequate and had already made as many of us happy in 1950 as are happy today. That additional leisure, if spent wisely, may well have "bought" us the happiness our additional consumption has not. Instead we have chosen more stuff over more leisure, working the same amount (actually *more*) to produce and consume ever greater amounts of, increasingly, disposable goods that must be replaced, leading to more extraction, production, and consumption. What constitutes real wealth, real well-being? Disposable income spent on disposable goods, or disposable time spent on genuine goods, those endeavors that make life meaningful and contribute to our flourishing and the flourishing of our communities and environments?

Despite the general trend, there have been some experiments with reduced workloads and the effects on social well-being were fairly dramatic. Perhaps the best-known example in the United States was the work reform instituted by W. K. Kellogg during the Depression. Kellogg put his workers on six-hour days and offered thirty-five hour's pay for the resulting thirty-hour workweek.[71] At the same time he built parks, sports fields, garden plots, and other recreational amenities in the communities in which his workers lived. This strategy immediately produced 400 new jobs, and productivity rose so quickly that soon Kellogg was getting the same amount for those thirty hours that he was previously getting for forty hours.[72] Not only did Kellogg's business flourish, but interviews with employees during the '30s suggest individuals and communities were also flourishing as a result of the plan.

> Researchers who interviewed the townspeople found that their interests had grown and changed: they now asked themselves, "What shall I do?" [as neighborhood parks, community centers, churches, and YMCAs all flourished, supported by the liberated townsfolk] not just "What shall I buy?" Indeed, workers looked back on the eight-hour day with a shudder. "I wouldn't go back for anything," said one. "I wouldn't have time to do anything but work and eat."[73]

The commitment to the thirty-hour workweek didn't begin to erode until the death of W. K. Kellogg, and persisted in some form into the 1980s. After returning to a forty-hour week, the workers reported that volunteerism went down and crime went up; they all lamented the shift and looked back fondly to the six hour days in which "you still had the energy to do [more than work]," and in which they were "much happier than . . . young families today, who have so much more stuff but never seem to have time."[74] Our hectic commitment to long work hours has real consequences for both individuals and for the community. Robert Putnam's *Bowling Alone* documents in extensive detail the decline in civic participation and engagement in the United States, and the attendant loss of "social capital" and impoverishment of our social lives.[75]

The various distortions in our social fabric, our tendency toward both *hyper*-individualism and *hyper*-consumption, are linked to a skewed economic and political narrative that equates gross domestic product (GDP) with social "health." No American politician of any stripe is willing to suggest that growth can be bad, or even that it is ambiguous. The chorus from the left and right is "business is business and business must grow," as one children's book mockingly puts it.[76] But the GDP doesn't really measure the well-being of a nation or society because it doesn't account for negative social and environmental externalities or unpaid costs. The GDP goes up when we produce things, but it does not discriminate whether the production responds to or results in desirable things. Among the great boosters of GDP one would have to include war, divorce, illness, natural disasters, crime, and pollution. All these things add to the GDP because we must produce things to address them: weapons, second homes, medical treatment, relief and rebuilding, security systems, and various environmental clean-ups. Needless to say, a growing GDP is entirely compatible with growing inequality and injustice. It's also compatible with social and environmental disaster in pursuit of the lowest apparent cost, at expense of dramatically higher genuine cost.

In pursuit of a very specific sort of efficiency and GDP, a bite of a typical American meal somehow travels around 1,500 miles to get to the plate (or fast-food package) from which it is eaten. Carlo Petrini recounts an absurd situation in which Piedmont—a region of Italy long renowned for its cuisine, especially the *peperonata* based on the local Asti peppers— now imports cheaper, mass produced, but gastronomically inferior peppers from Holland.[77] What is grown in Piedmont now that local farmers have abandoned peppers, having been undercut by Holland? Tulip bulbs that are shipped to Holland, which is famous for its tulips! This bizarre situation is far from unique. Seventy-five percent of the apples consumed in New York City come from either overseas or from the West Coast, despite the fact that New York State produces ten times the number of apples consumed in New York City.[78] What's going on here? "None of this makes much sense except by the standards of lowest-price economics"[79]—lowest *apparent* price on the shelf that is, not lowest *actual* cost including all the externalities related to the product, its waste, the people making it, the cultures involved in its production, and the environment in which it is made. The problem is that, in general, the classical economic approach is "enthralled with mathematical models that only operate in conditions that do not exist."[80] In the real world we must contend with limited resources and limited sinks, imperfect information, negative externalities (some of which we have not yet identified) related to people, cultures, and environments, inadequate or asymmetrical information, and, of course, irrational actors.

Simplicity and the Environment

The contributions of simplicity to environmental flourishing are so numerous and so obvious as to need no explanation. Many of the externalities that affect social well-being also impact environmental well-being. The inexpensive computer screen at the local "big-box store" is priced so low not only because of the unsafe and unjust working conditions of the people who source the materials and assemble the product, but also because the unregulated (or unenforced) resource extraction, production, and waste disposal. These environmental externalities affect people, but they also impact ecosystems and other species. We're simply consuming too much, too quickly, and too inefficiently.

Studies suggest that a global population of 6 billion, a figure that is now well in the rearview mirror, would require between 1.3 and 2.1 global hectares (gha) of productive resources per person, depending on how the calculations are done.[81] As the population grows, the amount of productive resources available per person generally decreases. But even with a stable population the more than 9.0 gha per person consumption of the United States is an unsustainable use of the environment. All told, humanity's current footprint exceeds the Earth's capacity by about 50 percent—that is to say that we collectively use 1.5 Earth's worth of resources.[82] This overconsumption is most pronounced among the affluent of the world. For example, if everyone consumed in the manner of an average Canadian citizen, we would need 4.3 Earths.[83] If everyone lived like the average citizen of the United States we would need more than 5 Earths. Our current trajectory puts us well along the road toward overshoot and collapse. Just how far along that road is a matter for heated debate; in any case it is clear that there simply are not enough resources to consume, or sinks to absorb the waste of that consumption, for us to continue on our current path. The unsustainable consumption of the global north is exacerbated by both the growing world population and the increasing affluence of formerly impoverished people. Consumption and population are two faces of the same problem, and because population expands by geometric or "exponential" growth, collapse could arrive relatively quickly.

Imagine a very large fish tank capable of supporting 200 fish. Now populate that tank with two fish and let loose geometric growth: the population grows from two, to four, to eight, to sixteen, to thirty-two, to sixty-four, to one hundred and twenty-eight. At this point the tank looks well-populated but still well within its limits. There are more than enough resources for all the fish. However, in the course of a single generation we move from this state of abundance (128 fish in a tank that can sustain 200) to collapse (256 fish competing for resources that can only sustain 200) and catastrophic die off. While this oversimplified case does not address the malleability of the Earth's carrying capacity—due to technological improvements, changes in consumption patterns, and so on—it is a stark reminder of how quickly overshoot and collapse can arrive in a system that, like the finite, spherical Earth, is ultimately limited.

There are other consequences of our extravagance and binge consumption as well. Industrialization has put over 100,000 man-made chemicals into the environment.[84] Almost all of these chemicals are unregulated and unmonitored. Only a fraction have ever been tested for potential harms to humans, animals, or the environment, and safe occupational exposure limits have only been set for a few hundred.[85] What are these chemicals doing to different life forms and systems? In most cases the answer is, "we don't know." Some of them may be harmless, but we seem to discover serious problems with alarming frequency, and with 100,000 chemicals and counting the odds are that we are releasing some substances that are going to cause trouble. When we do bother to test these chemicals we do so with a massive dose, isolating one chemical at a time, for a relatively short period of time. All this makes sense in terms of designing an easily testable experiment; however, it is exactly the opposite of how exposure happens in the real world: moderate doses, of multiple chemicals at once, over a lifetime. Modern industrial society is conducting a massive, irreversible, and largely unmonitored experiment in which the biosphere and everything in it are the subjects.

One of the more well-known of these ongoing experiments with the life-support systems on which we depend is anthropogenic climate change. The fact that greenhouse gasses are accumulating in the atmosphere and changing the climate is beyond dispute, as is the fact that the primary driver of this change is human activity, principally the burning of fossil fuels but also things like changes in land-use. While the process of anthropogenic climate change is well-established and well-understood, there are uncertainties associated with climate change that make simplicity a critical environmental virtue. It's not clear when and to what degree climate change might trigger "feedback loops" or self-reinforcing phenomena. For example, changing climate causes a loss in sea ice, which leads—because open blue water has a lower albedo (or reflectivity) than ice and consequently absorbs more solar radiation—to further warming. Similarly, a warming climate causes the melting of permafrost in the northern hemisphere, which leads to the decay of organic material that has long been frozen solid (and thus protected from decay). This decay releases carbon dioxide (CO_2) and methane (CH_4), both potent greenhouse gasses, which perpetuates, reinforces, and exacerbates the warming of the climate. Such feedback loops, in turn, increase the likelihood of passing some critical "tipping point" beyond which there is no hope of returning to status quo. The melting of permafrost is again a useful example, if we pass the tipping point at which large quantities of permafrost melt and decay, the resulting release of greenhouse gasses into the atmosphere will make any mitigation on the human side moot. Permafrost holds something around 1500 billion tons of CO_2 and CH_4, roughly double the total amount currently in the atmosphere (including all human contributions).[86]

Climate change and its impacts on the environment are directly related to human extravagance. Greater simplicity would mean less consumption and, in an economy based entirely on the burning of fossil fuels at every stage of production and distribution, less consumption means fewer greenhouse gasses emitted. Simplicity is especially critical here because climate change is unlike other environmental crises in one special respect. Many common environmental crises happen because something goes *wrong*—someone intentionally does something wrong and avoidable like dumping effluent into a river rather than disposing of it safely in order to save money—and that wrong is often addressed as people undergo "benign demographic transition," the process by which increasingly affluent populations tend to have fewer children (itself good for the environment) and become more environmentally concerned. But climate change doesn't happen because someone does something wrong; it is a problem that happens when things go "right," when we produce and consume goods, which is necessary for survival and flourishing. The harm is unintentional. Moreover, climate change actually accelerates as more people become more affluent and consume more goods, a sort of *"malign demographic transition."* We cannot consume our way out of climate change by consuming differently— as we consumed our way out of acid rain by choosing products without chlorofluorocarbons (CFCs)—because all consumption in our economy produces greenhouse gasses.

The twin pressures of population growth and more consumption are at the root of many environmental crises: the decline of wilderness areas, loss of biodiversity, degradation of ecosystem services, and so on. The degree to which our extravagant consumption has remade the planet—through increased greenhouse gasses and the resultant climate change, through ocean acidification, through urbanization and sprawl, through agriculture, through the release of untested industrial chemicals and GMOs—has led some scholars to refer to the current age as the *anthropocene*: the age of man, the time in which human consumption and technology has become the single most important driver in environmental change.

The transition to the anthropocene has been sped up by the development of a fossil fuel economy, beginning with the steam engine and continuing through contemporary dependence on coal, oil, and natural gas, not only for energy but for a bewildering array of products: plastics, fertilizers, solvents, food preservatives, asphalt, tar, clothing, electronic components, refrigerants, paints, insecticides, and others. The entire modern world is built upon and sustained by fossil fuels, which are finite and becoming increasingly scarce. We have grown and prospered based on the extravagant use of one-time, non-renewable resources rather than renewable resources based in natural biology, solar energy, and so on. When the oil runs out, the lights go off, the music stops, and the party is over. That might sound dramatic, and there are other possibilities beyond a peak oil crash. But those alternatives will require more than just doing things differently; they will require doing more with less. This is because we've become dependent on an easy source of energy that is not yet replaceable and is fast being depleted. Energy return on investment (EROI) is a measure of how much new energy we get for each unit of energy spent mining or producing the energy. Some estimates suggest that EROI for finding new sources of oil dropped from a whopping 1200:1 in 1919 to 5:1 in 2007, and the EROI for the production of oil and gas dropped from 20:1 to around 11:1.[87] While some renewable power now compares favorably with fossil fuels—solar is approaching 7:1 and wind is 18:1—all of these fall well short of the gratuitous inheritance of more than 100:1 oil on which our post-war economic boom was made.[88] The long and the short of it is that the days of investing one unit of energy to develop several score units are gone. We'll need sustainable agriculture, renewable fuels, smart design, alternative materials, and changes in urban development. But, in addition, we are simply going to need to consume less; we're going to need to cultivate simplicity. It should be clear by now that this is not a bad thing; simplicity is a virtue we ought to cultivate for our own good, even if it were the case that we could avoid the environmental crisis without simplicity. Ideally such simplicity will be adopted willingly, even enthusiastically, as part of a narrative of flourishing, especially given the individual and social benefits enumerated above—but it will have to be adopted in any case. We can adopt simplicity as a virtue that will enrich our lives and contribute to our flourishing, or we can adopt it as a necessary sacrifice. The former is clearly preferable to the latter, but systems of extraction, production, waste, and renewal will balance out one way or the other. The question is are we going to do it the "easy" way (choosing a new narrative about the human *telos* and remaking our social, political, and economic institutions to reflect it) or the "hard" way (famine, disease, resource wars, and so forth)?

Thoreau's Narrative

Arguments for simplicity can be made on the basis of facts, data, and statistics culled from psychology, sociology, economics, surveys, polls, and so forth; but narratives remain one of the essential forms by which we make arguments for virtues and commend them to others. Although I've drawn on a wide range of sources in this chapter, the case for simplicity is ultimately grounded in Thoreau's account, and in light of my overall arguments about narrative and environmental virtue it is worth pointing out that *Walden* is also a fine example of the self-conscious use of narrative to exhort us to virtue. Indeed, while there are many other examples of narratives that extol certain virtues and which are used to begin the process of cultivating those virtues in their readers, *Walden* gives us perhaps the best case study of a narrative that argues both for an environmentally sensitive account of virtue and for the power of narrative in the communication and cultivation of virtue.

Thoreau's own stylistic choices suggest a deep-seated belief in the power of narrative to make his argument. His early writings, argues Phil Cafaro, resemble " 'hero pieces,' in which an exemplary life teaches moral lessons."[89] In them we find "an ancient conception of virtue that combines moral integrity with intellectual and physical abilities in a comprehensive ideal of human excellence. Arguing for such a conception of virtue [is] the main goal in *Walden*. . . ."[90] Cafaro argues that Thoreau casts himself—or the literary image of himself as presented in *Walden*—as the hero of the story in the course of identifying the real challenges that he and his contemporaries face: not the challenges of warfare or of discovering new (physical) worlds, but the challenge of resisting ill-conceived conformity and of settling into America in a way that preserves the newness of the "New World."[91]

If one goal of *Walden* is to argue for a certain conception of human flourishing—that is to say, a certain conception of the virtues and how they relate to a good life—a second is to serve as a narrative exhortation and inspiration for others to conduct similar experiments in their own lives. While it's true that Thoreau makes more traditional arguments in some of his work, particularly in shorter efforts like *Life Without Principle* and *Resistance to Civil Government*, in *Walden*, his greatest and most important work, he employs narrative as an essential component of his paean to simplicity. This is most obvious in the structure, style, and genre of *Walden* itself, which is a narrative account of Thoreau's two years at Walden Pond condensed into the story of a single year. The story begins during the summer with Thoreau's own personal "independence day," on which he moves to Walden Pond, and ends, poetically, in the spring, signifying his rebirth.

Thoreau's commitment to narrative is also evident in the chapter on "Reading."[92] In this chapter, he argues for a strong connection between reading—living as a "student and observer"—and doing. Elsewhere he is exceptionally harsh in his estimation of a detached studiousness that defrauds us of experience, since such detachment is likely to lead to only "improved means to an unimproved end."[93] However, here he seems at pains to point out the connections between literature, when read well, and virtue.

> To read well, that is, to read true books in a true spirit, is a noble exercise, and one that will task the reader more than any exercise which the customs of the day esteem. It requires a training such as the athletes underwent, the steady intention almost of the whole life to this object. Books must be read as deliberately and reservedly as they were written.[94]

When we read in this way, we open ourselves up to the power of narrative to influence life, a power that stems from the proximity of narrative to life. "The written word is the choicest of relics. It is something at once more intimate with us and more universal than any other work of art. It is the work of art nearest to life itself."[95] Good books, read well, can make us better people. Books do not replace life—"[students] should not *play* life, or study it merely, while the community supports them at this expensive game, but earnestly live it from beginning to end"[96]—but they do influence and form us. Here, perhaps, Thoreau is not too far from his friend Emerson, who insists that books are primarily for inspiration rather than idolization.[97] Good and responsible reading is never easy. First, assuming we do not yet possess the virtues to which we aspire, we need books that will shake us from our lethargy and indolence: "We need to be provoked [by books]—goaded like oxen, as we are, into a trot."[98] Once inspired to change, we must "laboriously seek the meaning of each word and line" as we prepare to "emulate [our] heroes."[99] *Walden* itself is intended to serve just such an inspirational purpose, as if Thoreau is asking, a bit mischievously, "[L]ook what simplicity has done for me! What might it do for you, if only you gave it a chance?"

The Challenge of Postmodernity

"Would you tell me, please, which way I ought to go from here?" "That depends a good deal on where you want to get to," said the Cat. "I don't much care where—" said Alice. "Then it doesn't matter which way you go," said the Cat.

—Lewis Carroll, *Alice's Adventures in Wonderland*

Si fueris Rōmae, Rōmānō vīvitō mōre; si fueris alibī, vīvitō sicut ibi (If you are in Rome, live in the Roman way; if you are elsewhere, live as they do there).

—St. Ambrose's advice to St. Augustine

The Imprecision and Variability of Virtue Ethics

Following the discussions of virtue and flourishing in the previous chapters, it shouldn't be too difficult to discern a major difficulty for the virtue ethics approach—a difficulty that stems from the imprecision of virtue ethics and its acknowledged variability, and one that narrative might seem to exacerbate.

Virtue ethics, we saw, does not admit of the sort of precision we associate with math or geometry, which allow for genuine proofs. Nor does it seek the degree of precision common to certain physical sciences, which can avail themselves of empirical data backed up by repeated experimentation. Virtues elude precise definition. When speaking of virtue, we must content ourselves with conclusions that are true "for the most part."[1] Moreover, because virtue requires, in addition to the right action, other criteria such as feeling the right emotion during the commission of the action, it can be difficult to discern whether or not someone has truly acted virtuously. And, even more problematically, in a post-Freudian world we must acknowledge that the self is never fully transparent to itself. Therefore, it can be difficult to discern whether or not one has truly acted virtuously oneself![2] It's true that taking pleasure in a virtuous act is a useful indicator of having acted with genuine virtue, but it's easy to see how one might question whether or not one really "got it right," so to speak. In addition to the imprecision of virtue ethics, we must contend with its flexibility and variability. Virtues are context and agent sensitive. That is to say, what "counts" as courage differs from situation to situation and from person to person. The virtuous mean, says Aristotle, is relative to the person acting.[3] So in addition to the uncertainty stemming from the limited precision of virtue ethics, we also have to recognize that any precision we can achieve is destabilized to some extent by the fact that it applies differently to each person and situation.

However, if virtues can only be defined in broad strokes, are grasped by perception, and are relative to the individual, how are we to avoid full-blown relativism in which we are unable to compare different actions and judge them as more or less virtuous? How can we compare different accounts of human flourishing and judge them to be more or less accurate or complete? Are environmentally insensitive accounts of human flourishing as true as accounts that are environmentally sensitive? If there are no universal or objective criteria to which virtuous actions must conform, can *any* decision, act, or lifestyle "count" as appropriately virtuous merely because the agent in question feels she is acting virtuously?

Aristotle is well aware of this problem. We saw in Chapter 2 that he does not intend to suggest that each individual should be the sole judge of her own virtue, which *would* be like having the fox guard the henhouse. Rather, he suggests the mean that characterizes virtue must be rational; it's not simply a subjective feeling or inclination. Moreover, given that different people might, with good intentions, apply reason differently in trying to determine the virtuous mean, Aristotle further qualifies things through reference to the *phronimos*. Practical wisdom (*phronesis*) helps a person to make good judgments with respect to human conduct, and it plays an especially important role in cases that present novel or difficult ethical problems. In Chapters 1 and 2 we noted that universal rules tend to work best precisely when we need the least guidance. Almost anyone can follow a rule in situations that are relatively clear-cut. *Phronesis* is the ability to deal with complex and ethically ambiguous situations in which it is not clear what the relevant rules are or how they should be applied— when two ethical guidelines come into conflict, or when one is faced with an unavoidable choice between evils, or in a radically novel situation for which past experiences have not prepared us. Of course, these are precisely the sorts of decisions with which we will be increasingly confronted as environmental degradation accelerates.

As we confront problems like climate change we will be tempted to employ new and often untested technologies such as genetic engineering, nanotechnology, and various forms of geo-engineering. However, here we are in uncharted waters. While facts and data will certainly help where they are available, and educated scientific hypotheses will provide some sense of the costs and benefits where data are lacking, none of this will adequately guide our actions absent a good dose of *phronesis*. We will need both intelligence and creativity *and* the wisdom to use them well as we move forward: good scientists, engineers, economists, politicians, and activists to be sure, but only if they are also good people. The dangers of the former without the latter are all too obvious. History and literature are littered with cautionary examples of people who were good (that is, skilled or effective) scientists or politicians without being good (that is, virtuous) humans.

The Postmodern Condition

Aristotle's response to the threat of relativism, *phronesis* and the *phronimos*, no doubt seemed reasonable to him and to his contemporaries; they had the good fortune of having, or believing they had, *phronimoi* in the community to which they could point.[4] It is for this reason that Aristotle often begins by citing examples from his community. He notes the "general agreement" about the importance of *eudaimonia* and concludes, "we must consider happiness [*eudaimonia*] in the light not only of our conclusion and our premises, but also in light of what is commonly said about it."[5] Having come to some preliminary conclusions about virtue, he pauses to consider his view in light of the wisdom of his tradition: "Now some of these views have been held by many men and men of old, others by a few eminent persons; and it is not probable that either of these should be entirely mistaken, but rather that they should be right in at least some one respect, or even in most respects."[6] His faith in his tradition and the consequent pattern of turning to examples and beliefs in the community is repeated in the attempt to circumscribe *phronesis*: "Regarding practical wisdom [*phronesis*] we shall get at the truth by considering who are the persons we credit with it [that is, the *phronimoi* in the community]."[7]

However, while *phronesis* remains central to any account of virtue ethics, in the contemporary philosophical and cultural landscape I don't believe we can deploy a strict Aristotelian account of *phronesis* as if that would answer the charge of relativism. Thus, relativism remains a serious problem for any virtue ethicist in our "postmodern" age. Indeed, while certainly not without historical precedent, the lure of relativism is perhaps symptomatic of our time. The threat of relativism, with which philosophers have always grappled, has been exacerbated by globalization, which brings into contact and conflict a great many different "grand narratives," and by postmodernity, which, partly in response to globalization, undermines the very notion of a grand narrative.

Globalization

Our world is, in many ways, larger than Aristotle's. Despite his erudition, he was aware of at most a small fraction of the world and the diverse societies that inhabited it. But the largeness of our world is deceptive in certain respects. It's true that we are aware of cultures thriving halfway around the world, even those tucked away in geographically remote locations. But it's also true that we can get on an airplane and, in less than a day, disembark in Delhi, Caracas, or Cape Town. Indeed, I can speak instantaneously with friends in Tokyo, London, Malaga, or Chamonix. Thanks to the Internet I can even speak to several far-flung friends simultaneously, with live video feeds, without any of us having to leave our respective homes. The forces of technology and globalization have conspired to "shrink" our larger world such that, despite its size, we are confronted much more directly and much more frequently with otherness—the strange, foreign, alien, or unfamiliar. Even relatively homogeneous societies like those found in Japan and Scandinavia are beginning to give way to more diverse contexts brought on by immigration and global markets. While there remain insular pockets of uniformity and narrow provincialism, they are slowly but surely being eroded by urbanization and information technology. The former literally brings different people together, while the latter accomplishes the same thing virtually. Most major cities have become melting pots unlike anything Aristotle could have imagined, even with the relatively cosmopolitan trade contacts of ancient Athens. And the global melting pot phenomenon is not something confined to macro phenomena. Take, for example, my immediate family, which remains modest in number even when accounting for myself, my wife, our parents, siblings, and in-laws. Nevertheless, my family includes people with roots in the United States, Ireland, China, Iran, England, and Sri Lanka—several of whom are either expatriates or immigrants in their current country of residence—and people who consider themselves Catholic, Protestant, Hindu, Jewish, secular humanists, and "other."

Although various sorts of nationalism and racism persist, today it is much more difficult to think of foreign people as "barbarians" who are somehow subhuman and whose "culture," such as it is, both reflects and reinforces that inferiority. Today, we tend to see difference as difference rather than difference as deficiency. We not only know that diverse cultures exist; we know that they flourish. While Chinese culture is different from American culture, few Americans would think of Chinese culture as fundamentally deficient or less human.[8] Indeed, most people admire certain aspects of foreign cultures. In the wake of the triple catastrophe of the 9.0 earthquake, tsunami, and nuclear disaster in northeast Japan in March 2011, newspapers around the world marveled at the stoic endurance and community resilience of the Japanese people, and the absence of the rioting, looting, and criminal opportunism seen in the wake of other disasters in other locales.[9] Even when we do object to differences in another culture or tradition, rational people generally do not construe it as a sign of ontological inferiority, as if people from the different culture or tradition are somehow intrinsically subhuman—although genocides, ethnic cleansings, and the like illustrate all too clearly that we have not entirely escaped such sectarianism.

In addition to the regularity with which we encounter others and otherness in contemporary culture, globalization is paradoxically undermining the difference of that otherness in at least two important ways. First, we are becoming more comfortable with difference. Global migration has created melting pots—or salad bowls, choose your metaphor—like Toronto and Los Angeles, resulting in societies in which differences are both more common and less extreme. They are more common because people in such environments are confronted, daily, with "foreign" cultures. As a consequence, they tend to be more comfortable with diversity and difference, having become accustomed to encountering a variety of different cultures, religions, languages, and cuisines on a regular basis. The 2000 Census identified an astonishing 224 different languages, not including variant dialects, spoken by residents of Los Angeles.[10] Nevertheless, these differences are also less extreme in the sense that, living in close proximity, different traditions tend to influence each other and exchange characteristics. The Los Angeles gourmet "food truck" craze, which has now spread to many other cities, began with a truck selling Korean barbeque tacos, a mélange or fusion that could only have arisen in a global city.

Second, we are becoming more like each other. Global economies ensure that some cultural or economic features are more or less pervasive, exerting a homogenizing effect on cultures. The speed with which international news travels, as well as the amount and ubiquity of it, makes the potentially foreign more familiar. Likewise, the rise and expansion of international commerce—of the richest one hundred economic entities in the

world today, fifty-one are international corporations[11]—means that many
goods, services, and above all brands have become near omnipresent. For
example, according to one estimate, McDonald's operates over 31,000 locations, in over 119 countries on 6 continents, employing over 1.7 million
people, and serving around 60 million people *each day*—a neon beacon of
familiarity in any number of otherwise foreign landscapes.[12] The McDonald's brand, as well as the industrial food system that supports it, exists as
an increasingly common touchstone for people's daily experience in cultures
across the world. While a person will still encounter major differences in
traveling from New York to Prague to Singapore, she will also encounter a
wide variety of familiar phenomena, from Levi's to MacDonald's, Toyota to
Nokia. This is to say nothing of perhaps the most influential of all cultural
exports: the enormous influence exerted by American movies, television,
and advertising, which together paint a very specific, and not uncontrover-
sial, picture of human flourishing. As more people around the world aspire
to live like Americans—at least in terms of affluence, consumption, and
the like—and more corporations exert a truly global influence with their
brands and images, cultural differences inevitably begin to erode.

One consequence of the increasing trend toward globalization is that
in the marketplace of ideas different, even contradictory, conceptions of
the "good life" come into contact. These so-called "Grand Narratives"
(or metanarratives)—the overarching systems that give meaning to our
world—are called into question by other, competing grand narratives. A
Christian, for example, sees the world in terms of the Christian Narrative
and her beliefs, convictions, and assumptions with respect to the good,
the true, the beautiful, and the real reflect this perspective. In certain
times and places, a Christian might have lived her entire life without
encountering a significantly different narrative. However, today someone
inhabiting a Christian metanarrative is likely to be aware of, and increasingly likely to have personal encounters with, others whose narratives
are Jewish, Muslim, Buddhist, Hindu, or atheist, to say nothing of non-
religious metanarratives focusing on socialism, democracy, or capitalism,
as well as those focusing on national or ethnic identity. Some of these
narratives can coexist—one might be a German Christian socialist or an
Indian Hindu capitalist—but others contradict each other. The existence
of other metanarratives in close proximity—real and virtual—held by
other intelligent and sincere people inevitably leads a thoughtful person
to realize that her perspective, her metanarrative, is shot through with
contingencies. If she had been born elsewhere or otherwise she would very
likely see the world in terms of a different metanarrative, say Hindu or

Muslim rather than Christian, and her beliefs, convictions, and assumptions would reflect that perspective.

Postmodernity

The contact and inevitable friction between metanarratives has had a profound effect on the way people view the world. In his famous "report on knowledge," Jean-Francois Lyotard defined the postmodern condition as one characterized by "incredulity toward metanarratives."[13] The encounter between incommensurable metanarratives leads, predictably, to crises of identity and legitimation when one's faith in one's metanarrative begins to erode. Who am I? Why do I believe what I believe? Indeed, such crises undermine one's faith in the very possibility of a metanarrative. It's not just a question of whether or not *my* metanarrative is in fact right or correct, but a question of whether or not *any* metanarrative can be right or correct. Perhaps it is impossible to capture the complexity of the world in one global, all-encompassing metanarrative; perhaps all we can aspire to are local, regional, contingent micronarratives.

Jack Caputo argues that this situation presents a serious problem for virtue ethics in the Aristotelian tradition. *Phronesis*, he points out with characteristic brio, was a virtue of the "homogeneous, top down, aristocratic, rigidly closed little society" that was Aristotle's Athens; it assumes an agreement regarding ethical schemata and a univocal view of the right way to live that are simply lacking in the postmodern milieu: "Aristotle had a more settled view of things than [we do today]. Aristotle thought the main problem facing ethical judgment lay in the movement from the general schema to the concrete situation, but he did not think there was a crisis in the schemata."[14] Aristotle assumed, with justification, a high degree of correspondence between his own ideas about virtue and the ideas of his students and readers. If asked, they would praise the same virtues and, indeed, would likely come up with very similar "short lists" when discussing the identity of the *phronimoi*. Today, however, "even Aristotle . . . would have a tough time telling us who the *phronimos* is. . . ."[15] Another way of putting this is that a metanarrative, insofar as it is an overarching worldview or perspective, implies an account of the teleological goal of humans and a description of the flourishing with which virtue ethics is concerned. However, our incredulity regarding metanarrative leads to skepticism regarding any particular image of human flourishing and regarding any particular claim about habits and dispositions conducive to flourishing. No metanarrative, no *telos*. No *telos*, no virtue ethics.

Postmodern Temptations:
Hamlet's Indecision and Meursault's Indifference

So it seems that some of the standard problems for virtue ethics—how to identify the operative model of flourishing, how to identify the virtues that constitute that model, and how to cultivate those virtues in oneself—are severely exacerbated by postmodernity. Today, many people are aware, to some degree, of the contingency of their own metanarrative preference and, as a consequence, their confidence in the very idea of metanarrative has been shaken. Of course, each person still chooses or falls into a metanarrative, for it's hard to see how one could get by without a characteristic "way of viewing the world" so that it "makes sense." However, lacking any objective, unbiased confirmation that our particular choice is the correct one, we also recognize the contingency of our choice and the inescapability of the hermeneutic circle.[16] We never make our choices, including our choices for various micronarratives and metanarratives, starting from an objective and unbiased view. Indeed, we cannot do so.

We are haunted by the idea that our metanarrative perspective is something we inhabit as a result of a simple accident of birth and circumstance. Though many people still long for an objective and certain confirmation of the Truth of one Grand Narrative or another, and a fair number of people pretend that they have such confirmation, postmodern philosophies of paralogy assure us there is no perspective that could offer such a guarantee. As Caputo points out, there is no "privileged access to The Secret [that is, an 'objective' meta-perspective, a transparent *arche*, or an ultimate *telos*]."[17] And, absent such privileged access, an increasing number of people are persuaded by the consequent: "the secret is, there is no Secret."[18]

Which narrative shall we embrace? Despite the ways in which our world is shrinking and the degree to which globalization is exerting a homogenizing force on culture, relative to Aristotle's view of things our world is still characterized more by heterogeneity than homogeneity, and relative to the general agreement between Aristotle and his intended audience there is much less consensus about the good life and how to achieve it. We must choose amongst a bewildering array of perspectives, in a situation where there appears to be no broad agreement about the schema for the good life or the *phronimos* who embodies it. We've gone from negotiating the differences between Athenian and Spartan views of virtue, flourishing, and teleology, to suspecting, or fearing, that there may well be significant, perhaps irresolvable, disagreements about virtue and flourishing among myriad different cultures, societies, religions, and worldviews, all in a context in which there is no *telos*, objective truth, or unbiased perspective with which we can adjudicate between them.

There are, however, various ways to deal with the inescapability of the hermeneutic circle, alternative ways of inhabiting this contingency and uncertainty. Some people try to ignore or deny the self-referential and contingent nature of their metanarrative preference. Others choose a metanarrative, but do so in a way that is obviously provisional, even ironic. Still others attempt to fully embrace the contingency, abandoning any real attempt to justify competing interpretations. Overall, we might say that there is a spectrum of responses to postmodern "undecidability" ranging from fervent denial to zealous endorsement, and passing through various shades in between.

Shades of Relativism

I've suggested that relativism poses a problem for virtue ethics, but haven't really defined what that means. Relativism can mean many different things, and some stripes of relativism are less problematic than others; indeed, some sorts of relativism are not problematic at all. Few people, for example, bother to argue seriously about the objectively best cuisine—*de gustibus non est disputandum*. The problems arise when the near-universal open-minded tolerance with which we evaluate and discuss cuisine is applied, without reflection or modification, to moral and ethical discourse where, as MacIntyre reminds us, *de gustibus est disputandum*.[19] Therefore, we have to be clear about (1) which sort or sorts of relativism are problematic or dangerous and (2) what, if anything, virtue ethics might say about the matter.

On one level, relativism may be a merely descriptive claim about the way things are. Looking around the world, or back through history, is seems to be the case that different cultures have different ideas about ethics and morality. Key components of virtue ethics like the purpose or goal of a human life (our *telos*), the image of a good person (expressing our view of *eudaimonia*), and the virtues or excellences that contribute to being good and reaching our goal (*arete*) lie in contested terrain. On a purely descriptive level, there seems to be good circumstantial evidence favoring the relativist. However, some versions of relativism take this a step further. Starting with the meta-ethical claim that there are no universal moral or ethical standards, they argue that there is no way of reliably adjudicating between two incompatible moral or ethical systems. Postmodern undecidability implies, I take it, both descriptive and normative relativism: that different societies and different elements within any society *do in fact have different interpretations* of culture, tradition, morality, and so on, and, in addition, that these empirical differences are a predictable consequence of the fact that there *are no universal moral principles or ethical standards* that would enable us to justifiably prefer one interpretation to another.[20]

But even this charge must be further specified, for normative ethical relativism can itself take several forms. One might endorse, for example, a very robust sort of relativism, claiming judgments such as those made by virtue ethics are absolutely relative, differing from individual to individual with no external basis for approbation or reprobation whatsoever. This sort of relativism down to the level of the individual—which we might call subjectivism, since it suggests that standards are unique to each individual subject—bleeds into, or at least courts, nihilism. If there is no larger truth in light of which we can distinguish different actions, then no action is better than any other action and all claims about ethics and morality are equally (un)true. It is this sort of relativism that MacIntyre addresses under the rubric of Emotivism: the doctrine that "all evaluative judgments and specifically all moral judgments are *nothing but* expressions of preference, expressions of attitude or feeling, insofar as they are moral or evaluative in character."[21] If Emotivism is true, there is no way to rationally adjudicate between competing moral claims and discussion will, suggests MacIntyre, be entirely interminable (and, I'd add, almost entirely worthless and meaningless).

One problem with full-blown ethical relativism—especially once we realize that this includes razing to the ground all metanarratives, the very idea of metanarrative—is that it seems to imply one of two very dangerous consequences. Remember that, in the field of virtue ethics, we are concerned with identifying the *telos* of human flourishing, the goal toward which we should strive and the mold in which we should form ourselves. However, if there are no goals that are intrinsically good (nihilism) or if all such goals are equally (un)justifiable (relativism-qua-subjectivism), then it is very difficult to see how we can set goals at all for self-development. Won't we fall into something like Hamlet's indecision or Meursault's indifference? Either the perpetual cry of "What should I do?" or the plaintive sigh of "It doesn't matter what I do."

A healthy dose of skepticism regarding claims to truth, especially universal or quasi-universal truth, is an important part of the philosophical project. The problem arises when the skepticism itself becomes the first, last, and only principle, when the hermeneutics of suspicion becomes detached from the hermeneutics of affirmation. In their allergy to affirmation, certain postmodern thinkers resemble W. K. Clifford, who William James rebuked for avoiding error first and seeking truth second "like a general informing his soldiers that it is better to keep out of battle forever than to risk a single wound."[22] James is no dogmatic absolutist; he believes that truth is in some sense a moving target. However, he also makes an important distinction between two epistemological impulses—avoiding error and seeking truth:

> There are two ways of looking at our duty in the matter of opinion,—ways entirely different, and yet ways about whose difference the theory of knowledge seems hitherto to have shown very little concern. *We must have the truth*; and *we must avoid error.*——[T]hese are our first and great commandments as would-be knowers; but they are not two ways of stating an identical commandment, they are two separable laws. Although it may indeed happen that when we believe the truth A, we escape as an incidental consequence from believing the falsehood B, it hardly ever happens that by merely disbelieving B we necessarily believe A.[23]

The desire to seek truth is associated with those willing to employ the imagination and other creative capabilities—whether they happen to be scientists, mathematicians, novelists, or poets. The desire to avoid error is evident in those who accept only facts and, paradoxically, those who think there are no facts. Those who accept only facts demand "proof" before assenting to anything, often without a clear understanding of what that would mean, and those who reject all facts think nothing is reliable and so never assent to anything. In contrast to those who seek truth, neither is willing to run the risk that comes with any wager, whether it is hermeneutic, scientific, or otherwise. In the search for truth, including ethical truth, the point is to "enter the fray and take sides,"[24] not as part of a precipitous or ill-conceived rush to judgment, but as part of a considered, humble, wise, and genuine wager—a wager made all the more urgent in the case of virtue ethics by the fact that the point is to live well *now*, in the life we have. The problem with an unwavering commitment to avoiding error rather than seeking truth is simply that it will not get you anywhere. Skepticism is useful, even essential; however, elevated to the level of first commandment it is a non-starter.

> We all know objective truth is not obtainable . . . but we must still believe that objective truth is obtainable; or we must believe that it is 99 per cent obtainable; or if we can't believe this we must believe that 43 per cent objective truth is better than 41 per cent. We must do so because if we don't we're lost, we fall

into beguiling relativity, we value one liar's version as much as
another liar's, we throw up our hands at the puzzle of it all, we
admit that the victor has the right not just to the spoils but
also to the truth.[25]

The hermeneutics of suspicion is a welcome antidote to unreflective
and dogmatic deference to tradition. However, the radical commitment
to suspicion and acute allergy to affirmation, which are characteristic of
some manifestations of postmodernity, leads to a situation in which certain thinkers view all truth claims—even when those claims are humble,
tentative, provisional, open to revision, and so forth—as radical betrayals
tantamount to dogmatism. Ultimately, of course, everyone judges, chooses,
and acts. We cannot remain still, and cannot avoid choosing. Nevertheless,
for radical postmodern skepticism, in which relativism or nihilism is not
a dark night of the soul but rather the darkness of one blind from birth,
choices are ultimately made without a real reason, without why. They judge
because they *must*, rather than because they *should*, viewing judgment as a
(unfortunate) necessity rather than as a (fortunate) gift. Here, judgment is
a necessity rather than a virtue, and postmodern skeptics can never quite
bring themselves to make a virtue of this necessity.

But, of course, there are other kinds of relativisms. A somewhat less
radical position, a sort of contextualism, argues that no action is demonstra-
bly good in a way independent of its context. That is to say the goodness
of any good action is relative to the context in which it is performed, a
context that includes the culture and tradition in which an agent finds
herself. This position is not so radically relativist as subjectivism, because
there are rational grounds for criticizing a person's behavior or beliefs insofar
as they are appropriate for, or work, or correspond to beliefs about behavior
in a given context. So, we could legitimately rebuke someone for acting in
a way that is wrong, if by wrong we mean "wrong in the context of this
culture or tradition." However, this position remains relativistic insofar as
it claims there are no justifiable grounds for criticizing or condemning a
behavior in one culture from the perspective of another culture, and no
grounds for making such a condemnation in an absolute sense.

Finally, however, one might argue that a great deal of morality and
ethics is indeed contextual, but that there are some "contexts" that are in
fact universal parts of the human experience and so constitute de facto
universal moral and ethical truths, applicable to any human society in any
place at any time. Such a position attempts to capture something of both
the absolutist and relativist positions. With the absolutist, it maintains that

there are some universalizeable moral and ethical truths. However, in contrast to a simple absolutism, it maintains that such universality is not closed; there is always more to discern, discuss, understand, and say. Moreover, such universality does not apply to all ethical claims. Indeed, many ethical claims will be highly contextual in nature. Therefore, aligned with the relativist, this "ethical pluralist" maintains that there are many moral and ethical claims that can only be understood, and are only "true," in the context of their embeddedness in a particular time, place, culture, and context. Here the question is not "are morality and ethics relative or absolute," but rather "which aspects of ethics and morality are absolute and which are relative"?

Ethical pluralism allows that there are infinitely diverse ways in which cultures can articulate flourishing and virtue, but also that there are some ways of conceiving of these things that are, nevertheless, worse than others or flat-out wrong. Like points on a number line—on which we can simultaneously affirm that there are an infinite number of points between, say, four and five, and nevertheless know that numbers three and six are outside of this range—there are limits to legitimate accounts of virtue. Interpretations of virtue are infinite in the sense that there are innumerable ways to legitimately conceive of flourishing and virtue, but they are not infinite in the sense that human flourishing and virtue are ambiguous enough to admit of *any* definition, without restriction.

"Postmodern" Virtue Ethics

As we've seen, the challenge of relativism is nothing new. Aristotle knew well that a purely subjective account of ethics would be hopelessly incoherent. Thus, his account of virtue was closely tied to both rationality and the commonsense wisdom of his community and tradition, as well as the *phronimos* who embodied both. But postmodernity has exacerbated the temptation to relativism—whether people give in to that temptation in the form of descriptive relativism, normative relativism, cultural contextualism, ethical subjectivism, or some other form of ethical relativism.

So how have contemporary virtue ethicists, who do not share Aristotle's metaphysical biology or limited and static view of culture, respond to this challenge? A full account of the vast literature addressing nihilism and relativism is neither possible nor necessary. It should be adequate to address some of the most important responses to relativism made by the various thinkers whose work will inform the narrative environmental virtue ethics which I seek to develop.

Nussbaum's Neo-Aristotelian Defense and the Capabilities Approach

Aristotle's deference to the customs of his culture and his reliance on the ideal of the *phronimos* can't work for contemporary virtue ethics, but perhaps a neo-Aristotelian reading of his work will. Such is the position Martha Nussbaum defends.[26] She argues, sticking closely to Aristotle's own work, that virtue ethics need not be as relativistic as some would suggest.

Nussbaum begins by pointing out, correctly, that many contemporary virtue ethicists seem willing to abandon the project of justifying, and even the hope of identifying, "a single norm of flourishing life for all human beings and [to rely], instead, on norms that are local in both origin and practice."[27] This is curious, she suggests, because despite the high degree of flexibility built into his theory of ethics, Aristotle himself was nevertheless a defender of a single, objective account of human good, at least in the sense that such an account would be "justifiable by reference to reasons that do not derive merely from local traditions and practices, but rather from *features of humanness that lie beneath all local traditions* and are there to be seen whether or not they are in fact recognized in local traditions."[28]

Aristotle does this, writes Nussbaum, by identifying certain spheres of action in which all human beings are situated and in which they will all have to make choices. If all humans must make choices within these spheres, it seems reasonable to consider what would constitute a good or a bad choice. It is true that answers to such questions may differ fairly radically; however, even if we end up disagreeing about the characteristics of a good or bad action within a certain sphere—say something very basic, like enduring pain—we are, at the very least, *talking* about the same thing. Claims about virtues (dispositions to make good choices within a given sphere of action) are, it seems, not so broad as to constitute incommensurable discourses. We are often addressing the same phenomenon even when we disagree about it. This "thin" account of virtue—whatever consists of acting and choosing well within a certain sphere of action—suggests that we are not so bad off as to find ourselves in some situation of radically "post-Babel, pre-Pentecostal" incommensurability or untranslatability. While it's true that translation is never perfect and without loss or betrayal, across time and culture human beings share various "grounding experiences" by virtue of being the sorts of beings we are and the condition in which we find ourselves. These grounding experiences—such as bodily appetites and pleasures, social relationships with others, and fear of important damages like death—establish the objective spheres of action and form a touchstone to which we should return when engaged in ethical debate.[29] Ethical progress, suggests Nussbaum, generally occurs in the context of careful reflection on these grounding experiences and attitudes and responses to them.

This initial insight regarding grounding experiences and spheres of action was developed more fully as the "capabilities approach" to human development and ethics, which Nussbaum articulated with economist Amartya Sen and others.[30] Briefly, the capabilities approach provides a philosophical foundation for "a bare minimum of what respect for human dignity requires," arguing that "the best approach to this idea of a basic social minimum is provided by an approach that focuses on *human capabilities*, that is, what people are actually able to do and be."[31] A good life requires, at a minimum, the ability to develop and exercise these essential human capabilities. In her *Women and Human Development: The Capabilities Approach*, and again in *Creating Capabilities*, Nussbaum lists ten central human functional capabilities: life; bodily health; bodily integrity; senses, imagination, and thought; emotions; practical reason; affiliation; other species; play; control over one's political and material environment.[32] This list is neither exhaustive nor fixed; nevertheless, it represents a valid and useful way of approaching ethics, and one that is resistant to extreme forms of relativism.

However, the notion of ethical progress suggests that we cannot settle for a thin account of virtue that simply acknowledges that there are better and worse ways to act in various spheres. Virtue ethics requires—especially if we hope to grapple with either ethical progress or comparing incommensurable ethical schemas—a more robust, "thicker" account that addresses virtues in greater detail and in concrete circumstances. Such accounts would flesh out our initial identification of spheres of action and our desire to act well within them by describing in greater detail what it means to act virtuously in these spheres, giving examples of various contexts in which such action would be called for, examples of succeeding or failing to act virtuously, paradigms of virtuous or vicious dispositions, and the like.

This need for greater detail and concrete circumstances is one of the reasons that narrative plays such an essential role in the articulation of environmental virtue ethics. As we will see in subsequent chapters, it is through narratives like Thoreau's *Walden*, Leopold's *Sand County Almanac*, Muir's *My First Summer in the Sierra*, and Abbey's *Desert Solitaire* that we add flesh to the thin account of environmental virtue. These narratives and others like them propose a substantially thicker and more detailed description of human flourishing in a sustainable environment, and link that flourishing to the dispositions, actions, emotions, beliefs, and practices that support and contribute to it.

It is, of course, true that the fact that we are reflecting on a common sphere of action (at the thin level) does not insure a single response or agreed upon conclusion (at the thick). It's also true that there is no "innocent eye," unbiased view, or God's-eye perspective from which we can adjudicate in an absolutely objective manner between conflicting claims regarding virtue. However, this need not be fatal for virtue ethics, for we can still maintain that the specification of a given virtue might give rise to a disjunction resulting in a "plurality of acceptable accounts" without allowing that *anything* at all might fall within the range of acceptable accounts.[33] Indeed, this is just what we ought to expect from a position like Aristotle's, which believes in a universal truth but which is keenly attentive to concrete circumstances, including those of history and culture. Likewise, the fact that we cannot escape the hermeneutic circle, that there is no "view from nowhere," does not imply, as some relativists assume, "that all world interpretations are equally valid and altogether non-comparable, that there are no good standards of assessment and 'anything goes.'"[34] The relativist often overstates her case, failing to adequately demonstrate why we could not say, for example, that certain ways of addressing the human desire for autonomy are better than others. She also tends to "understate the amount of attunement, recognition, and overlap that actually obtains across cultures."[35] So while virtue ethics is rightly allergic to monolithic and absolutist accounts of morality, it need not, on that account, slide into full-blown relativism. Indeed, it seems most amenable to what I have referred to as a pluralistic account, which seeks to steer between the Scylla of absolutism and the Charybdis of relativism.

Naturalism and Sandler's Pluralistic Teleological Account

Sandler's pluralistic teleological approach was addressed in some detail in Chapter 2, but it should be obvious that, like Nussbaum's capabilities approach, Sandler's account of virtue has the benefit of foreclosing certain sorts of relativism. The pluralism of his approach means that while there are multiple ways to conceive of human flourishing and the virtues that contribute to it, at least some conceptions must be definitively rejected: "The pluralistic teleological account allows that there are innumerable ways for people to make their way in the world virtuously."[36] It leaves open "the majority of life courses, careers, roles, and projects" and underdetermines any specific account of how a specific agent will behave in a specific context.[37] It allows for the possibility of virtues that are specific to certain people due to their relationships with others, their job, their age, their role, and so on. However, despite this enormous flexibility, "some projects and life courses will be ruled out."[38] Sandler means to apply this rejection both at the level of the individual (he rules out, for example, the life of a gangster or grifter) and at the level of cultural practice.

> According to the pluralistic teleological account, a character trait is a virtue to the extent that it is conducive to a person in a world like ours realizing ends grounded in her own good, the good of other human beings, and the good of environmental entities with inherent worth. Neither the pluralistic teleological account nor the substantive specifications of the virtues that follow from it are simply reflections of cultural practice or personal preference or desires.[39]

The point is not to defend any sort of cultural absolutism, but to set up a defense against cultural relativism. As with the case of individuals, there are innumerable ways in which to conceive of virtue and human flourishing within the diverse cultures of the world; but that innumerability does not mean that any way of conceiving virtue and human flourishing is accurate or acceptable.

Much of what was said of Nussbaum's capabilities approach could also be said of Sandler's pluralistic teleological approach, at least insofar as they both foreclose the possibility of the most radical forms of relativism. However, growing out of the naturalistic approach, Sandler's account adds a certain natural and biological grounding of which we should take notice. The basic commitment to naturalism in Sandler's account lends itself to certain interpretations of human flourishing while precluding others. Under the naturalistic assumption, writes Sandler, questions about how we should live "are questions about how we should live as the biological beings that we are, given the particular world we are in"; while not reducible to biology, "they are not questions . . . *independent* of the facts about human beings and our environment."[40] While Sandler's own approach moves beyond the naturalistic approach in significant ways, it remains committed to naturalism and so can avail itself of basic natural limits on what might count as flourishing and what might pass for a virtue.

Under either the capabilities approach or the pluralistic teleological account, the discussion of virtue must take into account the *type of being* that we are. Therefore, biological—as well as anthropological, psychological, and sociological—data will be a useful complement to philosophical reflection. Articulating human flourishing and the virtues that contribute to it remains a fundamentally *philosophical* task, but it is a task in which philosophy can, and should, draw on appropriate insights from other disciplines.

MacIntyre and the Conflict of Traditions

Alasdair MacIntyre, we've seen, attempts to reestablish the idea of a *telos* by thinking of "human" as a "functional concept." Just like "watch" or "farmer," the concept of "human" entails certain functions that can be performed well or poorly, which means that the Emotivist and relativist claim that morality is nothing more than expression of individual preference— "hooray for honesty!"—is false. Nevertheless, MacIntyre's earlier work in *After Virtue* was heavily criticized for conceding too much to the relativist position. In it, he seemed to suggest that there was, ultimately, no way to adjudicate between competing cultural accounts of virtue, falling into a cultural relativism even as he defeated individual or subjective relativism.

In *After Virtue*, MacIntyre concludes by asserting that "goods, and with them the *only grounds for the authority of the laws and virtues*, can only be discovered by entering into those relationships which constitute communities whose central bond is a shared vision of and understanding of the goods."[41] Given the diversity of those communities and their respective visions of the human *telos*, human virtues, and human goods, it seems clear that MacIntyre was at this stage willing to concede quite a lot (although not everything) to the relativist. However, in light of criticism, he addresses this too-easy concession to cultural relativism in *Whose Justice, Which Rationality?* as well as in essays such as "Moral Relativism, Truth and Justification."[42]

Moral relativism, generally, is a response to "the discovery of systematic and apparently ineliminable disagreement between the protagonists of rival moral points of view, each of whom claims rational justification for their own standpoint and none of whom seems able, except by their own standards, to rebut the claims of their rivals."[43] The disagreement is often not only about moral and ethical content—virtues, vices, ideas about the human *telos*, and so forth—but, even more problematically, also about the very standards of justificatory reasoning that should be used to adjudicate disagreements. The disagreement includes disagreements about how to address disagreement. However, the disagreement not only suggests—with or without justification—some level of descriptive relativism, it also illustrates that the rival standpoints are committed to the idea of truth and justification, for otherwise there would be no disagreement.

Moral and ethical disagreements arise because the various claimants in the dispute are making claims, on some level, to truth. This, in turn, means that these various claimants are committed to some idea of rational justification that is not merely internal to their respective beliefs, a standard of justification that would apply to, and potentially sway, even those who do not currently hold the beliefs in question. Rational justification and truth are not synonymous, of course, but the former is only intelligible in terms of the latter—the attempt to rationally justify something implies a commitment to the idea of truth.[44] MacIntyre argues that attempting to rationally justify a moral standpoint also commits one to the following theses: (1) that the account of morality which one is defending is not fatally harmed by its own hermeneutic situatedness, that it not only describes how things *seem* to its adherents but also, in some significant way, describes how things in fact *are*; (2) that moral standpoints incompatible with the belief in question are somehow flawed, that is they can and should be replaced by a rationally superior standpoint; and, crucially, (3) that if further inquiry—reflection, discussion, debate, experience, and so forth—reveals that the moral standpoint being defended is incapable of exhibiting its "argumentative superiority" to its rivals, it should itself be replaced by some superior account.[45] In other words, commitment to rational justification means commitment to truth. The commitment to truth, along with assertions about one's own tradition, commits one to the belief that one's present standpoint is superior to its rivals, and that any rival traditions that are fundamentally incompatible with it are in error. However, the commitment to truth also implies that if reflection proves one's current standpoint inadequate it should be abandoned for something superior.

So, MacIntyre finds himself left with two conflicting claims. First, we cannot transcend our locally constituted moral point of view; there is no escaping the hermeneutic circle. Second, moral progress will require that a person holding a given moral standpoint is capable of transcending that standpoint in order to critique it. What to do?

In the attempt to engage another tradition—which already assumes we have left behind an unreflective sort of absolutist belief in our own tradition—we often begin by characterizing the foreign tradition in the terms of our native tradition. In doing so, we reject anything in the former that is incompatible with the central theses of the latter, although more open-minded individuals may allow that the foreign tradition has something to contribute in terms of "marginal and subordinate questions."[46] However, genuine discourse with another tradition requires something more: the recognition of "difficulties" and even "insoluble antinomies" in one's own tradition and willingness to "ask whether the alternative and rival tradition may not be able to provide resources to characterize and to explain the failings and defects of [one's] own tradition more adequately than [one], using the resources of that tradition, [has] been able to do."[47] Doing so requires, at least, three things. First, those engaged in rational justification of their own moral or ethical standpoint must also acknowledge that doing so commits them to a certain idea of truth which, in turn, commits them to show-ing how the resources of their standpoint are intelligible, and potentially convincing, to those who occupy rival standpoints. Second, transcending one's own moral or ethical standpoint requires that one is both able and willing to systematically critique it in a way that identifies its own limita-tions and difficulties. Finally, such transcendence requires the "ability to put in question the conceptual framework of that particular standpoint from within the framework itself by the use of argumentative resources not so far available within that framework, but now made so available" through the encounter with alternatives.[48]

In other words, what we need is a meaningful encounter with otherness.

~

It's all well and good to suggest that we must see things from alternative per-spectives, and that doing so is a prerequisite for the search for truth, for self-critique, for the cultivation of virtue, and for authentic self-understanding. However, while suggesting this is easy, perhaps even intuitive for certain people, understanding how this is possible is significantly more difficult, and actually doing it more difficult still. How do we gain an alternative perspective from which to examine and critique a perspective we currently endorse? How can we see things from the point of view of another person or a different tradition? The best resources for understanding how this is possible—and, happily, for actually doing it—come from the field of *nar-rative*; and it is narrative and its application to self-cultivation, virtue, and ethics which will occupy us for the remainder of this work.

Philosophers of narrative provide us with rich resources for articulat-ing just how exchange, translation, interpretation, dialogue, critique, and understanding are possible between diverse individuals, cultures, and tra-ditions. In addition, narrative proves indispensable for understanding self-identity and, therefore, for understanding self-transformation, the process by which someone becomes a new person, as when one strives to become virtuous. Indeed, certain capabilities Nussbaum champions (imagination, for example), as well as many of the "higher-order" criteria enumerated by Sandler (especially a "meaningful life" and "the realization of any non-eudaimonistic ends"), are phenomena that we understand, in large measure, through the use of narrative. This is, obviously, even more the case with an approach that gives a central place to tradition, narrative, or imagina-tion, as is the case of the work done by MacIntyre, Ricoeur, and Kearney.

None of this is to suggest that inhabiting a strange perspective or tradition is easy, or that narrative will provide us with a clear and unproblematic language with which to understand, communicate, and foster virtue, especially environmental virtue. Far from it. Inhabiting an unfamiliar perspective or tradition requires, writes MacIntyre, a "rare gift of empathy as well as of intellectual insight."[49] Only through "the exercise of philosophical and moral imagination [may] someone . . . on occasion be able to learn what it would be to think, feel and act from the standpoint of some alternative and rival standpoint, acquiring in so doing an ability to understand her or his own tradition in the perspective afforded by that rival."[50] Nevertheless, the relative rarity of empathy, intellectual insight, or narrative imagination is not due to some essential failure in human nature. These gifts, like many others, are ones we can *cultivate*, and now we must turn to considering how this is possible, for our ability to improve ourselves and live better lives, as well as to create a better environmental future for our children and grandchildren, depends upon it.

Narrative Theory

Stories and Our Lives

How many a man has dated a new era in his life from the reading of a book?

—Henry David Thoreau, *Walden*

The cultivation of virtues depends on narratives, vision, and the power of examples.

—Louke van Wensveen, *Dirty Virtues*

Life is not what one lived, but what one remembers and how one remembers it in order to recount it.

—Gabriel García Márquez, *Living to Tell the Tale*

Narrative, it seems, will play a major role in our understanding and articulation of the human *telos* and the virtues that contribute to it. However, before we go on to consider the role of narrative in virtue ethics, we should pause briefly to survey some important work in the philosophy of narrative. While philosophical attention to narrative has been episodic at best, concern with the nature of narrative and its effect on those who practice it is long standing, reaching at least as far back as Plato's *Republic*. Relatively few thinkers, however, have made narrative a primary focus of their work, among them are Paul Ricoeur, Richard Kearney, Martha Nussbaum, and Wayne Booth.[1]

The strongest case for a narrative component in virtue ethics begins with the argument that identity itself is fundamentally narrative. Paul

Ricoeur provides us with the most detailed account of the role of narrative in identity, and it makes sense to begin with his account. Next,
we'll consider Richard Kearney's treatment of narrative epiphanies and the
limited sense in which vicarious narrative experience can be better than
direct experience. Third, we'll turn to Martha Nussbaum, who highlights
a number of phenomena crucial to good judgment and ethical sensitivity that are overlooked in standard philosophical accounts, but which are
characteristic of narrative and virtue ethics. Finally, Wayne Booth's work
will flesh out some guidelines regarding what it means to read responsibly,
so that we may, ultimately, *live* more responsibly.

Paul Ricoeur and Narrative Identity

Because the cultivation of virtue involves training, developing, or making
a certain sort of person, it is inextricably tied to the idea of self-formation
and self-transformation. The former takes place any time we are establishing
character traits, dispositions, or patterns of behavior, and is most evident
in the moral and ethical education of children. The latter takes place any
time we attempt to change established character traits, dispositions, or
patterns of behavior, the paradigmatic example of which is when, to use a
suitably literary metaphor, a person "turns over a new leaf" and becomes,
or begins to become, someone new. However, before we can address what it
means to form or transform oneself we need to come to some understanding
regarding what a *self* is.

Who am I? This is, perhaps, *the* philosophical question. Answering
it is arguably a universal human desire or need. No other question is so
immediate, so compelling, and yet so frustrating. Socrates confessed that,
at least at times, it obsessed him to the exclusion of all other concerns:
"I can't as yet 'know myself,' as the inscription at Delphi enjoins, and so
long as that ignorance remains it seems to me ridiculous to inquire into
extraneous matters."[2] The list of similarly befuddled philosophers or thinkers is long and distinguished: Plutarch, inquiring into identity more generally, developed the paradox of the Ship of Theseus; Augustine declares his
bewilderment at his own nature in the *Confessions*; Boethius loses and finds
himself in the *Consolation of Philosophy*; Descartes' *Meditations* called into
question his very existence; Locke tied identity to consciousness as opposed
to substance; Hume argued that introspection finds nothing more than a
bundle of perceptions; Buddhism rejects the idea of any fixed self; and
Nietzsche suggests that the idea of a "doer" is a fiction added to the deed.

This long-standing human and philosophical concern has, not surprisingly, generated an extensive body of literature and thinking on the subject of personal identity. Fortunately, we can circumvent a great deal of this material because so much of it has failed to recognize one crucial distinction: the distinction between *what* we are and *who* we are. The work of Paul Ricoeur is particularly instructive here, especially as articulated in *Oneself as Another* and in the three volumes of *Time and Narrative*.[3]

> The problem of personal identity constitutes, in my opinion, a privileged place of confrontation between the two major uses of the concept of identity. . . . Let me recall the terms of the confrontation: on the one side, identity as sameness (Latin *idem*, German *Gleichheit*, French *mêmeté*); on the other, identity as selfhood (Latin *ipse*, German *Selbstheit*, French *ipséité*). Selfhood, as I have repeatedly affirmed, is not sameness. Because the major distinction between them is not recognized . . . the solutions offered to the problem of personal identity which do not consider the narrative dimension fail."[4]

This simple distinction indicates the significance of narrative for virtue ethics: virtue ethics is unintelligible without a clear account of identity, and identity is unintelligible without a clear account of narrative. More on the former in the next chapter; here we must focus on the role of narrative in identity.

When we inquire into identity, what is it that concerns us? It's true that in some cases we might be concerned with the whatness of a thing, especially when we are talking about things as opposed to people. However, even in the case of a person we might be concerned with the whatness of identity in trying to determine, for example, whether a person will be susceptible to certain diseases or responsive to certain treatments by mapping her DNA. In such a case we are after something like whether or not one thing is susceptible to degradation by another other thing or responsive to repair by yet another sort of thing. However, the abstraction evident in this example and the awkward language used to express it reveals the limited, though not insignificant or unimportant, sphere of *idem*-identity for addressing persons. It's useful within a certain limited range, but in general it is not what we are after when we think about identity. While it's true that we are sometimes concerned with questions of *whatness*, most of our thinking about and concern with identity is something that we can only address by asking questions of *whoness*. Most the time—and certainly with respect to any question of virtue—we are after the who of an individual rather than the what, the *ipse* rather than the *idem*.

Ricoeur's concern, like my own, is with identity as a lived selfhood rather than as an abstract sameness. I am concerned with the practical issues stemming from the question "who am I" rather than theoretical issues related to identity over time (e.g., "when I wake up, how do I know I am the same person who went to sleep the night before"). Viewed in this way, it becomes quite clear that there is an inescapable narrative aspect to identity. For each individual, her life story is an attempt to hold together her diverse acts, feelings, and thoughts into the coherence of one narrative subject that perdures over time. "*Who* am I?" "*Who* is responsible?" "*Who* is she?" Such questions are invariably answered with narratives that tell, in greater or lesser detail, the story of the agent:

> To state the identity of an individual or a community is to answer the question, "Who did this?" "Who is the agent or author?" . . . To answer the question "Who?" as Hannah Arendt has so forcefully put it, is to tell the story of a life. The story tells us about the action of the "who." And the identity of this "who" therefore itself must be a narrative identity.[5]

Ricoeur does not ignore the aspects of identity that carry the sense of "unchanged over time" or "the quality of being identical." Both *idem*-identity (sameness over time) and *ipse*-identity (selfhood, self-sameness, self-constancy) are significant. However, the static permanence of *idem*-identity, the quality of a thing being identical with itself is, I submit, less philosophically interesting than the more mutable qualities of identity captured under the rubric of *ipse*-identity. What we are certainly matters, but it is who we are that really concerns us in our deepest hearts.[6]

Of course, the fluidity of *ipse*-identity is not without limits. It is shaped and constrained by history, culture, tradition, and environment. Moreover, because *idem*-identity and *ipse*-identity are not unrelated, there are examples of phenomena in which they seem either to overlap or diverge in ways that will have significance for a narrative account of virtue. Two areas to which Ricoeur draws our attention are worth mentioning here: character and keeping one's word.[7] Character is "the set of lasting dispositions by which a person is recognized," representing an area in which *idem* and *ipse* overlap to a large degree.[8] What begins with an action can become a habit and eventually an established disposition or trait, each of these descriptors designating a more and more settled and fixed state. Actions are not fixed at all, which is why we might dismiss a given action, virtuous or vicious, as a "one off" or something "out of character." Habits are more settled, but can still be modified. A character trait, however, is both internalized and settled enough that we feel comfortable identifying the person possessing it in terms of that trait. For example, when we say that someone is an environmentalist, or is frugal, or is caring with respect to nature, we are asserting that these characteristics are part of who she is. This, incidentally, is why the translation of *hexis* as "habit" can be misleading. Aristotle has in mind something more deep-seated and settled than a behavioral quirk. Character represents the closest thing to an overlap of *idem* and *ipse*; it represents the "what of the who."[9] Promising, in contrast, represents a different kind of stability over time, self-constancy, that exists solely within the sphere of *ipse*. Here, the permanence of self is asserted against observable changes over time. It is the assertion that "I will hold firm" in the face of changes in situation, context, inclination, and so on.[10]

Narrative identity, ultimately, is a manifestation of the need to mediate between sameness and difference, to bring concordance to the discordance of happenings over time through the use of something like plot.

> It is thus plausible to endorse the following chain of assertions: self-knowledge is an interpretation; self interpretation, in its turn, finds in narrative, among other signs and symbols, a privileged mediation; this mediation draws on history as much as it does on fiction, turning the story of a life into a fictional story or a historical fiction, comparable to those biographies of great men in which history and fiction are intertwined.[11]

Narrative Refiguration: Stories that Change Our Lives

Together, character and promise-keeping push philosophical questions of identity into new territory, from the fundamental philosophical question "who am I?" to its unspoken, but equally important, correlate "who will I be?" In the case of promise-keeping this connection is clear. Can we really answer questions of identity without coming to terms with the constancy, or lack thereof, evident in our formal and informal promises about who we will be? However, for all its supposed fixity, the permanence of character is no less concerned with the future of the self. The permanence of *idem*-identity, as well as the intrusion of that sort of permanence into *ipse*-identity in character, seems to suggest that, while virtue ethics might well articulate a means of ethical formation, the possibility of ethical *trans*-formation is at best remote and at worst chimerical. Why is it that, despite increasingly dire evidence about environmental catastrophe, and despite widespread public opinion that something must urgently be done, relatively few people undertake the process of transforming themselves to become environmentally virtuous in significant ways? How can we overcome the ossification of character in order to become better people?

Here we must return to the idea of narrative identity, which bridges the fixity of character, where *idem* and *ipse* overlap, and the mutability of *ipse*, where the gap between them is evident. For, as Ricoeur says, "what character has sedimented, narration can redeploy."[12]

> Unlike the abstract identity of the Same . . . narrative identity, constitutive of self-constancy, can include change, mutability, within the cohesion of one lifetime. The subject then appears both the reader and the writer of its own life, as Proust would have it. As the literary analysis of autobiography confirms, the story of a life continues to be refigured by all the truthful or fictive stories a subject tells about himself or herself. This refiguration makes this life a cloth woven of stories told.[13]

Here we see why narrative is critical for virtue ethics. When I change the person I am—as when I attempt to become virtuous—I am "refiguring" the narrative that I am. It is the ability of a self to be refigured that constitutes narrative's special power for virtue ethics. This is possible because narratives are *both* descriptive *and* prescriptive. There are no ethically neutral narratives—especially when seen from the more expansive perspective characteristic of the virtue ethics approach—and each narrative exhorts us, as the sculpted torso of Apollo did Rilke, "you must change your life!"[14] Indeed, narrative accomplishes this transition so well that Ricoeur claims narrative constitutes the "natural transition between description and prescription."[15] The prescriptive aspect of narrative, along with the narrative aspect of identity, gives us a situation in which narrative itself plays a central role in the refiguration, or transformation, of a life. Ricoeur's formula is "describe, narrate, prescribe—each moment of [this] triad implying a specific relation between the constitution of action and the constitution of the self."[16]

How exactly does this work? Ricoeur describes metaphor and narrative in terms of *mimesis*, which he views through an Aristotelian rather than Platonic lens—that is, in terms of imitating action rather than imitating nature. His understanding of *mimesis* follows a tripartite model. First, in order to comprehend any narrative, we must have a preliminary understanding of human action. Ricoeur calls this prefigurative understanding "*mimesis*$_1$" and describes it as having three main components: structural, symbolic, and temporal. We approach any narrative with an understanding of structure that allows us to make sense of the "what," "why," "who," "how," "with whom," and "against whom" of any action, and to link these categories to each other.[17] Thus, we can grasp, for example, that "Ahab pursues Moby Dick to avenge the loss of his leg" and that "Thoreau went to the woods in order to live deliberately and to learn what life had to teach." We also have a symbolic preunderstanding of narrative that confers the "initial readability of an action"—that, for example, a raised hand is hailing a taxi as opposed to voting or greeting someone (each of these actions using the same movement of the hand).[18] In addition to the descriptive aspect of symbolic preunderstanding—and of the greatest importance for narrative's application to virtue ethics—there is a normative aspect of symbolic understanding that allows us to attribute *value* to actions and to agents, pointing toward the implicit ethical quality of any narrative. The urging to "change your life" implicit in a narrative may roar like Whitman's "barbaric yawp" or whisper *sotto voce* like E. E. Cumming's "little voice," but it is always present in some way. Ricoeur argues that "there is no action [and therefore no narrative *mimesis*] that does not give rise to approbation or reprobation, to however a small degree, as a function of a hierarchy of values for which goodness and wickedness are the poles."[19] Finally, we have a temporal preunderstanding that, among other things, helps us to understand the role of temporality in action. We can grasp the development of an action—how actions unfold over time as related to other events—and understand, for example, that John Muir left his job and home after nearly losing his eye in an accident.

$Mimesis_2$, in turn, is the configuration or "emplotment" of the narrative. This includes: (1) the "organization of the events," not as a series of sequential happenings, but as components of an intelligible whole that "transforms the events into a story" with meaning or purpose; (2) bringing together heterogeneous elements such as "agents, goals, means, interactions, circumstances, and unexpected results"; and (3) mediating the temporal characteristics that allow the aforementioned synthesis of the heterogeneous.[20] The result is that it is the reader who does the work of emplotting the narrative. The heterogeneous elements of the narrative must be organized by the reader so that they make sense as a narrative.

> It is the reader who completes the work [of emplotment] . . . [The written word] consists of holes, lacunae, zones of indetermination, which, as in Joyce's *Ulysses*, challenge the reader's capacity to configure what the author seems to take malign delight in defiguring. In such an extreme case, it is the reader, almost abandoned by the work, who carries the burden of emplotment.[21]

Rather than finding the narrative whole cloth in the words of the text, the elements of the narrative must be organized and connected by the reader. Indeed, in some sense the author herself is merely the "first reader" of her own narrative.

Finally, $mimesis_3$ takes place at the "intersection of the world of the text and the world of the hearer or reader," allowing the narrative to reach its fulfillment.[22] Hearkening to *Anwendung* (application) in Gadamer's work or to *mimesis-praxeos* (representation of action) in Aristotle's, $mimesis_3$ marks the point at which the narrative changes, refigures, or transforms the reader. Herein lies the real power of narrative for our purposes: the power to refigure our lives. Reading stories involves more than merely an exercise in historical curiosity or whimsical fantasy. Narratives allow us to see things from different perspectives. When we read stories we enter new worlds and try out new identities—worlds and identities that may, and in some sense always do, reshape the world and identity with which we began the story.

So, our identities are, in large part, narrative identities. And our understanding of any narrative is dependent on the existing store of narrative understanding at our disposal when we first encounter and interpret it. Our understanding will evolve with each narrative we encounter, changing both our retrospective sense of the narratives we already know and the prospective possibilities for narratives we will encounter in the future. All this makes perfect sense when we think of narratives in more than purely aesthetic terms. Most readers have had the experience of a "life-changing book." Nevertheless, it will still strike some people as odd to suggest that, for example, reading a book can help to make you a better person, although this wasn't always the case. Wayne Booth points out that until quite recently people took it for granted that there was a "direct connection between stories read and probable effects on conduct—on character."[23] However, skeptical contemporary readers will require some arguments and examples on behalf of this extraordinary narrative power.

Richard Kearney and Narrative Epiphanies

How is it that narrative can change a life? In the case of fiction, stories are made up; they are "make-believe," while life is "real." We think of fiction as the child's account of her daydream in which she flies on a horse to dine in France with talking animals, while non-fiction is clear and logical account of what her father did at work. However, while nonfiction professes objectivity it too *re*-presents something that is not actually present and, therefore, gives us, at best, reality at one remove. As Plato points out, art does not give us the real thing but rather a copy or imitation of the real thing.[24] Similarly, to use an environmental example, Jack Turner claims it was "Muir's mistake" to think that his experience of the wild could be reproduced and made available through things like Sierra Club outings.[25] Experiencing the wild indirectly through guided trips into relatively domesticated areas gives us only a mediated experience, a semblance of the real thing, an abstraction. If that is the case, it stands to reason that "traveling" to a place through narratives and photographs would be even more mediated—an indirect, desiccated, bloodless abstraction. Dealing with such abstractions blurs the boundaries "between the real and the fake, the wild and the tame, the independent and the dependent, the original and the copy, the healthy and the diminished."[26] This, to some degree, can account for our fascination with the picturesque, odd, or bizarre in art and nature writing, at least since the Romantics.

Thus, to the reality of life we contrast both the make-believe of fiction and the counterfeit of nonfiction. For this reason Ricoeur had to contend with the claim that "stories are recounted and not lived; life is lived and not recounted."[27] Indeed, on the face of it, the idea that narrative actually presents reality seems like a stretch. Isn't any story detached, by its very nature, from the reality it is trying to re-present? It may be true, as Richard Kearney suggests, that to understand something about courage we tell the story of Achilles—or, perhaps, some other modern virtuoso of courage—but reading about the siege of Troy or the slaughter on Omaha Beach and Pointe du Hoc is a far cry from actually experiencing either battle. The "as-if" experience of narrative differs from the visceral experience of lived reality in ways that are both theoretically and practically significant. As Kearney himself points out, in reference to the obscenity trial surrounding Joyce's Ulysses, "no one was ever raped by a book."[28] The vicarious experience of engaging a narrative is not the same as the direct experience of reality; unlike the repetition of actual virtuous acts prescribed by Aristotle, no amount of reading about courage will fully succeed in making someone courageous.

It is for this reason that Turner claims that we need "gross contact," intimate personal experience with actual wildness, in order to either grasp its truth or to appreciate and value it. Why? Because "we only value what we know and love" and, lacking precisely the visceral experience of gross contact, most people "no longer know or love the wild."[29] Experiencing wildness secondhand, as through narrative, leaves us with only the "abstract wild."[30] It is, perhaps, for this reason that Thoreau placed such a strident emphasis on the importance of personal experience. In a pithy apologia for speaking so much about himself he claims he is "confined to this theme by the narrowness of [his] experience."[31] Thus, he is in favor of "practical education," choosing to grow his own food and build his own shelter so as not to be "defrauded" of the experience by "resigning the pleasure of construction" to the carpenter.[32]

However, it was precisely the genius of Muir—as well as his successor, David Brower—that successfully induced many people to value and, after a fashion, to love places that they themselves would in all likelihood never see or experience in person. An uncompromising commitment to firsthand experience runs counter to a long tradition that assumes that narratives can affect character, as well as to the claims by numerous people that books have in fact changed their lives. While neither of these considerations constitutes an unassailable argument for the power of narrative in the sphere of virtue, it would be foolish to dismiss such claims without further consideration. Moreover, there are practical reasons to be concerned with the efficacy of narrative, especially in terms of environmental virtue. Virtues are cultivated, in large part, by engaging in certain actions. You cannot become a good carpenter without having things to build on which you can practice, and you cannot become a person who lives simply without practicing simplicity in your daily life. If certain virtues are often, or best, cultivated as the result of certain experiences with nature, what are we to do in a context in which many people are excluded from the experience in question?[33] Take Turner's concern with wildness. If truly valuing wildness depends on loving it, and loving it depends on gross contact with it, then wildness and wilderness will be lost. Not everyone has the luxury to take off weeks, months, or years to immerse themselves in nature. Even if they did have the time, many would not have the inclination to do so. Moreover, even if they did have the time, inclination, *and* means to do so, in an already over-populated world so many people seeking gross contact with a wild ecosystem would surely overwhelm and destroy it.[34] The desire for gross contact with certain manifestations of wilderness or wildness can be destructive. Stegner muses about one of his own favorite places in the Unita Mountains: "Places as perfect as this should be as secret as they are inaccessible. They cannot stand advertising, because we have a habit of destroying what we love."[35]

Even if a person has access to the sphere or arena in which a given virtue is practiced, she needs guides or exemplars for how to act virtuously. Just because a person has access to dangerous circumstances and chooses to act in them does not mean she will become courageous. Acting in danger-ous situations might produce courage, but it could also produce cowardice or rashness. A person who aspires to virtue is much more likely to hit the mark if she has someone to mentor or guide her, especially in her initial efforts. This could certainly come in the form of an actual mentor, such as Muir or Brower leading the Sierra Club outings. However, today most people lack firsthand experience with someone who has cultivated environmental virtues to a high degree. Having no experience of someone who lives or attempts to live sustainably, they have no model to follow.

Surely one possible answer to this dilemma is the concession that not all virtues are for all people. Some virtues are role-specific. Moreover, some people are simply not in situations that allow for the cultivation of certain virtues. If a person does not have access to an arena in which to practice a given virtue, she cannot cultivate it. Thus, when Aristotle discusses the virtue of "magnificence" he tells us "a poor man cannot be magnificent, since he has not the means with which to spend large sums fittingly."[36] Perhaps "environmental" virtues are similarly limited to those with the proper access and experience.

On one hand, it is no doubt true that one's virtue is limited by one's circumstance and that some people are simply excluded from some virtues. However, if we insist too strongly on this, we overstate the case. First, if magnificence is a virtue, it seems to be an unusual one.[37] Most virtues—simplicity, courage, generosity, hospitality, temperance, and so on—can be practiced, for all intents and purposes, by any human being. Second, assuming environmental virtues have some discernable benefit to the environment, it will be practically disastrous to limit those virtues to agents with the most direct experience of nature—farmers, restoration ecologists, wilderness explorers, and so on—and exclude urban and suburban citizens.[38] Everyone has some access to some aspect of "the environment" and, thus, to some of the virtues associated with it.

Nevertheless, experience remains a critical component of virtue ethics. This much seems certain. Aristotle argues that discussions of politics and ethics are not useful for those "inexperienced in the actions that occur in life . . . and it makes no difference whether he is young in years or youthful in character; the defect does not depend on time, but on his living [that is, his experience]."[39] Inexperienced people may well follow rules made by experienced people, but in such cases the inexperienced people are not strictly speaking virtuous, but are merely performing virtuous actions prescribed, in this case, by people who are virtuous.[40] The inexperienced do not, generally, understand the reasons for the rule and are unable to discern the contexts in which it should be bent or broken. *Phronesis* requires life experience that builds, over time, sensitivity to context, which in turn allows one to properly apply universal rules (which are a kind of ethical shorthand based on long personal or cultural experience) to particular situations (which are always unique and which, for that reason, may require bending or even breaking the rule in question).

Experience is also critical to the cultivation of virtue because virtues arise from specific sorts of activities. Aristotle argues, "states of character arise out of like activities. This is why the activities we exhibit must be of a certain kind; it is because the states of character correspond to the differences between these. It makes no small difference, then, whether we form habits of one kind or of another from our very youth; it makes a very great difference, or rather all the difference."[41] Becoming courageous is the result of practicing courageous actions, and doing so until acting courageously (including feeling the proper emotions and so forth) becomes a fixed disposition. The same thing holds true for all the other "moral" virtues, including environmental virtues. We become virtuous by experiencing things a certain way and, paradoxically, we experience things a certain way because we are virtuous.[42] So experience is critical in both the cultivation of virtuous character traits and the understanding that applies those traits to the diverse and complex situations we encounter in life.

The question is, do *narratives* provide us with *experience*?

Ricoeur's description of the threefold *mimesis* at work in narrative and identity argues that the narratives I read or hear change the narrative that I am (the *who* that I am as opposed to the *what* that I am). They do this, he says, by offering a sort of "as-if" experience in which we can try out, as it were, different possibilities in the "ethical laboratory" of narrative.[43] We use narratives to experiment with possibilities, exploring different situations and different ethical responses, projecting ourselves into stories and making judgments about the actions of characters. It is for this reason that there are no ethically neutral narratives.[44] As Kearney points out, "to understand what courage means, we tell the story of Achilles; to understand what wisdom means, we tell the story of Socrates; to understand what *caritas* means, we tell the story of St. Francis of Assisi"; and I'll add, with respect to environmental virtues, to understand simplicity, we tell the story of Henry David Thoreau; to understand attention and observation, we tell the story of Aldo Leopold; to understand love of wildness, we tell the story of John Muir.[45] These examples suggest that, in addition to exposing us to different ethical situations to which we might not have easy access in our day-to-day lives, narratives can also offer us models of virtue we would otherwise be unlikely to encounter—virtual, or "as if," *phronimoi* so to speak. Kearney continues by arguing that "the validity of Ricoeur's observation can be seen in the simple fact that while ethics often speaks generally of the relation between virtue and the pursuit of happiness, fiction fleshes it out with experiential images and examples—that is, with particular stories."[46] Compare Kant's *Critique of Pure Reason* to Aristotle's *Nicomachean Ethics* or to various works on environmental virtue. The ubiquity of examples in the works on virtue ethics, and their near complete absence in Kant, suggests something about virtue ethics. The point is not that the *Critique of Pure Reason* could have been written with myriad rich examples, the point is that good accounts of virtue *cannot be written without them.*

The power of narratives to help us "see things anew" can hardly be overstated. Indeed, while it is true that narrative accomplishes "less" than actual experience in many ways, it has numerous other salutary features, at least some of which may accomplish "more" than actual experience. Kearney goes so far as to claim that, at least in certain cases, while narrative experience is vicarious—that is, unreal on the face of it—"it is experience nonetheless; and one more real sometimes than that permitted in so-called reality."[47] He is not alone in his belief in the power of narrative. Authors, perhaps predictably, make similar claims. Dermot Healy writes, "I can still remember the liquid feel of . . . words for rain. How the beads were blown against the windowpane, and glistened there and ran. The words for rain were better than the rain itself."[48] Similarly, Ernest Hemingway wrote, in a letter to his father, "I'm trying in all my stories to get the feeling of the actual life across—not to just depict life—or criticize it—but to actually make it alive. So that when you have read something by me you actually experience the thing."[49] And James Joyce famously strove "to give a picture of Dublin so complete that if the city one day suddenly disappeared from the Earth, it could be reconstructed out of my book."[50] How could the words for rain be "better" than real rain? Can Hemingway and Joyce give us the "actual" experience each seeks to communicate? Surely the suggestion is not that we might water our crops with words, or that preserving stories about Bighorn sheep in the Sierra Nevada is better than preserving actual Bighorn sheep. What, then, are we to make of this claim?

As with "real" experience, narrative changes us, either by the incremental development of personal evolution or by the radical transformation of epiphany and conversion. Indeed, it has a particular facility for doing so. The "as-if" experience of narrative is still a type of experience, even if it differs from "actual, firsthand" experience. And as we will see, in developing practical wisdom (*phronesis*) the more experience the better. If some of that experience comes in the form of "as-if" experience, well and good; it is experience nonetheless. In addition, the imaginative play of narrative and the "synthesis of the heterogeneous" that are part of emplotment are capable of highlighting paradoxes, emphasizing essential truths, and revealing hidden mysteries that might otherwise be missed. This is as true of commonplace narratives we use to relate, recount, and remember our own actions as it is of "high" literary novels, which is why narrative plays an indispensable role in our understanding of and reaction to direct experiences, including habituation. In the chaos and rush of certain experiences, or in the busyness of everyday life, or in the idleness of reverie, we can miss essential truths that only come to light later, in the retelling. As the Reverend John Ames puts it, in his end-of-life reflections in Marilynne Robinson's *Gilead*, "I believe there are visions that come to us only in memory, in retrospect."[51]

In other words, "direct" experience is not quite as direct as it appears. We miss in the moment of experience what we find—in retrospect, as we retell the story of what we experience to others or to ourselves—to be essential about the experience. Simply put, narrative can help us to focus on things we would ordinarily overlook and, in so doing, transform the "simple contingencies of everyday life . . . into narrative epiphanies."[52] Emily Brady notes that imagination—and the same could be said for narrative—can intensify experience and in so doing play an exploratory, projective, ampliative, or revelatory role.[53] Returning to Dermot Healy's claim, we might say that the words for rain are "better" than the rain itself insofar as the words, the story or narrative, can be, at least in some cases, *more* effective than actual experience at bringing about the life-altering insights that amplify our concern, increase our understanding, or drive personal transformation. Rain simply falls; it *does* things in the world, but it doesn't *mean* anything. It takes narrative to suggest that rain is good or bad: that rain is "hard on loving" or foretells death;[54] that rain is disinterested, falling equally on the just and the unjust (Matthew 5:45); that "rain is grace;"[55] or that it "speaks" and is "joyful."[56]

Martha Nussbaum and the Judicious Spectator

It is precisely because a text can actually teach us something beyond "facts" regarding the persons, places, and events of the story that narrative is able to facilitate understanding beyond the mere accumulation of information or data points, something approaching, perhaps, wisdom. Martha Nussbaum makes a variety of arguments on behalf of literary imagination, which she sometimes calls "fancy," in *Poetic Justice* and *Love's Knowledge*. In many crucial respects Nussbaum's arguments buttress those made by Kearney and Ricoeur, further supporting the case for narrative's refigurative power.

Love's Knowledge

In *Love's Knowledge*, Nussbaum argues that form and content are not neatly separable, that literary form directly influences philosophical content.[57]

"Life is never simply *presented* by a text; it is always *represented as* something. This 'as' can, and must, be seen not only in the paraphrasable content, but also in the style, which itself expresses choices and selections, and sets up, in the reader, certain activities and transactions rather than others."[58] Literary texts, she argues, communicate meaning both directly, so to speak, through the meaning(s) offered by the plot, and indirectly, through the form in which they are communicated.

It's true that aspects of the former, more direct sort of communication—regarding specific claims about human goods, flourishing, and so forth—might be transmitted in other ways, including dry, logical, non-narrative argumentation. However, certain views can only be stated properly in narrative or poetic form.

> With respect to several interrelated issues in the area of human choice, and of ethics broadly construed . . . there is a family of positions that is a serious candidate for truth—and which deserves, therefore, the attention and scrutiny of anyone who seriously considers these matters—whose full, fitting, and (as James would say) "honorable" embodiment is found in the terms characteristic of . . . novels.[59]

The Greeks were well aware of the poetic perspective, which is deeply concerned with the broad question—central to virtue ethics—of how one ought to live and which, they thought, offered itself as a rival to philosophical arguments. For example, where many prominent manifestations of the latter insisted a good man could not be harmed by external events, argued for a clear hierarchy of goods, and taught that the passions must be thoroughly ruled and controlled by reason, the former tended to insist on the importance of contingency, external events, irreconcilable conflicting obligations, the variety and incommensurability of goods, and the significance of the passions.[60]

At times, Nussbaum seems to suggest that her comments regarding philosophy and literature apply to very specific novels (*Hard Times* or *The Golden Bowl* for example). In other instances her scope expands to include all realistic novels or the novelistic form more generally. For the most part, however, she is reluctant to adopt the broader view of narrative I intend to take in this work. Toward the end of "Form and Content: Philosophy and Literature" she does allow that "neither all nor only novels" meet the criteria for her arguments.[61] As long as the narrative in question is written in a style that gives sufficient attention to particulars and to the role of emotions, as well as involving its readers in the lives and possibilities of the characters, such a narrative will be ethically significant in the ways she argues.[62]

Given these criteria, she is reluctant to extend her advocacy to either what I have called the "thin" narrative forms or to "life itself." With respect to "thin," non-novelistic forms, Nussbaum suggests that they lack attention to particulars, emotional resonance, plot, or the intent to involve the reader and, therefore, that they do not have the same power as literary novels. However, it does not seem beyond the realm of possibility for a poem or movie—perhaps even a work of art or philosophical example—to draw our attention to ethically significant particulars, to connect us to the life of someone quite different from ourselves in a manner strong enough to "involve" us, or to invite us into friendship or to fall in love.[63] I'm inclined to extend the range of "narrative" well beyond the sphere occupied by the classic literary narrative to include a range of genres between the "thick" narratives rich with detail and a clearly articulated plot, and "thin" narratives that require that we, as readers, fill in the gaps so to speak. There is a spectrum of narrative force and efficacy.

Part of the problem with Nussbaum's analysis may stem from a general underestimation of the role of the reader or viewer in emplotment. Nussbaum occasionally speaks as if there is "a meaning," or "the meaning," of a given text. She writes of the "proper reading of the text" and is concerned with "intentions and thoughts that are realized in the text, and that may appropriately be seen in the text, not with other thoughts and feelings the real-life author and reader may find themselves having."[64] She continues, "I am interested, then, in all and only those thoughts, feelings, wishes, movements, and other processes that are actually there to be seen in the text."[65] Nussbaum is clear that she is not suggesting that the author herself would be the authoritative reader of the text, and it is certainly true that she moderates or balances any suggestion regarding "a" proper reading of a text with an appreciation for the role of the reader and the role of interlocution between readers, one that is congenial to the argument I am making here. However, her work on literature is peppered with occasional overestimations of the role of the text vis-à-vis the role of the reader.

This is, perhaps, what leads Kearney to suggest that Nussbaum lacks sufficient appreciation for the "hermeneutics of suspicion."[66] Texts have power. And precisely because that power is not always good and can, for example, dissimulate with respect to historical truth, it is incumbent on the reader to play her role in the creation of meaning in any narrative, to actively emplot by reading, as Nietzsche says, "slowly, deeply, looking cautiously before and aft, with reservations, with doors left open. . . ."[67] If the "proper" plot or "actual" meaning or message of a given narrative is *in the text* then the style of the text would be determinative and many of the non-literary forms of narrative that Nussbaum criticizes would rightly be excluded from the field of ethically edifying narrative. However, if the plot or meaning or message of a given narrative is *in the act of emplotment*, which takes place at the *intersection of the world of the text and the world of the reader*, then the style of the text is suggestive rather than determinative of the meaning and the scope of narrative power is significantly expanded. To borrow, and modify, a line from Thoreau, which gestures toward the intersection of life and narrative with which we are concerned: who can say what possibilities a narrative—novel, oral folktale, film, short story, poem, work of art, anecdote, or example—offers another?[68]

Nussbaum is also suspicious that "life itself" can do all the work of ethical formation, a suspicion I share. Why? First, because "we have never lived enough. Our experience is, without fiction, too confined and too parochial."[69] Each of us lives only one life, a life that may be cosmopolitan and adventurous or provincial and staid. However, without narrative even the most experienced and well-traveled person lives only a single life; with narrative, however, we can experience (in the "as-if" mode) many lives, many circumstances, and many places. Second, because "pure, uninterpreted life itself" is, to use an appropriate play on words, a fiction. "Life itself," insofar as we understand it, is already emplotted. Or, as Nussbaum asserts: "all living is interpreting; all action requires seeing the world as something. So in this sense no life is 'raw,' and (as James and Proust insist) throughout our living we are, in a sense, makers of fictions."[70] To be clear, I am not suggesting that narrative can replace life; rather, I am suggesting that life—life as we understand it, experience as we use it to explain, predict, and plan, and actions insofar as they are meaningful—is always already tied up in narrative. The narrative core of life is as true for the more active lives of Muir, Abbey, and Turner as it is for the bookish and academic James and Proust. Another way of putting this is that, insofar as "life itself" *does* have the literary power Nussbaum identifies, it is because life itself is understood in terms of the various narratives in which I find myself caught up. There is no "life itself" that isn't already narrative, because as soon as we reflect on the meaning of any action or experience we emplot it in terms of our life's narrative. Finally, Nussbaum points out, as I've suggested above, that the focus of narrative gives it a normative force absent in "normal" experience.

> In the activity of literary imagining we are led to imagine and describe with greater precision, focusing our attention on each word, feeling each even more keenly—whereas much of actual life goes by without that heightened awareness, and is thus, in

a certain sense, not fully or thoroughly lived. Neither James nor Proust thinks of ordinary life as normative, and the Aristotelian conception concurs: too much of it is obtuse, routinized, incompletely sentient."[71]

Narrative, arguably, gives us more and deeper experience. Deeper, because it can bring things into sharper focus than regular life. More because, through it, we can experience additional lives beyond the one we each get to live and breathe, and because narrative allows us to experience things we would never actually encounter in our everyday lives. Such experiences are of the "as-if" variety, but they remain experiences.

Nussbaum enumerates a number of characteristics associated with the vicarious experience of narrative, but I don't want to suggest that she offers us a good model for environmental virtue. Indeed, I'm not even suggesting that the narratives she offers and the examples she uses offer us good archetypes of virtuous living. I think her sense of the scope of ethically beneficial narrative is too narrow—repeatedly returning to the novels of James and Dickens, and to Greek tragedy—and that she focuses on a limited, if essential, set of virtues: the virtues associated with empathetic judgment.[72] Virtue, especially environmental virtue, requires many additional narrative voices, especially those attended to the natural world and our place in it (Thoreau, Muir, Leopold, Carson, et al.); it also requires that we incorporate narratives, however virtuous, into the work and play of actual living in the complex, dirty, wondrous world in which we find ourselves. The virtues of empathetic judgment that Nussbaum finds in certain novels are surely important, but they represent only a small fraction of the larger account of a virtuous life.

Still, her account of the benefits and powers attributable to the literary form are useful here. This is because Nussbaum argues that the ethical power of the literary form is aligned with a particular ethical approach: the Aristotelian ethical view.[73] She addresses, in particular, the literary appreciation for (1) the noncommensurability of valuable things, (2) the priority of particulars, (3) the ethical value of emotions, and (4) the ethical relevance of uncontrolled happenings.

Virtue ethics in the Aristotelian tradition is fully committed to the uniqueness, multiplicity, and noncommensurability of ethical goods and "this emphasis on the recognition of plural incommensurable goods leads directly and naturally to the perception of a possibility of irreconcilable contingent conflicts among them"[74]—that is to say, the possibility of tragedy. On the virtue ethicist's account we cannot simply compare ethical goods "scientifically" in terms of some single metric that we would then seek to maximize, as is the case with utilitarianism. The lack of one particular kind of ethical good, say friendship, cannot be compensated for by a surplus of a different ethical good, say temperance, as if temperance and friendship were merely containers for various amounts of some third thing such as "pleasure," "happiness," or "virtue." Rather, as Aristotle points out, friendship is a unique sort of ethical good that cannot be simply exchanged with other sorts of ethical goods: "without friends no one would choose to live, though he had all other goods."[75] Nussbaum argues that literary novels are "committed more deeply than other forms to a multiplicity and fineness of . . . distinctions" between valuable things, and therefore that they are natural allies of the Aristotelian ethical view.[76] "The novelist's terms are even more variegated, more precise in their qualitative rightness, than are the sometimes blunt vague terms of daily life; they *show us vividly what we can aspire to* in refining our (already qualitative) understanding."[77] Novels are also particularly adept at capturing the reality of conflicting attachments and obligations—including the reality of forced, tragic decisions—on human flourishing. Nussbaum's arguments here are entirely congruent with Kearney's belief in "narrative epiphanies" and Emily Brady's suggestion that imagination can play an "ampliative or revelatory" role in our understanding. I suspect many philosophers who are also lovers of poetry and literature have felt at one time or another that a particularly fine poetic or literary work captures certain truths more faithfully than their own philosophical arguments.[78]

The attention to particulars characteristic of novels is another feature that makes them congenial to the Aristotelian ethical schema. Virtue ethics is highly sensitive to the particular context in which any action, virtuous or vicious, takes place. Thus, Aristotle argues that virtue must be concerned not only with the act but also with a host of other factors related to the act. His point could be summed up succinctly by saying that virtue must be sensitive to the particular context taken broadly to include all the relevant features of the agent, of other people involved, and of the wider environment in which the agent acts. Novels, argues Nussbaum, have a particularly fine "responsiveness to the concrete"—that is, to the relevant particulars—which works to cultivate in us the gift of ethical "improvisation."[79] Ethical improvisation is the ability—characteristic of *phronesis*, as well as narrative imagination (Kearney) and judicious spectatorship (Nussbaum)—to wisely and virtuously apply universal rules (e.g., do not lie) to particular situations (e.g., Kant's famous case of the murderer at the door). Such improvisational skill also prepares us to imagine and cope with new and unexpected ethical situations or features, to appreciate the context-embeddedness of ethically relevant data or phenomena, and to honor the ethical significance of human relationships, including special relationships with particular people such as one's spouse or child.[80]

The sensitivity to context and particulars characteristic of novels also means that these literary forms are particularly adept at drawing our attention to the ethical relevance of uncontrolled happenings. Novels recognize that surprises, unforeseen reversals of fortune, forced choices between evils, unavoidable tragedies, and other harmful situations can and do impact the ability of persons to flourish.[81] A certain philosophical perspective—seen, for example, in Plato's dialogues and in various Stoic philosophers—holds that a good person cannot be harmed. Thus, Marcus Aurelius tells us, "living and dying, honor and dishonor, pain and pleasure, riches and poverty, and so forth are equally the lot of good men and bad. Things like these neither elevate nor degrade; and therefore they are no more good than they are evil."[82] Now there is, I believe, certainly a kernel of truth in Stoicism that we should not abandon; nevertheless, Nussbaum is correct to point out that we miss something significant, essential even, if we insist too strongly on the imperviousness of the good person.

It's true that the virtuous person can bear the "slings and arrows of outrageous fortune" far better than the vicious person, and that her virtue and her wisdom are indeed shield and armor against the blows we all, to some extent, endure. However, it is also true that a naïve or rigid insistence on the protection provided by these defenses overstates their efficacy or, more likely perhaps, under-appreciates the true extent of the tragedies and horrors that can be visited on a person by fate. I'm inclined to agree with Gabriel Marcel on this point, when he asserts that it is a hallmark of authentic philosophy that it addresses, or at least does not deny, the tragic aspects of our existence.[83] Marcel was concerned with the tragedies of the human condition, the most acute of which is the mortality of those we love; however, we could easily point to tragic environmental examples: the extinction of certain species as a result of excessive, or simply thoughtless, human consumption and pollution; the disappearance of unique or rare wildernesses or ecosystems; and many other similar examples.

The virtuous person can no doubt shrug off minor misfortunes, and even more significant setbacks will not really impact her well-being; however, the vulnerability of all persons to real tragedy must be recognized. How do we differentiate between those obstacles and challenges that should be born without complaint, perhaps even joyfully, and those for which we should have genuine sympathy? There is no formula, since each instance is unique. Only experience—actual or "as-if"—can develop in us a sensitivity to the ethical significance of uncontrolled happenings that will allow us to distinguish the merely inconvenient from the actually challenging, and both of these from the authentically tragic. The context-sensitive nature of novels and narrative helps to foster this sensitivity.

Poetic Justice

The fourth ethical power of the literary form that Nussbaum finds aligned with the Aristotelian ethical view, the ethical relevance of emotions, is addressed in depth in *Poetic Justice*.[84] There she addresses the role of emotion in rational judgment, specifically in cases of legal judgment but more broadly as relevant for any good citizen. Novels in particular, says Nussbaum, contribute to our ethical education and ethical judgment.

There is a widely held assumption that fiction, storytelling, imagination, and similar phenomena are at odds with rationality. This prejudice is not always, or perhaps even often, conscious, vocal, or militant; however, people don't need to argue that "imagination is irrational" in order to act as if this is the case. Each time we are asked to view an ethical case "objectively" or "dispassionately" the implication is that emotional connection with the people in question, imaginatively considering what it would be like to be in their shoes, to play their part in their narrative, is antithetical to rational assessment of the case. However, Nussbaum argues that storytelling and the use of literary imagination are not opposed to rational argument; rather they are, at least in some cases, an essential part of it. How so?

"Fancy" is Nussbaum's term for "the ability to see one thing as another," which Ricoeur addresses under the rubric metaphor.[85] And, critically, the perspective associated in any "seeing as" is always implicitly normative. "See the world this way." "Change your life!" These exhortations go hand-in-hand. Ethically, this is connected to the ability to see oneself in the shoes of another, and therefore, says Nussbaum, with important virtues like charity, generosity, and justice. The use of narrative, or literary, imagination encourages us to concern ourselves with the lives of people who may be very different from us, including their ethical choices, their characteristic view of the world, and their conception of human goods. As Ricoeur and Kearney suggest, we enter imaginatively into the lives of these people and experience things "as if" we were there. Nussbaum argues that novels allow us to "imagine what it is like to live the life of another person who might, given a change in circumstance, be oneself or one of one's loved ones."[86]

One of Nussbaum's key contributions, for the present project, is her assessment of "judicious spectatorship" in the context of novels, narrative, fancy, and imagination. Building on the work of Adam Smith in *The Theory of Moral Sentiments*, Nussbaum sketches an image of a judge whose characteristics form the paradigm for public rationality.[87] The judicious spectator is, precisely, a spectator: "he is not personally involved in the events he witnesses, although he cares about the participants as a concerned friend."[88] That is to say—with Aristotle, Kearney, and Ricoeur—the narrative "reader" must have sufficient distance from the events she is "witnessing"; however, despite this distance or spectatorship, among the most important ethical faculties of the judicious spectator is "the power of *imagining vividly* what it is like to be each of the persons whose situation he imagines."[89] Thus, judicious spectatorship—like Kearney's narrative imagination, or Aristotle's account of *catharsis* in poetics—requires both distance and proximity, disinterestedness and interestedness, the detachment required by "objectivity" (or, better, justice and fairness) and the involvement required by empathy.[90] In fiction, we encounter people who are sufficiently like us—sharing common human problems, hopes, and fears, as well as familiar physical and moral attributes—to generate interest in their lives and ethical choices, but who are also different enough from us—in terms of their concrete circumstances and history—that we are able to maintain the distance proper to good judgment.[91] As Kearney says, "we need to be sufficiently involved in the action to feel that it matters" but must also maintain "sufficient distance [in order to] grasp the meaning of it all."[92]

Therefore, narrative does not ask us to look at things objectively in the sense that we would view the case "from nowhere," without any perspective or place, but rather to look at things from another, different perspective. The a-historical, a-cultural, a-temporal, dis-placed view from nowhere is a fiction in the pejorative sense—a fiction that leads us astray rather than aright. This does not mean that we should not strive for objectivity in the sense that we should not allow our idiosyncratic perspective on the world to unduly or unjustly color our perception of a case, only that we should not deceive ourselves into thinking that our various perspectives can be shed and abandoned like a cocoon after metamorphosis, without residue. Nor should we believe that the more closely we approximate to some quasi-objective, inhuman, robotic assessment the better our judgment will be. That sort of objectivity is not only impossible; it is undesirable. Nussbaum argues compellingly that reason works best when supplemented with emotion. Emotion and narrative imagination (fancy) are not synonymous or interchangeable with reason or logic, but they are ways of perceiving and so contribute to, rather than simply distort, our rational assessments.[93] The formulaic use of reason, detached from particularity and blind to others, leads only to "programmable" systems or blueprints for action, which are neither ethical nor just.[94] Narrative imagination is an essential element in good decision making or judging (Nussbaum), in self-understanding

(Ricoeur), in ethical action (Kearney), and in the cultivation of virtues, environmental and otherwise.

In asking us to consider what it would be like to be another person in another situation, literature asks us to focus on the possible. And in nurturing our appreciation for and understanding of possibilities, narrative seems directly related to developing virtue and vice, both of which are possibilities for any one of us. However, despite this emphasis on possibility, novels are deeply concrete, concerned with specific people, with specific prospects, in specific circumstances, places, and environments. Nussbaum points out that this concern for the concrete means that narratives mediate between the universal and the particular.[95] This means that narrative provides a paradigm for ethical reasoning, which is also concerned with mediating between universal and particular, and with applying general rules in very different particular contexts. Critically, given the postmodern condition addressed in Chapter 5, they are able to do so in a way that is "context-specific without being relativistic."[96] Narratives, taken together, suggest that there are myriad ways of succeeding or failing in the pursuit of the good life; however, every narrative implies that there is a right way—or are right ways—of going about this and, crucially, that there are wrong ways of doing so. In addition to the delicate balance of detachment and involvement-by-fancy good judgment requires sensitivity to the facts of the case, precedent, dimensions of the judge's history and perspective that might distort judicious spectatorship, as well as critical judgment and philosophical argumentation.[97] This pluralistic commitment of narrative—which denies both a single unambiguous Truth and the idea that any truth is as good as any other—stems directly from the diversity of narratives. Narrative wisdom is, by its very nature, collaborative and comparative; it depends upon what Wayne Booth calls "coduction."

Wayne Booth and Coduction

A corollary of the argument that narrative plays a central role in the cultivation of virtue is the suggestion that there are good and bad books, not artistically good or bad—though those judgments are, of course, also legitimate—but *ethically* good or bad. Some books might push us toward environmental virtues (perhaps *Walden*, *Under the Sea-Wind*, or *Sand County Almanac*) and others might be misleading or harmful, encouraging environmentally vicious ideas, emotions, or behaviors (one thinks of Glenn Beck's *An Inconvenient Book: Real Solutions to the World's Biggest Problems* and, with Harriet Parke, *Agenda 21*). True, we still need to differentiate between genuinely pernicious books, which I suspect are relatively rare, and bad reading, which I fear is somewhat more common. Nevertheless, we can't avoid the full implications of the notion that books change us.

In *The Company We Keep: An Ethics of Fiction*, Wayne Booth seeks to rehabilitate the practice of ethical criticism as distinct from aesthetic criticism, particularly with respect to narrative and fiction. Where aesthetic criticism asks about the artistic value of the work, ethical criticism asks about the value of the work in terms of how it might influence the character or behavior of a reader.

Booth reminds us that the belief that artistic works, particularly narratives, have important ethical significance was once a commonplace: "until the late nineteenth century almost everyone took for granted that a major task of any critic is to appraise the ethical value of works of art."[98] This is, no doubt, in part because the ethical assessment of narratives leads almost inexorably to the discussion of "ultimate questions": among them the nature of right and wrong, good and evil.[99] However, more recently, ethical criticism has fallen on hard times. The reasons for this shift in critical practice from the "aesthetic and ethical" to the merely aesthetic are no doubt complex; however, Booth identifies four factors contributing to the demise of ethical criticism.[100]

First, the supposed fact/value split argues, following Hume, that one cannot derive an "ought" from an "is," that is to say claims about what is (fact) and claims about what ought to be (value) are separated by an unbridgeable chasm.[101] If we take the fact/value split seriously, all judgments of value will come down to personal preference and the Emotivist thesis, with which MacIntyre grapples, wins the day. A second, parallel factor is a change, which has now achieved the status of dogma, in what it means to "prove" something sufficiently to say that we "know" it. If proof requires indubitable demonstration, I'm not sure we can progress much past the near-tautological *cogito* of the Second Meditation, prior to the semicircular argument by which Descartes "wins back the world."[102] There are many examples of this demand for proof. A number of sources have lamented the so-called "CSI effect," whereby real-world jurors now expect proof "beyond a reasonable doubt" to mean "demonstrable and irrefutable proof" backed up by massive amounts of the high-tech scientific evidence, much of it completely fictional, seen on the eponymous television series.[103] A less extreme, but much more pervasive, example would be widespread belief that science deals only with facts, while ethics and similar fields deal with mere opinion or preference. The third contributing factor, as we saw in Chapter 5, is our acute awareness of the contingency and variability of our judgments, especially with respect to aesthetics and ethics. Each of us recognizes that, were we born elsewhere or otherwise, we would very likely have quite different assessments of aesthetic and ethical value. Finally, Booth points to "the rise of theories that elevated abstract form to the top of every aesthetic pyramid," suggesting that form, rather than content, should be the sole focus of criticism.[104] Taken together these trends suggest strongly that ethical evaluation is, at best, a private and idiosyncratic endeavor. There are, of course, rejoinders to each of these claims, but they remain, in varying degrees, influences on our perception of the ethical value of art.

However, it's also true that the decline in ethical criticism has been neither uniform nor universal. Booth notes many times that we all engage in ethical criticism, often without thinking about it or even recognizing it. We all judge, for example, the actions of characters in novels, histories, or biographies to be appropriate or inappropriate, good or bad, laudable or shameful. This phenomenon is evident in a broad spectrum of examples. Think of teenagers in a movie theater involuntarily shouting out "don't do that!" as their cinematic counterparts open the door on a dark and stormy night to investigate the strange noises outside, just after the phone lines have gone dead. We make similar judgments whenever we see, hear, or read a story. These judgments are often more restrained, perhaps even unconscious or semi-conscious when compared to adolescent outbursts in a cinema; but when readers of Kazuo Ishiguro's novels grapple in various ways with the stoic or phlegmatic dispositions of his characters, trying to understand why they act as they do, they inevitably make judgments about their character.[105] No narrative, no reading, is ethically neutral.

But the ubiquity of ethical criticism—despite the trends enumerated above, which often undermine our conscious recognition or endorsement of it—raises problems of its own. Much of the discussion of the ethical value of narrative, including the discussion in this work, focuses on the salutary aspects of narrative, the possibility that reading good books and reading them well can help, in some way, to make us better people. However, if we allow that people may judge certain narratives to be ethically enlightening, and that they have plausible reasons for doing so, we must come to terms with the opposite possibility: that there may be works that we judge, with good reasons, to be aesthetically pleasing but morally pernicious, perhaps more pernicious precisely because aesthetically pleasing. Thus, a fifth factor in the decline of ethical criticism is the fear that it is the first step on a slippery slope leading, inevitably, to censorship.[106]

Booth is no fan of censorship, whether self-imposed or enforced by external authority.[107] However, the idea of protecting oneself from harm— by choosing certain things rather than others—or of society choosing to protect its members—by mandating or prohibiting certain options—is much more complex than a binary choice between advocacy and censorship with the unreflective assumption that the former is good and the latter bad. We need look no further than commonplace, accepted, and frequently praised efforts by parents who prohibit or impose narratives with particular ethical significance in the education of their children.

I'd argue that there is a spectrum of options with respect to endorsing or opposing narrative on ethical grounds: assigning or requiring (as when a professor assigns a book for a class, or when the Pledge of Allegiance is required in U.S. public schools); vigorous advocacy (books or works of art the popularity of which we actively promote); support (books we find edifying and which we would recommend); acceptance (all examples to which we give little or no thought); toleration (books or works of art we find distasteful, but which we are willing to accept, perhaps because we recognize that tastes differ and others may find value in art which we do not see); vigorous condemnation (book or works of art we find to be ethically pernicious, which we criticize both privately and publicly, encouraging our friends to avoid); and censorship or prohibition (examples of censorship or attempted censorship are too numerous to list here).

There are a number of philosophically and sociologically significant questions to be asked here; however, for the moment let's stay focused on the most common objection to ethical criticism: the specter of censorship. Bracketing for the moment the sticky issue of potentially justifiable censorship—for example, withholding the names of victims of certain sorts of crimes or protecting young children from certain narratives—it's safe to say that in free and democratic societies censorship is generally viewed very negatively. If censorship is bad, must we abandon ethical criticism? Or can we argue passionately against the ethical harm done by certain aesthetic works without insisting that they be censored? Have political correctness and the belief that claims about ethics, virtues, and value are mere statements of opinion pushed us so far toward relativism that we can no longer engage in ethical criticism?

The problem, arguably, is that those who openly embrace ethical criticism are often those who *do* endorse some forms of censorship, strengthening the association between the former and the latter. This happens because ethical criticism, like many other intellectual and imaginative tasks, can be undertaken in a fundamentally lazy way. Too often ethical criticism is nothing more than a statement of opinion, an overgeneralization of a purely subjective assessment that moves, unreflectively, from a judgment about "a good" to a claim to have found "The Good," seeking to form a universal rule solely on the basis of individual personal experiences.[108] The problem with these too-quick generalizations is not that they move from particulars to universals, but that they move from a certain sort of particular (a single instance or personal experience) to a certain kind of universal (a rule that is no longer context-sensitive in its application, which does not admit of alternative interpretations, and to which there are no exceptions).

However, while it is undeniably true that some proponents of ethical criticism are also advocates of some forms of censorship, that some readers may undertake emplotment without sufficient imaginative engagement or with a vicious disposition, and that narratives can be, and have been, used to support base, barbarous, or wicked ends, it's not at all clear that the problem lies with imagination, narrative, or ethical criticism. What we see in these instances of over-zealous criticism, deficient emplotment, or vicious narration is not a defect in fancy, or imagination, or narrative refiguration but rather "a defect in human beings who do not exercise that type of fancy [or imagination, or refiguration] well, who cultivate their human sympathies unequally and narrowly. The remedy for that defect seems to be, not the repudiation of fancy [or imagination, or emplotment/refiguration], but its more consistent and humane cultivation."[109] Such a remedy is to be found in an alterative form of ethical criticism, one that does not over-generalize by relying solely on individual experience and one that does not overreach in seeking to establish universal and immutable rules or judgments.

Our judgments of narratives should never take place in a vacuum. Or, since they cannot, perhaps we should say that we ought not proceed as if they do. The responsible critic consciously compares and evaluates her judgment of a narrative in the context of all the other narratives and experiences in her personal "library." However, precisely because our own experience is relatively narrow, the responsible critic also engages in conversations with other readers, evaluating her interpretation and judgment in light of the interpretation and judgment of her interlocutors. Thus, evaluation proceeds by comparison—doubly so, since we compare narratives to other narratives, and interpretations to other interpretations—rather than demonstration. And, thus,

> [t]he logic we depend on as we arrive at our particular appraisals is neither deduction from clear premises, even of the most complex kind, nor induction from a series of precisely defined and isolated instances. Rather it is always the result of a direct sense that something now before us has yielded an experience that we find comparatively desirable, admirable, loveable or, on the other hand, comparatively repugnant, contemptible or hateful.[110]

Booth calls this "logic" of ethical criticism coduction: "a thoroughgoing particular engagement with this narrative, considered neither as based on nor leading to general rules but as an ever-growing awareness of what is humanly possible [and, I would add, praiseworthy or blameworthy] in some one kind of endeavor."[111] The "co" of coduction indicates that our judgments always take place in the context of and in dialogue with a community of interpreters. Of course, this opens important questions regarding the people with whom we choose to coduce. While we can, and too often are, wrong about what is best for us, it does not follow that any other individual will necessarily see more clearly what is best for us.[112] Here again, practical wisdom and hermeneutic responsibility will play decisive roles. Both entertaining all other interpretations and choosing only those interpretations that reinforce one's own reading are genuine pitfalls. Some interpretations can, and should, be excluded as beyond the pale, so there will be some hermeneutic discrimination at work. However, if responsibility requires rejecting the interpretations of radical outliers, it also requires that we sail beyond the safe harbor of our own interpretation, exposing ourselves to interpretations that contradict and challenge our own and engaging them in dialogue that is both charitable (in the sense of being genuinely open to the foreign interpretation) and critical (in the sense of critically evaluating both the foreign interpretation and one's own).

This process is open-ended. There is no point at which we can say we have arrived at the single, immutable interpretation or judgment of the ethical value of a narrative. We must remain open to the possibility that new experiences, additional interlocutors, new interpretations, or additional narratives will shed new light on the narrative in question, and potentially change our judgment. The task of hermeneutics is never complete. Because of the structurally open nature of coduction, its judgments and the arguments in support of it aim at something like plausibility, to use Ricoeur's term, rather than proof or demonstration. Such judgments transcend mere subjective opinion—"what we are after is not just a view of moral education that makes sense of our own personal experience, but one that we can defend to others" with good reasons and rational justifications[113]—but fall short of apodictic certainty. The good coductive judgment is the *most plausible* interpretation *at the present*. This does not mean that coduction is a statistical endeavor whereby we "add up" the interpretations of the various coducers to arrive at an "average."[114] Rather, recalling that Aristotle warns us that different disciplines admit of different degrees of exactitude, it is simply a consequence of the nature of hermeneutics. This shouldn't trouble us, because in our actual lives, we generally do not demand "proof" for our beliefs. In real life we set more sensible goals for ethical reasoning, and we frequently meet them.[115]

Objections: The Return of Relativism and the Excesses of Imagination

There are a number of potential objections to the narrative approach to virtue introduced above and further developed in the next chapter. Without claiming to be comprehensive, here I want to address a number of the most obvious and powerful objections. The first two objections revisit topics already addressed: first, that narrative cannot replace firsthand experience and, second, that narrative exacerbates the problem of relativism, which constantly haunts virtue ethics. An additional set of objections raises new issues: first, that narratives distort reality, which is better captured by science, and second, that facts, not narratives, should be the basis for judging and acting.

Narrative Cannot Replace Experience

A common supposition is that narratives give us reality at one remove, so to speak. This claim is as old as philosophy. Plato famously argued that art, especially in the form of poetry or narrative, is a corruption of the truth, and he therefore restricted its presence in his ideal state. On his account narrative is an imitation of things and events, which are themselves, in a sense, just imitations of the reality of the forms, which is itself derivative of the Good. So narrative is, at best, a glimpse of reality and truth at three removes.[116] This position, as well as the aforementioned view of the significance of context and uncontrolled events, led the Greeks to view poetry and philosophy as offering different and competing accounts of life and how it ought to be lived.

It seems both common sense and commonplace to assume that narratives, whether they present themselves as fiction or non-fiction, are "not the real thing." Narrative is read or written, heard or told, not actually lived; life is lived, not recounted.[117] Who would want a copy of reality, however skilled the forgery, when reality itself is available? Why would we wrap ourselves up in something that is not the real thing when we could, instead, experience the real thing? The preceding accounts of Kearney's and Nussbaum's work clearly illustrate the extent to which the "as-if" experience of narrative is nonetheless an experience, one that is valuable and which, in some qualified sense, might be "better" than real experience. However, with respect to virtue ethics, a new and problematic issue arises. It may be true that narratives can make us reflect, teach us things, and so on. But the sharpest point of the objection for an environmental virtue ethics is the claim that the "as-if" experience of narrative can never replace the "actual" experience of life when it comes to habituation, a cornerstone of most accounts of virtue.

On one level, we must immediately concede that "as-if" experience is not unabridged experience, so to speak, and cannot on its own perform the full work of habituation. No amount of reading about temperance or simplicity can fully habituate a person to either virtue, including all the practices, dispositions, emotions, and nuanced judgments that are part of it. There is an inescapable *practical* element in the cultivation of virtue, which requires actual, not "as-if," experimentation, effort, and training. Nevertheless, narrative does play a role in the identification, articulation, and understanding of virtue—a role that is indispensable to the full, accurate, and convincing articulation of virtue ethics. Think here of the way narrative helps to articulate a vision of virtue and flourishing in Thoreau's *Walden*.

Narrative also plays a role in the actual cultivation of virtue. Turner has it right when, following Hume, he argues that "reason alone is insufficient to move the will."[118] What then, is a more reliable source of motivation? With respect to environmental dispositions, Turner argues that "most of us, when we think about it, realize that after our own direct experience of nature, what has contributed most to our love of wild places, animals, and plants—and even, perhaps, to our love of wild nature, our sense of citizenship—is the art, literature, myth, and lore of nature."[119] This in the context of a book that rails incessantly about the inadequacy and danger of "mere concepts and abstractions." The conclusion, it seems, must be that narrative, while falling short of the visceral reality of "gross contact," surpasses in some significant way the sterility of abstraction. It throws a bridge—the bridge of "as-if" experience—across the gap between abstract theorizing and concrete experience.

Narrative Exacerbates Relativism

A second objection argues that the infinite varieties of imaginative variation and emplotment, as well as the ambiguities inherent in narrative wisdom, substantially *exacerbate* the challenge of relativism with which we dealt, provisionally, in Chapter 5. There we saw the ways in which Nussbaum, Sandler, and MacIntyre frame possible responses to a strong relativism from the virtue ethics perspective. Nevertheless, relativism continues to be a challenge against which we must remain on guard. Doesn't the diversity of narrative give us even more versions of flourishing and virtue, more options to choose from, all without any clear method for comparing and ranking alternatives? It seems like this diversity would exacerbate postmodern incredulity about metanarratives that purport to frame and answer big questions like the nature of human flourishing. How are we to distinguish the "good" narratives from the "bad" ones? Those that encourage genuine virtue, environmental or otherwise, from those that are misleading or deceptive, presenting vice in the guise of virtue? The preliminary responses offered by Nussbaum, Sandler, and MacIntyre provide us with valuable resources to combat relativism, but a brief word on relativism is in order from the perspective of narrative itself.

Does narrative itself encourage relativism? It certainly seems radically opposed to absolutism. While there are myriad examples of regimes or individuals using a single, absolute metanarrative to dominate or oppress, the narrative method outlined above—framed by coduction, multiple readings and re-readings, open-ended interpretation, and purposeful engagement with alternative, counter-narratives—is allergic to such monolithic and absolutist discourse. As the fictional Diego Alatriste cautions: "Never trust a man who reads only one book."[120] But this only digs the hole of relativism deeper, for now we have a diversity of narratives, with no objective way to rank them, and a method that asks us to consciously embrace this diversity.

The possibility of adopting a relativistic approach to narrative, or having one's relativism encouraged by narrative, is undeniable—just as relativism remains an alternative in philosophy, culture, and morality. Nevertheless, viewed broadly, it is clear that narrative is most closely aligned with the pluralist position for which I have been arguing rather than either the relativist or absolutist positions that are its antitheses. How so?

First, a narrative approach to virtue ethics suggests that descriptive relativism is not as obvious as it seems. There are certain narratives that certainly appear to have very broad cross-cultural appeal and resonance— *King Lear*, the *Odyssey*, and the *Bhagavad-Gita*, for example.[121] Although there is a great deal of diversity amid narratives, there is also a fair bit of consistency or harmony, including with respect to what makes life fulfilling. Moreover, one need not look very hard to discover some more or less universal narrative themes. Take the "Golden Rule," which can be found in some form in Christianity, Judaism, Islam, Greek thought, Buddhism, Confucianism, and Hinduism. That sort of breadth certainly seems, for all practical purposes, universal. One might object that "do unto others as you would have them do unto you" is insufficiently thick, incapable of being unpacked in such a way that it could support a robust ethical system, and therefore inadequate for supposing that there might be universally held aspects of ethics. But in fact the golden rule plays a quite central role in many major ethical perspectives. One story tells of Rabbi Hillel, who was challenged by a skeptic promising to convert if he could be taught the entire Torah while the Rabbi stood on one leg. The Rabbi lifted his leg and said "What is hateful to you, do not do to your friend. This is the entire Torah; the rest is interpretation, which you must go and learn" (Babylonian Talmud, *Shabbat*, 31A). Likewise, the Apostle Paul writes, "Serve one another . . . in works of love, since the whole of the Law is summarized in a single command: Love your neighbor as yourself" (Galatians 5:13–14). And the *Analects* of Confucius tell us, "Zi Gong asked, 'Is there one expression that can be acted upon until the end of one's days [that is, one word that can serve as a guiding rule]'? The Master replied, 'There is *shu*: do not impose on others what you yourself do not want.'"[122]

One plausible reason for the ubiquity of certain ethical themes is the homogeneity of the human condition. That is to say, there are universal ethical truths that stem from universal aspects of the human condition. Humans flourish in distinctively human ways and certain narrative themes articulate virtues that respond to the broadly human, rather than the specifically Japanese or French or Columbian context. There are similarities in diverse human narratives precisely because they are *human* narratives expressing *human* hopes and fears, needs and desires. And I would maintain that if we are searching for nuanced treatment of the "grounding experiences" that humans from diverse backgrounds share, there is no better place to look than in great narratives. Of course, any articulation of, for example, the golden rule will still need to be interpreted and applied, and the devil is in the details. Nevertheless, the ubiquity of narratives focused on this rule of ethical reciprocity suggests that narratives can indeed give us insight into universal aspects of ethics.

In addition to contesting broad claims about descriptive relativism, an emphasis on narrative tends to make radical normative relativism much less attractive. Indeed, Nussbaum argues that narrative itself is opposed to relativism. Why? First, because interpretations are, in fact, limited by preunderstanding—circumscribed by tradition and culture—and by the structural limits imposed by the narrative itself. And both preunderstanding and structure are influenced by responsible coduction. Only an abusive distortion could interpret, for example, *Walden* as a paean to the virtues of groupthink, unrestrained consumption, urban sprawl, and corporate domination of community life. If common sense were not enough to demonstrate this, any reasonable attempt at coduction would. Coduction also works to erode and undermine less obviously abusive interpretations, as does dialogue with science, personal experience, tradition, and philosophical argumentation.

Moreover, our very reaction to narrative suggests that it is not aligned with relativism. Recall again the ethical judgment solicited by any narrative: "There is no action that does not give rise to approbation or reprobation, to however a small degree, as a function of a hierarchy of values for which goodness and wickedness are the poles."[123] Action—and thus narrative, which imitates action—"can never be ethically neutral."[124] That is to say, each individual narrative implies that there is a right and a wrong, or at least that there are better and worse actions. Thus, adopting a narrative approach to virtue actually downplays rather than encourages a relativistic perspective. We judge, almost without our consent, acts that are narratively recounted to be good or bad, suggesting that all responses are not equal, as exaggerated relativism would have it. The approbation and reprobation called for by every narrative imply—even when such judgments are tentative or uncertain—that some actions are better than others, some visions of the good life are better than others, and, thus, that some perspectives are more true than others. As Kearney notes, the "concreteness" of fictive examples fleshes things out in a way unlike the cold detachment of pure theory. Narratives put a *face* to ethical questions and, environmentally, I'd add that they also *place* ethical questions, grounding them in a specific context and environment.[125] It is one thing to entertain, intellectually, the possibility of the cold indifference of the stars[126]; it is another thing entirely to assert that it does not matter whether or not this person here before us is raped or murdered, whether this specific species goes extinct, or whether this particular place is paved over and developed. This is why Meursault—the protagonist of Camus's *L'Etranger* for whom all acts are equally uncompelling—is not heroic, but inhuman.

I often use a humorous example from the Coen brothers' movie *The Big Lebowski* to illustrate the untenable nature of nihilism and exaggerated relativism to my students.[127] In the movie, a trio of self-proclaimed nihilists—caricatures of German postmodernists who traipse around LA insisting, "We're nihilists! We believe in nothing!"—perpetrate a kidnapping hoax. In a climactic confrontation with the movie's main subject, the "Dude," and his friends Walter and Donny, the nihilists demand payment. At one point, Walter screams, "There's no ransom if you don't have a f--king hostage! That's what ransom is. Those are the f--king rules!" To which the disappointed nihilists ultimately whine, "But that's not fair!" Walter, justifiably indignant, shouts, "Fair?! Who is the f--king nihilist here?" The point, with apologies for the language, is that no one maintains his or her nihilism, or relativism, in the face of perceived injustice. Nihilism and relativism may be intellectual temptations, but they are not lived ethical standpoints.[128] No person being victimized thinks, "My attacker's interpretation of this situation is not congenial to mine." Victims of injustice cry out, and ought to cry out, against injustice. Radical normative relativism is something that one can entertain in the abstract; but in concrete, or narrative, situations it seems less plausible and is much less palatable.

If such narrative insights suggest that descriptive ethical relativism is only true within certain limits and that an exaggerated type of normative ethical relativism is nothing more than a bogeyman, then what virtue ethics really has to come to terms with is a less radical relativism, a "contextualism" that insists that we cannot speak clearly about virtue and vice abstracted from concrete situations. Narrative pluralism recognizes the multiplicity of goods, as Nussbaum reminds us, as well as the inescapable possibility of those goods coming into tragic conflict; it also recognizes that the goodness or badness of events, phenomena, or actions is often dependent on context.[129] Here again, however, narrative has something to say about the limits of relativism. The influence of context ranges from virtues that are highly situational, even context- or role-specific, to virtues that seem to be universal or near-universal, and every shade in between. At the risk of pedantry, we could point again to the "quasi-universal" narratives that seem to undermine an overly broad affirmation of descriptive relativism. No doubt that these common narrative themes are ubiquitous, in part, because of the common human condition, a "universal context" to which they respond, which is perhaps a narrative way of getting to the commonalities implied in Aristotle's teleological biology, the naturalistic focus on the "type of being" that we are, or the human capabilities that are the focus of Nussbaum's work. Indeed, a common theme in responding to the four objections raised in this chapter is that insights from other disciplines and ways of knowing can and should inform discussions of virtue—as they have for Sandler and Nussbaum. Natural sciences, social sciences, personal experience, and philosophical reflection all work alongside narrative in circumscribing virtue and flourishing; but narrative remains an essential component without which science and experience would not be complete. And narrative itself suggests that virtue and flourishing, while contextual and therefore pluralistic, are not relative in the strong sense. Such a pluralistic perspective can be illustrated, as I suggested in the previous chapter, through a mathematical analogy. On a number line, there are an infinite number of points between four and five; nevertheless, we know that three, six, seven, etcetera are not included in this range. Similarly, while there is an infinite diversity of ways in which to be virtuous—narratives about virtue are structurally open ended—that does not mean that any action at all is virtuous. Some things are, rightly, beyond the pale.

Thus, contrary to some claims, a narrative approach to virtue is not really allied with, or indeed even congenial to, relativism. Of course, taking a stand against relativism in literature means passing ethical judgment about good books and bad books, or about good emplotment and bad emplotment. We are still faced with the difficulty of either reconciling or choosing between incompatible ethical claims arising from different narratives. Such competing claims are not always minor differences in opinion. Moreover, as Katie McShane points out, we also have to deal with the reality of "pernicious narratives that are very effective at getting people to do very stupid things."[130] One thinks here of cornucopian stories of infinite growth on a finite planet, conspiracy theories about a global takeover by the United Nations under the influence of Agenda 21, narratives focused on the denial of anthropogenic climate change, or, in non-environmental discourse, of specious accounts of race superiority, historical revisionism, Holocaust denial, and the like.

However, the preceding account—along with input from Nussbaum, Sandler, and MacIntyre in the previous chapter—suggests that there are resources to help us root out pernicious narratives. This process will never be infallible. As we've seen many times in the course of this study, there is no simple formula for clearly identifying good books and bad books; there are, however, guidelines. First, we must keep in mind that within the field of narrative we are aiming at plausibility rather than proof. Oftentimes we cannot prove ethical claim A is superior to ethical claim B, but, recognizing the degree of specificity appropriate to ethics, we must content ourselves with successfully arguing that A is more plausible than B. Second, we must remember that responsible ethical narration and interpretation are both open-ended and social in nature. As Nussbaum cautions, "we need to exercise critical judgment in our selection of novels, and to continue the process of critical judgment as we read, in dialogue with others."[131] Coduction helps us to sharpen our arguments for plausibility, opens us to unseen alternative interpretations, and develops the habit of and skill in discernment that will help us apply virtues in context and wisely differentiate between competing ethical claims. Third, in addition to coducing with respect to common narratives, we should consciously engage unfamiliar or foreign narratives (and in so doing engage otherness). The unfamiliar and foreign will shed light upon the familiar—as Ricoeur says, the shortest path from self to self is through the other. Engaging otherness in the form of other narratives will, again, force us to clarify why one account is more plausible than another; it will also open us to novel perspectives detailing alternative, perhaps more plausible, accounts of virtue and flourishing. This does not mean we need to give equal time or weight to all perspectives, a distortion evident in the blind application of something like the "fairness doctrine" in journalism. We *do* need to challenge ourselves with opinions, perspectives, and narratives different from—even disagreeable, antagonistic, or repugnant to—our own. But while in certain cases it is difficult to tell where to draw the line, legitimate lines are drawn. We generally *don't* make time for phrenologists to rebut civil rights attorneys on news programs. Nor do we consult the fry cook at the local fast-food franchise for a second opinion regarding our doctor's advice about our cholesterol levels. Similarly, we ought not give equal weight to the opinions of random political bloggers or non-scientific specialists (for example, those with an MBA, JD, or a PhD in Education) on the physical facts about climate change when considered alongside the opinions of climate scientists. Finally, because narrative resources cannot, on their own, do away with relativism, we must also make use of other complimentary practices such as careful attention to one's actual experiences and the experiences of others, judicious listening to wisdom traditions, and so forth. We should also avail ourselves of other "non-narrative" ways of knowing including science, ecology, psychology, economics, and more. Engaging these alternative perspectives will help to counterbalance misrepresentations, distortions, and omissions that narrative alone might pass over. Our judgments about narratives, just like our judgments about persons, will never be certain and beyond revision. Nevertheless, we can and do make such judgments, and we can and do recognize when we, or others, judge well.

Narrative Distorts Reality

A third objection suggests that, rather than simply distancing us from reality, narratives actively distort reality. At least since Descartes, we've rearranged our thinking to privilege certain methods and certain conclusions.[132] Sometimes, of course, that privilege is justified, but not always. In terms of environmental discourse—whether metaphysical, epistemological, or ethical—there tends to be a strong presumption that scientific inquiry is the standard for truth. This presumption explains, on some level, the attractiveness of naturalistic accounts of virtue. What is a naturalistic virtue? It's a characteristic that helps us to flourish as the kind of material and biological beings that we are. But all too often narratives play fast and loose with biology and other scientific disciplines. If virtues are grounded, in part, in biology and ecology, and if narratives tend to get the biology and ecology wrong, then narratives will be dangerous ways of understanding virtues.

Let's begin by looking at some of the ways in which narratives do get the science wrong. When discussing environmental issues, narratives are notoriously anthropocentric, viewing non-human nature through a blatantly human lens or projecting human affairs—values, virtues, concepts, concerns, and so forth—on to non-human nature. Narratives often manipulate their subjects by either exaggeration or understatement, and frequently sentimentalize or demonize aspects of nature.[133] This might seem a purely epistemological issue, and so foreign to a discussion of virtue, until we realize that the way in which we conceive of nature affects our understanding of it as well as our possibilities for flourishing within it or as part of it.

Marcia Eaton points out a classic example of such distortion, one so influential and so convincing that it fairly closes the case on narrative: Felix Salten's *Bambi*.[134] Today, few people (at least in those countries within the expansive reach of the Disney Corporation) can "look at a deer or a picture of a deer and not imagine it as the innocent, noble creature that Salten depicts."[135] *Bambi* is a prime example of the way in which people project human virtues onto non-human animals, casting some in roles that are noble (the pacifism and nonviolence of Bambi's mother), heroic (the courage of the eponymous mongoose in Kipling's *Rikki Tikki Tavi*), or friendly (the perpetual "smile" of Flipper the dolphin) and others in roles that are base (the spotted hyenas in *The Lion King*, another Disney project) or vicious (the voracious malice of the shark in *Jaws* or, more classically, of Ahab's nemesis in *Moby Dick*).[136] While many such narrative projections are aimed at children, they remain very strong influences on adult perceptions of nature, and are strengthened by the many narrative documentaries aimed at older audiences, including *Winged Migration*, *March of the Penguins*, *One Life*, and innumerable National Geographic specials.[137] Returning to the paradigmatic case of *Bambi*, Eaton points out the problem: while the narrative is useful if one wants to teach children certain moral lessons—perhaps about nonviolence—it is totally false if one wants to teach children, or adults, about real deer in the real world, how they interact with and function within their ecosystems, how we relate to them, and how we should relate to them.[138]

Certainly we *do* use our imagination in our encounters with non-human nature. Kearney goes so far as to suggest that, just as narratives can help us to experience the lives of different human persons, "we can even transport ourselves into the skin of a 'non-rational' animal. What is impossible in reality is made possible in fiction."[139] Rachel Carson explicitly adopted this technique in her first book *Under the Sea Wind*, in which tells three stories *from the perspective of sea animals*: a sanderling, a mackerel, and an eel. In composing the book she "decided that the author as a person or a human should never enter the story, but that it should be told as a simple narrative of the lives of certain animals of the sea. As far as possible, I wanted my readers to feel that they were, for a time, actually living the lives of sea creatures."[140] This might appear to embrace the very sort of crass anthropocentrism that, understandably, concerns Eaton and others. But is that the case? Although our individual perspectives will inevitably color our interpretations, whether of other people or of nature, it does not follow that this coloring will necessarily be either vicious or fundamentally misleading. Our interpretations, our *human* interpretations, will always have an inescapable residue of anthropocentrism; however, just as narratives can open us to genuine, if complicated and partial, understanding of other human experiences and worlds (for example, the Holocaust or antebellum slavery in the United States), narratives can open us, provisionally and partially, to other non-human experiences and worlds.[141] Of course, we must remain ever vigilant against allowing our inescapably anthropocentric perspective from sliding into a naïve and vicious anthropocentrism. Nevertheless, this should not dissuade us from embracing narrative in a manner that is (1) humbly aware of its inevitable bias and, at the same time, (2) excited about its genuine ability to open us up to other worlds.[142]

This inescapably anthropocentric perspective is why Turner concedes that, "I don't think we can say why [certain animals do what they do] without using analogies and metaphors from human emotional life."[143] Addressing a sort of projection more central to the discussion of virtue, he writes,

> It is not popular now to attribute human characteristics and processes to wild animals, since it projects onto the Other our biases and perceptions and limits our view of their difference. But all description is merely analogy and metaphor, and as such is forever imperfect and respectful of mystery . . . We also fail to appreciate that many of our descriptions of human behavior are appropriations from wild animals: the lion-hearted hero, the wolfish cad, the foxy lady. And this suggests that life is a spectrum where unity is more pervasive than difference . . . It is no more odd to say that pelicans love to soar and do so in ecstasy than it is to say what we commonly say of human love and ecstasy: that our heart soars.[144]

Doug Peacock makes a similar point: "Humans are so strongly discouraged from comparing their lives with those of other animals. Yet everything I had experienced taught me that metaphor is the fundamental path of imagining, a first line of inquiry into the lives of other creatures that sheds light on our own."[145]

If we anthropomorphize nature we also biomorphize ourselves, so to speak—though that is perhaps not the perfect phrase for what needs to be indicated: the flattening out of relevant distinctions between ourselves and other forms of life. While it is no doubt true that the former is more common and more problematic, the sword cuts both ways. And both translations—human to non-human, and non-human to human—require careful navigation because, as Ricoeur points out, translation is a double betrayal.[146] The lion-hearted hero, wolfish cad, and foxy lady are metaphors, as are the noble deer and the heroic mongoose, and like all good metaphors they do get at something meaningful; however, we must be on guard against taking them literally. But while translation is dangerous, it is also necessary. As most of the philosophers working in narrative are at pains to remind us, albeit in different terms, there is no escaping the hermeneutic circle, no view from nowhere, no unbiased or innocent eye. When we speak about nature we do so in ways that reflect our own perspective, and this is as true of the vaunted objectivity of science as it is of narrative and other modes of inquiry.

Many environmentalists, who are generally more scientifically literate than the average person, align themselves (consciously or not) with that segment of the population for which science provides the gold standard— indeed, for some the only *real* standard—for knowledge and truth.[147] Thus, celebrated environmental philosopher Holmes Rolston III argues for the "superiority" of science, which provides the "definitive interpretation" of natural phenomena: "science corrects for truth."[148] However, the supposed unbiased and objective detachment of scientists has been critiqued from many angles, most famously by Thomas Kuhn in *The Structure of Scientific Revolutions*, but also by predecessors like William Whewell and Karl Popper.[149] While there is a temptation to regard science as the study of objective reality unsullied by opinion or bias, progressing inexorably toward the *really* real and the *truly* true, according to Kuhn science is not engaged in inevitable, teleological progress toward objective, ultimate truth.[150] "An apparently arbitrary element, compounded of personal and historical accident, is always a formative ingredient of the beliefs espoused by a given scientific community at a given time."[151] Whewell and Popper referred to scientific beliefs and positions as "idea-laden" or "theory-laden"—they are grounded on assumptions aligned with particular paradigms, to use the term favored by Kuhn.

Paradigm shifts—a phrase that has now entered our collective lexicon—do not happen because someone just sees the truth more clearly. Often "the new paradigm . . . emerges all at once, sometimes in the middle of the night, in the mind of a man deeply immersed in crisis. What the nature of that stage is—how an individual *invents* (or *finds he has invented*) a new way of giving order to data now all assembled—must here remain inscrutable and may remain so."[152] The transition from one paradigm to another is marked by "a *conversion* that cannot be forced"[153] and which cannot be justified by "proof."[154] However, while proof may be lacking, paradigm shifts are frequently shaped by *aesthetic* appeals to simplicity, suitability, neatness, elegance, or similar traits. Indeed, according to Kuhn, "the importance of aesthetic considerations can sometimes be *decisive*."[155] Recall, here, the role played by aesthetics in ethics, as in Aristotle's insistence on the *kalon* nature of virtue. In science, as in other modes of inquiry, there is no "raw data" or "pure given" unsullied by interpretation[156] and there is no objective decision procedure to guide us in choosing a new paradigm over the old one.[157] Seen in this light, science itself, at any point in its history, is merely one way to view the world; it answers some questions very well, and others poorly or not at all. I hasten to point out that this need not suggest relativism, which I've already rejected and which Kuhn repudiated as well. Science is a powerful tool, and it is an absolutely indispensable pillar of any sound environmental ethics, as writers like Thoreau, Muir, and Carson have demonstrated. However, if science does not provide a pure, unbiased, and objective view of the Truth, then we must ask ourselves whether and how science provides "the definitive" interpretation of nature or "corrects for truth."

While the scientific interpretation arguably reigns supreme in modern discourse, it is not without its own problems and limitations. The very detachment and disinterestedness that gives science its power opens it to charges of abstraction. Indeed, this tendency is part of what ecology, as a discipline, attempts to correct. Although abstraction is not bad or distortive *per se*, it can metamorphose, eventually succumbing to what Gabriel Marcel calls the "spirit of abstraction."[158] The spirit of abstraction should not be confused with science, nor with theoretical thinking, nor even with abstraction itself (for it is possible to abstract without succumbing to the spirit of abstraction), each of which, used properly, can be a helpful tool in our quest for greater knowledge and understanding of the world and our place in it. The spirit of abstraction is rather something along the line of losing the forest for the trees, seeing a part as the whole, perhaps even going so far as the reification of things or idolatry.

The power of abstraction lies in its ability to help us to understand—more precisely, with greater detail, and so forth—due to the focus that it allows. However, because abstraction can succumb to the spirit of abstraction, abstractions can lead to their own *mis*understandings. These misunderstandings are often tied to the abstraction itself, from looking at a thing in isolation, in a vacuum, rather than in context where it interacts with and depends on many other things in a complex web of relationships.

Instances of scientific misadventures stemming from abstraction abound. Take, for example, the deleterious effects of abstraction that result in the kind of "nutritionism" or "nutrition science" critiqued in Michael Pollan's *In Defense of Food*.[159] Nutritionism encourages us to "understand and engage with food and our bodies in terms of their nutritional and chemical constituents and requirements—*the assumption being that this is all we need to understand*."[160] Nutritionism is a reductionist approach to food that is born of an abstraction run amok, an abstraction that looks at parts (nutrients) and assumes that they collectively equal the whole (food). What's remarkable about this approach is not the obvious fact that it completely misses a number of significant things about production, preparation, and consumption of food—the social and cultural aspects, for example—but that it *also* misses the one thing at which it does aim: more healthful eating. It is nutrition science that brought us breakfast "cereals" that are nothing but corn soaked in sugar and "fortified" with "vitamins and minerals," which in turn helped to bring us the obesity, heart disease, cancer, and diabetes that go along with such nutrition-endorsed "edible food-like substances."

Such abstraction seem fundamentally at odds with the sort of comprehensive approach, sensitive to the complexities of each individual and context, that is a hallmark of virtue ethics. We should keep in mind that pure, "objective" scientific description would, perforce, be rigorously descriptive and value neutral. It would be silent at best, and relativistic or nihilistic at worst, with respect to value and virtue. Scientifically, there is no reason at all that the Earth is "better" with a climate of, on average, 14°C than it would be at 20°C; and, again from a purely descriptive and scientific perspective, the universe is no "better" with intelligent life than it would be without it. It is the incorporation of the dry, sterile, objective description of rain (in the examples above) into a narrative that initiates the first critical step toward an account of our relationship—actual, potential, aesthetic, and ethical—to rain and toward a prescription of how we should respond to rain. Scientific insight definitely has a part to play in our self-understanding and, therefore, in our understanding of virtue; but it is inadequate on its own. It's narrative that provides the bridge between description and prescription. And environmental virtue ethics, like all versions of ethics, is ultimately about prescription; it is, as MacIntyre reminds us, concerned with how we get from "who we are" to "who we ought to be."

Facts, not Fictions, Should be the Basis for Judging and Acting

A corollary of the claim that science, not narrative, is the discipline concerned with truth is the claim that facts, not fiction, should be the basis on which we judge and act. The response to this objection must, of course, echo the above argument that there is no perspective that is entirely free from interpretation. This is not to say that there are no "facts," but rather that the relationship between facts and interpretation is much more intimate, intertwined, and nuanced than is generally appreciated. However, even when we bracket the supposed objectivity of facts, we find that facts do not always have the motivational force that we attribute to them. Thus, if the line between science and narrative cannot be clearly drawn by crudely claiming one deals with objective facts, and the other with subjective interpretation or opinion, perhaps this is just as well. When it comes to modifying behavior—which must remain one of our central concerns in an environmental virtue ethics—facts, it turns out, are significantly less powerful than we generally suppose.

Recent research in psychology and political science illustrates well the limitations of using a purely factual-argumentative approach to change people's minds or behavior. Joe Keohane summarizes some of the relevant research:

> In a series of studies in 2005 and 2006, researchers at the University of Michigan found that when misinformed people, particularly political partisans, were exposed to corrected facts in news stories, they rarely changed their minds. In fact, they often became even more strongly set in their beliefs. Facts, they found, were not curing misinformation. Like an underpowered antibiotic, facts could actually make misinformation even *stronger*.[161]

Environmentalist David Brower used to quip that you can't reason prejudice out of people because that's not how it got in.[162] Philosopher Rosalind Hursthouse concurs: with respect to the inculcation of racism it is "vividly clear that 'the' way in which the training of the emotions shapes one's thoughts of generic good and evil cannot be divided neatly into the rational and the non-rational."[163] It turns out facts are less likely than we generally think to change opinions and beliefs about the world. And since our opinions and beliefs about the world shape, in large part, our desires, it stands to reason that we are not going to change our behavior without a change in our opinions and beliefs. As Aristotle notes, we have to *want to be* virtuous before we can *become* virtuous.

It would be tempting to conclude that the fault lies in a lack of education. Educated people, even when misinformed, should possess the critical tools to analyze their beliefs in light of new information. Indeed, this is one of the promises of education, especially in the liberal tradition.

That conclusion, however, would be incorrect: studies suggest that, at least in the case of political information, astute and well-informed thinkers were even less receptive to new information than their unsophisticated counterparts.[164] Although well-educated people may be correct in a large number of their beliefs about states of affairs, their justified confidence in this body of knowledge makes it almost impossible to correct them on the things about which they are completely wrong or misinformed. Their education and the fact that they are generally well-informed make them overconfident in even their mistaken beliefs.

This phenomenon, which Brendan Nyhan and Jason Reifler have dubbed "backfire," presents a real problem for those who believe that more accurate facts, more information in our already information-saturated society, is the panacea to our woes, ethical, political, or environmental.[165] Many studies have shown that material wealth, after a relatively low threshold, does not bring about substantially greater happiness. Nevertheless, it's far from clear—indeed, it is highly unlikely—that simply presenting the relevant academic studies will induce large numbers of people to abandon the "hedonic treadmill" of the rat race. Aristotle himself cautions us about overconfidence in the efficacy of arguments, pointing out that many people remain unmoved even by sound and reliable arguments.[166]

The majority of our opinions are based on unverified beliefs, whether those are beliefs about climate science or beliefs about the good life. Although Thoreau and Aristotle both, in different ways, remind us of the importance of personal experience, much of what we believe we believe based on what we glean from others—others' experience, others' empirical verification, others' expertise, the wisdom of tradition, and so forth. Most of this is communicated to us via narrative of one sort or another. The problem for the "cognitive approach," one based on argument and facts, is that our current beliefs dictate in large part what new information we will accept as fact. This phenomenon was recognized long ago by William James: "Our minds thus grow in spots; and like grease-spots, the spots spread. But we let them spread as little as possible: we keep unaltered as much of our old knowledge, as many of our old prejudices and beliefs, as we can. We patch and tinker more than we renew."[167]

Suppose a person spent a long time, a very long time, attempting to assemble a jigsaw puzzle. The puzzle, call it "The Cloud," has many thousands of pieces and is uniformly white, without any picture to distinguish the pieces. Moreover, "The Cloud" lacks any traditional shape that would give it sharp, discernable edges to facilitate solving the puzzle. Having sacrificed many months, perhaps years, our hypothetical puzzler raises the final piece to snap into the completed canvass, only to find . . . it does not fit. First perplexed, then frustrated, then quite angry, she tries various orientations of the piece in a vain attempt to get it to fit the rest of the assembled puzzle. However, in each and every orientation there is an extra bulge of material that prevents the last piece from fitting into any one of the final gaps. Clearly, reasons our puzzler, there has been an error at the factory and this puzzle is defective. After so much time invested, the puzzler is *highly* unlikely to scrap the entire effort and start over in order to figure out how and why this last troubling piece connects to the existing framework. After all, it is clearly the final piece that is defective (that is, "wrong") since the rest of the pieces already fit together in what appears to be—or appeared to be until the discovery of the ill-fitting piece—a well-organized unit. It's not hard to imagine that, in such a situation, the next step in the process would be to go to the kitchen for a pair of scissors to "fix" the offending puzzle piece in order to ensure that it fits in the way it was, obviously, supposed to. We would rather mutilate a new piece of information to make it fit in our cognitive puzzle than rearrange long-standing patterns in the puzzle to see if and how the new piece might fit.

Psychologist Jonathan Haidt is among those who emphasize the importance of confirmation bias, our tendency to look for data that support our existing views.[168] Reason, argues Haidt, operates less like a disinterested philosopher seeking truth and more like a lawyer or press secretary justifying policies. Our tendency toward confirmation bias is exacerbated by technological resources, as a quick Google search can find web pages supporting almost any position under the sun. Want to find "proof" that climate change is a hoax perpetrated by the United Nations in order to subjugate the United States? Google can help you "confirm" it. This leads Haidt to claim, "anyone who values truth should stop worshiping reason."[169] There is a difference between finding the truth and confirming a belief, and our reason works hardest at the latter. Individual reasoning is "post-hoc and justificatory."[170] What then is the solution? The only cure for confirmation bias is working in dialogue and debate with other people, which is precisely what happens in academic peer review, science, and narrative coduction.

James wrote about his "grease spots" in 1907, but the contemporary research confirms his insights regarding the way in which our knowledge grows. People, it turns out, are "motivated reasoners" who process information "defensively." An extensive body of psychological work "shows that humans are goal-directed information processors who tend to evaluate information with a directional bias toward reinforcing their pre-existing views."[171] If we want people to understand and accept new or different facts about the world—or, in terms of virtue ethics, if we want them to change their beliefs about human flourishing and the environment, and as a consequence change their behavior—we cannot rely simply on presenting cold bare facts that challenge the status quo. Facts fit into a certain worldview or perspective. Indeed, certain worldviews will preclude even recognizing certain things as facts at all. So presenting facts must be accompanied, or in some cases preceded, by addressing the underlying worldview of the target audience. But a person's worldview, like her personal identity, is fundamentally *narrative*. To get people to change their minds about, for example, climate change, it is necessary to address the underlying narrative into which facts about climate change fit or do not fit. Likewise, to get people to change their minds about what beliefs, opinions, behaviors, dispositions, and so forth are conducive to living the good life, we need to address the underlying narrative that articulates a more or less global vision of "the good life." Simply bombarding people with more information, more facts and arguments, is unlikely to have any effect. It is for this reason that Turner argues, "old ways of seeing do not change because of evidence, they change because a new language captures the imagination."[172] And Thoreau himself—Thoreau, indefatigable champion of the immediacy of personal experience and sucking the marrow from life—recognizes the power of narrative to give us living truth when he writes,

> A fact stated barely is dry. It must be the vehicle of some humanity in order to interest us. It is like giving a man a stone when he asks you for bread. Ultimately the moral is all in all, and we do not mind it if inferior truth is sacrificed to superior, as when the moralist fables and makes animals speak and act like men. It must be warm, moist, incarnated—have been breathed on at least. A man has not seen a thing who has not felt it.[173]

Narrative Environmental Virtue Ethics

If arguments were in themselves enough to make men good, they would justly . . . have won very great rewards. . . . [However,] while they seem to have power to encourage and stimulate [a few], they are not able to encourage the many to nobility and goodness.

—Aristotle, *Nicomachean Ethics*, X.9.

Truth is not that which is demonstrable, but that which is ineluctable.

—Antoine de Saint Exupéry, *Wind, Sand, and Stars*

Surely one of the novel's habitual aims is to articulate morality, to sharpen the reader's sense of vice and virtue.

—John Updike, *Hugging the Shore*

Introduction: Ethical Formation and Reformation

Virtue ethics is, at its heart, about ethical formation and reformation. It is, as MacIntyre says, about how each of us gets from "who I am" to "who I ought to be." Rosalind Hursthouse goes so far as to suggest that it is the only major ethical approach to take this distinction seriously and to address the complexities and difficulties associated with this transition:

[There is] a specially realistic feature of Aristotle's thought—that he never forgets the fact that we were all once children. To read almost any other famous moral philosopher is to receive the impression that we, the intelligent adult readers addressed, spring fully formed from our father's brow. That children form

155

part of the furniture of the world occasionally comes up in passing (about as often as the mention of non-human animals), but
the utterly basic fact that we were once as they are, and that
whatever we are now is continuous with how we were then, is
completely ignored.[1]

This all too common lacuna with respect to childhood formation is just as
glaring in the case of adult reformation. This is odd since we know that
moral subjects are something other than perfectly rational actors, that we
are motivated and defensive reasoners, that complete self-transparency is
an illusion, and that ethical formation is more complicated than simply
following rules for conduct. So, when either the letter or the spirit of an
ethical system suggests that simply following a single, universally applicable
rule—the Categorical Imperative or the Greatest Happiness Principle for
example—provides sufficient motivation or adequate action guidance, we
ought to be suspicious. Would that it were so! It would be much easier, as
a father, to simply drill my daughters until they commit to memory "actions
are right in proportion as they tend to promote happiness; wrong as they
tend to produce the reverse of happiness . . . [considering] not [your] own
greatest happiness, but the greatest amount of happiness altogether" or "I
ought never to act except in such a way that I could also will that my
maxim should become a universal law."[2] It would be easier to believe that
a single universal rule adequately captures the diversity and complexity of
ethical life, that applying such a rule would be relatively straightforward,
and that acting on the basis of that application would not take extraordinary effort. I would sleep easier at night.

But we've already seen some of the problems associated with overly
legalistic systems and facile reliance on universal rules: the lack of sensitivity to the particularities of context; dubious guidance in particularly vexing
situations; the difficulty in dealing with novel challenges; a general silence
with respect to a number of ethically significant environmental issues; and
so forth. To those problems we can add the charge that relying on such
rules "full stop" is bound to run into real problems with respect to ethical motivation or inspiration, ethical discernment, and ethical cultivation.
Recall C. S. Lewis's warning in *Mere Christianity*:

What is the good of drawing up, on paper, rules for social
behavior, if we know that, in fact, our greed, cowardice, ill
temper, and self-conceit are going to prevent us from keeping

> them? . . . [A]ll that [systematic and legalistic] thinking will be
> mere moonshine unless we realize that nothing but the courage
> and unselfishness of individuals is ever going to make any system
> work properly. . . .[3]

This is one reason that I do not ask my daughters to memorize regulations as if they—even when well-understood—will actually provide clear answers to complicated, and all-too-common, ethical conundrums, to say nothing of the lonely emergencies of life in which we are really put to the test. It's also why, as adults, we generally don't reflect on our own lives in terms of our obedience to regulations. We're much more likely to reflect in broadly narrative terms. Is that what I should have done or felt? What would I have done or felt if I were a better person, that is to say, if I were more virtuous? Even when we do compare our actions to some abstract rule or regulation, it's generally in terms of what a good person would have done in light of that rule or regulation. Follow it strictly? Bend the rule? Break the rule?

It's not that rules aren't useful; they *are*. But we don't want to put the cart before the horse. It's all too clear that a person—either a child or adult—is fully capable of memorizing, understanding, and reciting a moral law, credo, statute, catechism, honor code, or other rule for behavior and, in the very next moment, acting contrary to it. There are myriad reasons for the incongruities between thought and act: weakness of will, self-deception, "rational" justifications, selfishness, egoism, and so on. But the point is that rules, on their own, will not turn us into good people.

However, good people can make good use of rules. Rules, guidelines, adages, proverbs, and aphorisms—many, we should note, originating from or drawing on narrative—provide a useful ethical "shorthand" for expressing what a good person would generally do in most situations. "Be honest" is not the inflexible and unbreakable rule of practical reason that Kant supposes; rather, it's an abbreviated way of saying: "Honesty is a virtue, one of the characteristics that make good people good. It's important to be honest and a good person tells the truth in most situations, even in very difficult circumstances, although there are some uncommon situations in which a good person would dissimulate or even lie." All things being equal, we ought to tell the truth. But things—persons, motives, consequences, times, places, environments, conflicts, other incommensurable goods, and so on—are never really equal. That is why, according to Aristotle, practical wisdom is like the "Lesbian rule," a soft lead measuring rule that can bend and conform to measure irregular shapes, and in doing so measure more accurately, more truly.[4]

Rules of a sort can play a critical role in helping to guide our actions, especially those of us who are not yet virtuous. But how will we know which rules to follow? What of the objection that a person who is not virtuous would be completely incapable of discerning how to act virtuously and, therefore, incapable of habituating herself to virtue? Hursthouse offers a number of responses to this sort of objection. First, our hypothetical ethical aspirant could simply find a virtuous person and ask her for guidance in applying rules or choosing actions, a point akin to Aristotle's reliance on the role of the *phronimos*. This possibility, which Hursthouse suggests is "far from . . . trivial," also emphasizes the social nature of virtue and the fact that we "quite often seek moral guidance from people we think are morally better than ourselves."[5] In general, she rejects the idea that a person who is not fully virtuous will not, therefore, know what a virtuous agent should do. As we will see, one of the major reasons this is so is that narratives give us virtuous exemplars and accounts of their actions in various contexts even when we ourselves are not yet virtuous and have not yet experienced similar situations. Hursthouse also suggests that virtue ethics is able to offer rules of a sort, which she calls "v-rules," and that for this reason it is false to claim that virtue ethics lacks sufficient "action guidance" for us to determine what ought to be done in any given circumstance.[6] V-rules prescribe general ways of proceeding: "do what is honest" or, conversely, "do not do what is dishonest."[7] Although one might object that these rules are too wooly to be useful, requiring that we unpack the evaluative terms in which they are expressed, Hursthouse argues convincingly that this is no different from attempting to apply the categorical imperative or the greatest happiness principle. Both deontology and utilitarianism require extensive elaboration—of what constitutes rational preference, what distinguishes higher and lower pleasure, or the meaning of evaluative terms like beneficence—before offering any sort of useful action guidance, and the guidance they purportedly offer is invariably the subject of heated debate.[8]

Therefore, it's not that we should reject ethical rules, but rather that we need to *begin* somewhere deeper and more fundamental, and that we should be capable, when appropriate, of moving *beyond* them. One helpful way of articulating the relationship between virtue and rules can be found in the "little ethics" of Paul Ricoeur's *Oneself as Another*.[9] Ricoeur distinguishes between the ethical aim expressing the teleological perspective of what we consider to be good and moral norms expressing a deontological perspective that imposes itself in terms of obligation. His contribution lies in the creative interweaving of the Aristotelian and the Kantian in order to establish: "(1) the primacy of ethics over morality, (2) the necessity of the ethical aim to pass through the sieve of the moral norm, and (3) the legitimacy of recourse by the norm to the aim whenever the norm leads to impasses in practice."[10] In other words our ethical thinking should begin with the ethical aim, which expresses our understanding of the *telos* of human being, the good life, what it means to be a good person. From this rather broad and comprehensive picture we derive moral norms that flow from the ethical aim and which articulate duties and rules for conduct based on that aim. However, as we have seen, while such rules are useful in many ways they often fail us precisely when we most need guidance. In these lonely emergencies—when moral norms fail us because they are insensitive to the unique features of the particular case, or because the issue in question is entirely novel, or because we find ourselves caught in an inescapable, tragic circumstance—we can and must fall back on the ethical aim:

> A great part of *rational* deliberation will be concerned with ques-
> tions about whether a certain course of action here and now
> really counts as realizing some important value (say, courage
> or friendship) that is a prima facie part of [one's] idea of the
> good life; or even whether a certain way of acting (a certain
> relationship-type or particular) really counts as the sort of thing
> [one] wants to include in [one's] conception of a good life at
> all . . . For this sort of question, it seems obvious that there
> is no mathematical answer; and the only procedure to follow
> is . . . to imagine all the relevant features as well and as fully
> and concretely as possible, holding them up against whatever
> intuitions and emotions and plans and imaginings we have
> brought into the situation or can construct in it. . . . Among
> stories of conduct, the most true and informative will be works
> of literature, biography, and history; the more abstract the story
> gets, the less rational it is to use it as one's only guide. Good
> deliberation is like theatrical or musical improvisation, where
> what counts is flexibility, responsiveness, and openness to the
> external; to rely on an algorithm here is not only insufficient,
> it is a sign of immaturity and weakness.[11]

Moral norms or rules for conduct are useful shorthand that attempts to distill and condense what a good person would do; but when shorthand is inadequate to guide us we return to the broader and more complicated story that the shorthand was trying to summarize. This more fundamental ethical ground is to be found in a clear articulation of our image of a good person and the virtues or characteristics that shape her goodness. It is framed by a teleological sense of what it means to excel as a human being and is, more often than not, best captured, articulated, explained, and passed down in our narratives. This image of a good person must, I've suggested, include characteristics that contribute to her goodness viewed holistically, including, at least, her individual flourishing, the flourishing of the social groups of which she is a part, and the flourishing of the environment in which the first two sorts of flourishing take place, as well as what Sandler calls relevant "non-eudaimonistic" components of such goodness.

A fully developed environmental ethics should address not just what we should *do*, but also who we should *be*—describing the habits, dispositions, beliefs, emotions, and other characteristics which make a good person good, both in general terms and with specific reference to the environment. Thus, a fully developed environmental ethics must, at a minimum, include a very robust virtue ethics component. However, it turns out that virtue ethics is itself deeply tied up with narrative. So any virtue ethics— whether its emphasis is environmental, social, or individual—must deal with the role played by narrative in the identification, understanding, and cultivation of virtue. It is true that narrative never undertakes—or never responsibly undertakes—this work alone. Narrative plays a critical role, one that we ignore at our peril; but in addition to the inter-narrative dialogue of coduction, the narrative approach to virtue ethics should engage in an ongoing dialogue and debate with other approaches, whether they be philosophical, scientific, ecological, biological, psychological, sociological, anthropological, or otherwise.

∾

What, then, is the full extent of narrative's power in the context of environmental virtue ethics? Just how far can we push the notion of "as-if" experience, and what role does it play in the identification and cultivation of virtue? Keeping in mind the aforementioned engagements with other, complementary approaches to thinking about virtue, flourishing, and goodness, as well as all the ways in which narrative cannot replace actual lived experience, I nevertheless want to maintain that the reach and influence of narrative is quite expansive.

The clearest use of narrative is in the realm of moral and ethical education. Narratives can *inspire* us (i.e., arouse in a person the desire to be virtuous) and *motivate* us (e.g., to persevere in the cultivation of virtue). In addition to this exhortative function, narratives can help in the actual *transmission* of the virtues, handing down ethical experience and knowledge. We use narratives to *experiment* with possibilities, exploring different situations and different ethical responses. We project ourselves into stories and make judgments about the actions of characters. Such experiments serve several useful functions. First, narrative experiments help us to cultivate the habit of ethical *discernment*, differentiating between different ethical schemas, dispositions, responses, and so on. Second, these experiments help us to *understand* virtue, including which virtues "succeed" and which ones "fail" (that is, which ones are not genuine virtues). Because of this, narrative does more than merely illustrate virtue. It is one of the important ways in which we grasp what "works" in terms of flourishing. Therefore, narratives often help us to *identify* good role models and the virtues that make them good; they actually help us to *determine* what we view as flourishing and what we take to be virtuous and vicious. Finally, narratives are frequently a central part of the method by which we *apply* and *cultivate* virtues in our own lives. Because narratives provide us with "as-if" experience, they often constitute the first step, as it were, on the road to actually developing a particular virtue.

Ethical Education: Motivation and Transmission

Motivation

Henry David Thoreau muses, rhetorically, "how many a man has dated his life from the reading of a book?"[12] The answer, for Thoreau, is likely more or less equal to the number of people who read good books and read them well. Narrative in one form or another plays *the* central role in ethical inspiration and motivation.

Each of us has an image of the person we'd like to become. Whether that image is rough or detailed, fixed or fluid, it is one that has been profoundly shaped by the various narratives that make up our conception of the good life. But no notion of the good life springs fully formed from the head of the person who desires it. "Images" of the good life are actually narratives of the life we'd like to live. Some of the elements of this narrative may well be culled from the books Thoreau praised; but if other influences on our view of the good life come from movies, advertisements, television programs, news stories, talking with other people, and the examples found in our family and community, they are for that no less narrative in nature.

Take Cervantes's *Don Quixote*, an excellent example of thinking about the relationships between narrative, self-transformation, and virtue. Though many people are familiar with the comical aspects of the tale— tilting at windmills and so forth—*Don Quixote* is much more nuanced in its treatment of narrative, truth, and virtue than a clichéd or superficial reading might suggest. True, Don Quixote (born Alonso Quixano) "lost his wits" and "wrecked his reason" by his obsession with books of chivalry. However, Cervantes's grand mockery of the deleterious effect of books on common sense and reason is not directed at all books or stories per se. While Alonso Quixano decries on his deathbed the influence of "those detestable books of chivalry," it is primarily because they kept him from reading "other books, [that] might [have] enlighten[ed] [his] soul."[13] It seems that La Mancha's knight errant—a wonderful play on words—was led astray not by books, but by the wrong books or, more likely, by books read in the wrong way. Others seem to recognize this as well. After Quixote/Quixano loses his wits and testifies to the power of narrative by asserting, "I know who I am . . . and I know, too, that I am capable of being not only the characters I have named, but all the Twelve Peers of France and all the Nine Worthies as well. . . ."[14] His concerned friends Doctor Pero Perez the Priest and Master Nicolas the Barber do not burn all his books, or even all the books of chivalry. During the "inquisition" in Quixano's library, among the books they examine they choose to save more than they burn, although a great many others are consigned to the flames out of laziness and an unwillingness to read through everything.

Another lover of books who came to a tragic end inspired, at least in part, by the narratives that captivated him, was Christopher McCandless, the subject of John Krakauer's bestselling *Into the Wild*.[15] McCandless was fascinated by Emerson, Thoreau, Tolstoy, Pasternak, London, and other authors, which coupled with his idealism led him on a spiritual quest, rejecting social norms for a life as a "leathertramp" on the road and trail. Krakauer admits "it would be easy to stereotype Christopher McCandless as another boy who felt too much, a loopy young man who read too many books and lacked even a modicum of common sense," but is quick to add, "the stereotype isn't a good fit."[16] McCandless's story is more complicated than that. Like the fictional Quixote, McCandless spurned what he saw as the corrupt morality of the day in favor of a more demanding standard and a commitment to living out his beliefs. He rejected the stifling world of "abstraction and security and material excess" in favor of wildness and the "raw throb of existence."[17] If poor judgment played a part in McCandless's death on his "grand Alaskan adventure," so did simple bad luck. Ultimately, Krakauer and his friends—themselves well-regarded veterans of highly risky adventures—concede that their own youthful exploits could just as easily have ended in tragedy, and wonder that, had this been the case, they would have been mocked for their incompetence and failure, as was McCandless, rather than praised for their daring and success.

While the cases of Quixote and McCandless might be seen as poor examples in an argument designed to laud the role of narrative in the cultivation of virtue and in human flourishing, I don't think that's the case. First, on some important level Quixote and McCandless—not to suggest any invidious comparison between the two—*do* embody significant virtues. Despite his excesses, Quixote's commitments to love and justice, however often they misfire in practice, stand in stark contrast to the abusive, even brutal, vices of innumerable other characters in the tale (such as the Duke and Duchess). However, reluctant or casual readers are liable to miss these distinctions because our perception of the Man of La Mancha has been distorted by the many caricatures of a figure who was himself meant to be a parody. For his part, McCandless embodied a certain kind of spiritual seeking and belief in the power of an individual to reinvent himself, as well as a deep commitment to truth, a rejection of consumerism and materialism, a belief in self-sufficiency and perseverance, and a love of wild nature. Again, a casual familiarity with the story—or, in other cases, a curious blindness among a certain set of outdoor enthusiasts as to the striking, if general, similarities between McCandless and themselves—leads some people to miss the undeniably admirable aspects of his character.

Second, not all narrative inspirations lead to disaster. Far from it. Consider the role played by Thoreau's *Walden*, Muir's *My First Summer in the Sierra*, Brower's *Let the Mountains Talk, Let the Rivers Run* (or McPhee's account of Brower in *Encounters with the Archdruid*), Abbey's *Desert Solitaire*, and Peacock's *Grizzly Years* in inspiring generations of readers to enter the wilderness, cultivate a relationship with wild nature, and fight to preserve it. It would be easy to add Annie Dillard, Norman Maclean, Gary Snyder, Terry Tempest Williams, and others to this list. Moreover, even to the extent that these two examples, Quixote and McCandless, offer cautionary tales about the dangers of narrative inspiration—comic and tragic, respectively—they testify to the astonishing motivational and inspirational power of narrative.

Those of us who are avid readers will readily call to mind books that changed our lives; however, as books are only one manifestation of narrative, others will certainly be able to point to unwritten stories that served as a catalyst for change. St. Augustine, for example, was motivated by hearing the story of Victorinus, who was a person quite similar to Augustine: someone to whom he could easily relate. Like Augustine, Victorinus was an educated man. Like Augustine, he found aspects of Catholicism attractive. However, again like Augustine, though for different reasons, he was for a long time unwilling to make the leap to convert. Yet upon hearing the story of Victorinus's conversion, Augustine was persuaded that

he too might overcome his difficulties and that his own conversion was a
real possibility: "When Simplicanus, your servant, related to me [the story
of] Victorinus, I was on fire to imitate him, and it was *for this reason* that
he had told it to me."[18] Augustine's *Confessions* were no doubt written to
play a similar role for others; why else confess to God, who already knows
what is in our hearts?

Or again, consider Rosalind Hursthouse's conversion to vegetarianism, which came about not because of the philosophical arguments she
was reading in books, philosophical arguments she was deeply involved in
understanding, critiquing, discussing, and writing about. Rather, her gradual
move to vegetarianism was brought about by considering the attitudes that
informed and were reinforced by a flesh-based diet, and by reflecting on
those attitudes in light of the "interest and delight" she took in "nature
programmes about the lives of animals on television."[19] Realizing that these
two aspects of her self were in conflict and could not be maintained with
integrity, she concluded that she would rather be the kind of person who
took delight in narratives about the lives of non-human animals than the
kind of person who took delight in consuming non-human animals. "Without thinking that animals had rights, I began to see both the wild ones and
the ones we generally eat as having lives of their own, which they should
be left to enjoy. And so I changed."[20] Hursthouse was converted not by
philosophical argumentation, but rather by a change in the way she saw
herself and her actions in relation to the rest of the world, a change in
the story she told about who she was and what she valued.

Although such transformative stories are more common than we generally suppose—examples can be found in books, oral narratives, movies,
and so forth—we are most familiar with them when found in the context
of formal education, especially of children. This is not to suggest that
narrative is not useful in the (re)education of adults—I've argued just the
opposite—but rather to point out that we commonly think of narrative as
an essential tool in the education of children and, therefore, it makes sense
to begin by looking at the ways we use narrative in children's education.

When we tell children morality tales, part of the point is to motivate
them to be good, to instill in them the desire to become good people.
Aristotle tells us that anyone who hopes to benefit from ethical discussions
"must have been brought up in good habits."[21] Although the habituation
one undergoes as a child is critical, and may even be decisive, for forming our adult ethical selves, it would be silly to say that only people who
already have virtuous habits will benefit from the discussion of virtuous
habits. The point here, surely, is to be brought up as the sort of person
for whom goodness is a crucial concern. While we must certainly strive to

instill virtuous habits in our children, there is perhaps no more important thing to foster in them than the desire to be good and a willingness to work at becoming good, for without this general orientation the virtuous habits of one's youth are likely to be hard pressed when confronted with the temptations and complexities of adult life.

Transmission

Historically, of course, narrative has been the preferred tool for transmitting ethical values to children, both inculcating in them the general desire to be good (motivation) and giving them an account of what it means to be good (transmission). Rowan Williams, the former Archbishop of Canterbury, argues that the power of imagination helps us to remember "things could be different" and that "we learn this as children through fantasy and play."[22] Aesop's fables are among the more familiar examples of such "morality tales." Brief as they are, "The Crow and the Pitcher," "The Ant and the Grasshopper," and the "The Fisherman and the Little Fish" represent, respectively, narrative lessons in ingenuity, foresight and responsibility, and planning, patience, and moderation. When we hear "The Goose and the Golden Egg," we all realize that the point has nothing to do with animal husbandry or home economics, but rather that we should not be greedy, and that we should be content with and grateful for good fortune. Aesop's other fables perform similar duties with virtues such as industry, courage, benevolence, frugality, and appreciation, or vices such as inappropriate zeal, immoderate ambition, and excessive pride.

These classic tales are only a few among myriad, cross-cultural examples of children's stories formulated with the express purpose of ethical education. Take, for example, the Hindu *Panchatantra*, a series of animal fables similar to both Aesop's and the Buddhist *Jataka* tales. The aim of the *Panchatantra* is to instruct the reader in the principles of wise or advantageous conduct in life (*nīti*), focusing on two components of flourishing dear to the tradition of virtue ethics: social relationships and intellectual life.[23] Thus, in Book III we learn the importance of relying on the good counsel of others when the advice of *Ciramjivin* saves the crow kingdom from an assault by their rivals the owls, who are hamstrung in part because their king did not listen to *Raktaksa*, his own counselor. The *Panchatantra* is far from unique in the Hindu tradition, where didactic storytelling is so common that there is a specific name, *katha*, for the genre.

Similar tales can be found in almost every culture: the sacred narratives and mythology of Native American peoples, Irish myths, Chinese folk tales, African fables, and the motley patchwork of American folklore.

Critically, such tales often promote similar virtues: industry, cleverness, compassion, courage, humility, and so forth. The diversity of such examples—from America, Europe, India, China, and Africa—illustrates the genuine ubiquity of moral instruction via folktales, fairy stories, myths, and other narratives. Of course one might suggest, as did Plato, that narratives are used in the education of children precisely because their rational faculties are not sufficiently developed.[24] Children cannot rationally grasp the ground or foundation of normativity and so fables operate as a sort of stand-in until they can. Stories can tell children *what* to do, but they cannot really tell them *why* they ought to do it. Oh, stories offer children all sorts of "whys"—the comeuppance of the Boy Who Cried Wolf, for example—but none of these is the *real* reason why, which is fully captured only when one can rationally establish the genuine, fundamental ground of moral action. Lying is not wrong because one day you might be set upon by wolves and no one will believe you or come to your aid; lying is wrong because it violates the categorical imperative or because it leads to a decrease in overall utility; and when a person is old enough to grasp this she can put away childish things and kick away the narrative like the proverbial ladder. But this position both underestimates the power of narrative and overestimates the self-sufficiency of reason. We've seen that adults are not the simple mechanistic actors of rational-choice theory, that ethics does not conform well to the sort of inflexible legalism characteristic of some modern moral theories, and that narrative affects the ethical formation of both children and adults.

The diversity of the examples above—Augustine, Hursthouse, Thoreau, Muir, Peacock, Pasternak—is strong evidence that the scope of narrative instruction extends well beyond the nursery room. On reflection much of our folklore—passed down in the form of myth or fairy tale—contains distinctly adult themes and messages that would be entirely lost on children.[25] J. R. R. Tolkien argues that we are mistaken in supposing that "fairy stories" are for children, for upon consideration they are a quite serious business. Such tales are, as Tolkien sees it, stories *about* Faërie, the "perilous realm" in which the archetypal denizens—elves, witches, giants, dragons, and other fey or magical folk—exist. These stories do more than merely motivate us to "be good"; they transmit to us an understanding of what it means to "be good." The essential power of Faërie stories is to "make immediately effective by the will the visions of 'fantasy,'"[26] including the "strong moral element" that characterizes them and the "inherent morality"[27] they offer as a model. Thus, remarkably, "it is one of the lessons of fairy-stories . . . that on callow, lumpish, and selfish youth peril, sorrow, and the shadow of death can bestow dignity, and even some wisdom."[28]

Tolkien argues this effect is possible because despite their "arresting strangeness" these stories are to some degree aligned with reality. "History often resembles 'Myth,'" he says, "because both are ultimately of the same stuff. . . . If no young man had ever fallen in love by chance meeting with a maiden, and found old enmities to stand between him and his love, then the god Frey would never have seen Gerdr the giant's daughter from the high-seat of Odin."[29] While fairy stories and the like are no doubt fantastical, they also reflect and in turn affect reality: "there remains . . . a point too often forgotten: that is the effect produced *now* by these old things in the stories as they are."[30] Narrative reflects life, which in turn reflects narrative.

Some of the most influential moral teachings in the world have been communicated principally through narrative. Take the parables of Jesus— the Prodigal Son, the Good Samaritan, the Workers in the Vineyard, and many others—or the stories in the *Mahabharata*, especially the *Bhagavad-Gita*. The parable of the Good Samaritan makes a strong argument for the nature of specific virtues. The eponymous Samaritan comes upon the victim of the robbers, who has been left "half dead," stripped, and beaten in the middle of the road. Unlike the priest and the Levite who passed the victim without offering aid, the Samaritan "had compassion," bound his wounds, carried him to an inn, and paid for his convalescence. Given that readers have just been instructed to "love . . . your neighbor as yourself," who, asks Jesus, has "proved neighbor to the man who fell among the robbers?" (Luke 10: 25–37). The point of the parable is to illustrate and convey to readers the true nature of love and compassion, and to show them what compassion looks like in practice.

In a similar manner, the narrative of the *Bhagavad-Gita* teaches readers about the nature of renunciation. Arjuna, a warrior distraught at the prospect of entering a battle in which he will be forced to kill many of his mentors, friends, and family members, seeks counsel from Krishna, his charioteer and an avatar of the godhead. Krishna first advises him that it is his duty (*svadharma*) to fight because he is of the warrior caste and, second, that the deaths with which he is so concerned are in fact both inevitable and insignificant. While bodies can be destroyed—indeed the death of every living body is inevitable—the soul (*atman*), which is part of the godhead (*Brahman*), cannot: "There was never a time when I was not, nor you, nor these princes were not; there will never be a time when we shall cease to be" (*Bhagavad-Gita*, 2:12). Thus, right conduct involves discharging one's duty, without inappropriate concern regarding the consequence: "The hero whose soul is unmoved by circumstance, who accepts pleasure and pain with equanimity, only he is fit for immortality" (*Bhagavad-Gita*,

2:15) and "Perform all your actions with mind concentrated on the Divine, renouncing attachment and looking upon success and failure with an equal eye" (*Bhagavad-Gita*, 2:48). It would be difficult to overstate the influences of these two narratives: taken together the Christian and Hindu narratives currently influence—in varying degrees to be sure—the moral and ethical formation of close to half of the Earth's human population.[31]

Though most of the major (in terms of adherents) ethical systems communicate their wisdom and worldview via narratives of one sort or another, this is also often true of smaller, local, indigenous belief systems: Greek, Roman, and Norse mythology; Irish stories of Cú Chulainn in the Ulster Cycle and Fionn mac Cumhaill in the Fenian Cycle; the Songlines of the Aboriginal peoples of Australia; Maori knowledge (*wānanga*) passed down in tales (*kōrero paki*) and allegorical stories (*kōrero tairitenga*); the diverse stories coming out of various African traditions; the so-called Rhino Sutra (*Khaḍgaviṣāṇa Gāthā*) of Buddhism; the oral traditions of the First Nations of North America; and many others.

Some of the relatively less well-known narrative traditions are exceptional in terms of the power of their poetry: "In general the language of Native American oratory is remarkable . . . for its directness, its metaphors and vivid images, its comprehension of clashing worlds. These are the literary qualities that give these speeches their freshness, power, and poignancy; read them within the context of America's history and they take on an even deeper pathos."[32] *Black Elk Speaks*, perhaps the "single most widely read book in the vast literature relating to North American Indians,"[33] is an attempt to "pass on the knowledge of things that were sacred in the old ways of [Black Elk's] people."[34] The narrative is itself about the role of narrative in changing a life, the story of Black Elk's "Great Vision" and the story of how that story changed his life, transforming his relationship with the land, animals, and other persons. For example, after the vision, Black Elk can no longer kill animals for sport—when he does he becomes nauseated—since his new narrative worldview sees them as relatives who are themselves "holy."[35] Making this narrative available to a wider audience is supposed to communicate these "higher values" and "save [Black Elk's] Great Vision for men."[36] Oral traditions like these occupied the central role in Native American wisdom traditions, explicitly shaping and transmitting understanding of a wide variety of subjects. Native American author Thomas King writes,

> The truth about stories is that's all we are. The Nigerian storyteller Ben Okri says that "In a fractured age, when cynicism is god, here is a possible heresy: we live by stories, we also live

in them. One way or another we are living the stories planted in us early or along the way, or we are also living the stories we planted—knowingly or unknowingly—in ourselves. We live stories that either give our lives meaning or negate it with meaninglessness. If we change the stories we live by, quite possibly we change our lives."[37]

Ethical Experimentation: Discernment and Understanding

Inculcating a desire to be good and transmitting a certain vision of goodness or flourishing would be of limited use if we did not also develop the habit of and skill in recognizing, understanding, judging, applying, critiquing, and modifying the various virtues passed on to us by our tradition(s). Among other things this requires discernment (the ability to recognize virtue and vice, as well as a keen sensitivity to the nuance of context) and understanding (insight into the nature of flourishing, virtue and vice, and specific virtues and vices). Here too, narrative plays a critical role.

Discernment

Philip Pullman writes, in the introduction to *Citizen Ethics in a Time of Crisis*:

> . . . to see what virtue looks like, we need to look not to lists of laws and commandments, but to literature. Was a lesson on the importance of kindness ever delivered more devastatingly, or learned more securely, than Mr. Knightley's reproof of Emma in the novel that bears her name? Was the value of play in childhood (a profoundly ethical matter) ever more memorably conveyed than by Dickens's description of the Smallweed children in *Bleak House*? . . . The lesson of every story in which the good is illustrated is, as Jesus said after telling the parable of the Good Samaritan, "Go, and do thou likewise." The genius of Jesus—and Jane Austen, and Dickens, and every other storyteller whose tales are memorable—gives us no excuse to say we don't know what the good looks like.[38]

Literature—and, if we are to believe Rilke's *Archaic Torso of Apollo*, many other great works of art—exhorts us: "change your life!" All this flies in the face of the well-worn objection that virtue ethics is impractical because a

less than fully virtuous agent won't know what virtue looks like, and therefore won't know how to begin habituating herself to virtue.[39] True, we still
have the problem of adjudicating between competing images of virtue—that
is, the problem of relativism—but we've already seen that the relativistic
challenge can be met. Each narrative makes a case, in which the criterion
is plausibility rather than proof, for its own account of the human *telos*,
flourishing, virtue, and vice; and in so doing narratives commit themselves,
and us, to the belief that strong versions of relativism overstate their case.

How exactly does narrative cultivate and sharpen discernment? How
can it help us to develop the ability to "see" more truly—that is, with
greater wisdom—in situations of ethical significance? Discernment and wisdom are both the result of experience. Aristotle says that those who study
ethics and politics should have experience with life, and later says that
practical wisdom (*phronesis*) is related to having experience in the world: it
is concerned "not only with universals but with particulars, which become
familiar from experience. . . ."[40] So experience is a critical component of
being able to discern and judge well with respect to virtue and flourishing,
applying universal rules or patterns in the messy complexity of particular
situations. We've seen, however, that while narrative and life remain distinct, the "as-if" experience of narrative, in which we live "*in the mode of
the imaginary*," does provide us with a sort of experience.[41]

Because narratives are particularly attuned to the concrete and to differences in context, they help us to cultivate the gifts of ethical improvisation (Nussbaum), narrative imagination (Kearney), judicious spectatorship
(Nussbaum), and the like. Each of these skills is closely aligned with ethical
discernment, the ability: to recognize what, in a given situation, is ethically significant and what is not; to perceive the differences between two
similar accounts flourishing or virtue, or between similar actions, feelings,
or traits; and to fathom the significance of agency, ignorance, unintended
circumstances, unforeseen consequences, and tragedy.

Ricoeur calls narrative an "ethical laboratory" in which we can explore
different situations and different actions.[42] Kearney develops this point: "As
Aristotle was the first to acknowledge poetics teaches us essential truths
about human experience (unlike history which is confined to particular
facts); and these essential truths are intimately related to the pursuit of
possibilities of happiness or unhappiness—that is, the desire for the good
life guided by practical wisdom."[43] Narrative understanding is in the family
of practical wisdom precisely because both are concerned with particular
examples or illustrations of universal truths. "It is the function of poetry
in its narrative and dramatic form, to propose to the imagination and to
its mediation various figures that constitute so many *thought experiments* by

which we learn to link together the ethical aspects of human conduct and happiness and misfortune."[44] These thought experiments take place at the intersection of the world of the text and the world of the reader, though the emplotment is carried out by the reader. And it is precisely because we are involved in the emplotment of the text that we can be changed by a text.

Emplotting a narrative gives us an "as-if" experience of ways in which human action relates to happiness (*eudaimonia*) by illustrating the manner in which certain sorts of conduct lead to flourishing or decline. It proposes a certain picture or account, whether partial or thoroughgoing, of what it means to live well and of the role played by good or bad conduct, virtue and vice, in that flourishing. Emplotting a narrative can also give us an "as-if" experience of the ways in which human action, or suffering, relates to misfortune (tragedy) by illustrating the fact that, *pace* Plato and the Stoics, "happenings beyond the agent's control are of real importance not only for his or her feelings of happiness or contentment, but also for whether he or she manages to live a fully good life."[45] Human beings act, but they also suffer or undergo, which is why Ricoeur's description of humans as acting and suffering, and his attention to both aspects of this pair, is so appropriate.

Understanding

Ethical discernment naturally contributes to improved ethical understanding. The infinite variety of possible narratives and emplotments allows us to "practice" life imaginatively in order to see what works, which actions are most likely to lead to happiness or success, before we embark on the higher stakes performance of living our actual lives. Narratives allow us to live more, as it were, by experiencing things in the "as-if" mode. In so doing, we glean some of the wisdom that would be gained from actually experiencing those lives. Experience is a critical ingredient in practical wisdom, and more experience—whether firsthand or "as-if"—contributes to better understanding. As Nussbaum reminds us, when it comes to practical wisdom, "we have never lived enough."[46]

In addition to experiencing more, narrative allows us to experience otherwise, another essential component in the development of practical wisdom. It is not enough to have extensive experience if that experience is uniform, rote, or monotonous. It's certainly true that repeated experiences can, up to a point, deepen one's appreciation, understanding, and insight; however, the full flowering of practical wisdom requires that a person become familiar with diverse and variegated experiences that will expand her horizons and stretch her imagination. Fortunately, narrative provides us with more diversity than one could ever experience in a single lifetime:

"our experience is, without fiction, too confined and too parochial."[47] If one is a good reader—that is to say if one is willing to be inquisitive and adventurous in one's selection of narratives, open to what a given text has to say, active in coduction, and so forth—one can experience very different lives and circumstances. An affluent American citizen can experience what it is like to be an impoverished immigrant. An Israeli can experience life as a Palestinian refugee. An Indian Hindu can see through the eyes of a Pakistani Muslim. All these experience are, to be sure, experiences in the mode of "as-if," along with all the qualifications that entails. And even a rich library of narrative will inevitably fall short of actual experience in important ways. For example, reading about love in Shakespeare, Abelard and Heloise, Rumi, Brontë, and the like is clearly not the same as the experience of being in love. However, if we must remain on guard against overstating the significance of "as-if" experience, we should be equally on guard against understating it. For, in an important sense, that hypothetical library of "as-if" experience does expand one's horizon, familiarize one with what love looks like in practice, deepen one's understanding of love and what it requires, prepare the soil of one's soul for the actual cultivation of virtue, and even initiate and support the cultivation of that virtue.

Not surprisingly, fully understanding a virtue requires that we consider it in diverse contexts. It is not enough to know, even through personal experience, what courage looks like in a single instance. To see, or experience, or exhibit courage, even in an arguably archetypal situation—say, the Selma to Montgomery marches in 1965 or the landing at Omaha Beach in 1944—is still only to see, experience, or exhibit courage in one relatively narrow context. Individual examples, individual experiences, and even (most) individual lives are far too limited and routine to give one full insight into virtue. We need both more experience and more diverse experience in order for our understanding to have sufficient breadth and depth, and narratives (both historical and fictional) contribute to that library of experience. We need the courage of Hector turning to battle Achilles beside the springs that feed Scamander's stream outside Troy, of John Muir riding out a windstorm in the top of a Douglas spruce, of David facing down Goliath in the Valley of Elah, of Martin Luther nailing his *Ninety-Five Theses* to the church door in Wittenberg, of the Spartans and their allies standing shoulder to shoulder at Thermopylae, of Joshua Slocum on the first solo circumnavigation of the Earth, of Henry V and his men charging into battle on St. Crispin's Day, of Rosa Parks refusing to move to the back of the bus, of Julia "Butterfly" Hill sitting in Luna for 738 days, of Shackleton and the men of the *Endurance* braving the Southern Ocean, of Cú Chulainn standing against champion after champion from the army of Connacht, of Nelson Mandela refusing to negotiate for his freedom from solitary confinement on Robben Island, of John Hancock boldly and clearly signing the *Declaration of Independence*, of Frodo Baggins voluntarily walking to his doom in Mordor, of Galileo in publishing the *Dialogue Concerning the Two Chief World Systems*, of the forty-seven *ronin* of the Akō vendetta, of Beowulf and Wiglaf facing the dragon, and many, many others. And of course, notwithstanding the constructive role of narrative in the formation of virtue, we must never forget that we must practice courage in our own everyday lives by facing up to physical, intellectual, and social risks to the right degree, in the right way, at the right time, for the right reasons, and so on.

We need this diversity so that we can fully appreciate courage by viewing it in myriad particular manifestations, each with it's own unique constellation of actors, motives, consequences, other persons, environments, competing interests, conflicting obligations, and unforeseeable complications. Narratives aid us because they are especially adept at capturing the relevant differences between circumstances. With narrative we can describe with greater precision, greater sensitivity to nuance and detail, and greater focus on relevant motives, emotions, and the like. Fictional events can be imbued with a power and pathos it is difficult to find in ordinary experience, and this is true even in fictional accounts of ordinary experience. It's also true in narrative reflection regarding our own nonfictional experiences: events that we would pass over in actual life, unreflective and unaware, are revealed in their full significance in the retelling. It is only with the insight of hindsight that we come to understand the meaning of actions and events. At least in this sense, narrative accounts are more fully lived than many of the hours and days we actually pass under the sun.[48]

Interestingly—in the spirit of narrative engagement with other ways of knowing—contemporary neuroscience supports these claims, suggesting that we understand the real and the symbolic in strikingly similar ways. Our brains are actually hardwired in such a way that they conflate the fictive and the factual, the physical and the psychical, the literal and the symbolic, the physical and the metaphorical. The area of the brain activated by encountering physical decay like rotten food or spoilt milk, the insula, is also activated by the contemplation of shameful or "rotten" actions or people. In other words, we experience—at least at the neurological level— sensory disgust and moral disgust in much the same way because our brains don't really distinguish between sensory disgust and moral disgust. Robert Sapolsky writes, "When we evolved the capacity to be disgusted by moral failures, we didn't evolve a new brain region to handle it. Instead, the insula expanded its portfolio."[49] Sapolsky offers numerous other examples of studies

documenting this "literal-metaphorical confusion," which collectively suggest that, perhaps, "our neural circuitry doesn't cleanly differentiate between
the real and the symbolic."[50]

While this confusion can very obviously result in deeply problematic negative consequences—as when politicians use the language of moral
disgust to elicit a visceral response in their constituents, using instinctive
emotional responses to circumvent careful intellectual evaluation of a position—it can also result in positive outcomes since we can use symbolic
rapprochement to advance the cause of real-world reconciliation and coop-
eration. Annie Murphy Paul reports that a body of new neurobiological
research suggests "that individuals who frequently read fiction seem to be
better able to understand other people, empathize with them and see the
world from their perspective."[51] Moving beyond individual recognition to
national or cultural recognition, Robert Axelrod argues that "mutual symbolic concessions" that touch on "existential issues" are likely to be decisive
in the Israeli-Palestinian peace process: the recognition of Israel's right to
exist, apologies for the exile and dispossession of Palestinians in 1948, and
so forth.[52] Such concessions make no material difference in the negotia-
tions, but they do make important a symbolic difference and this symbolic
difference will arguably be the catalyst for change. Why? Because such
symbolic rapprochement is a necessary condition for more concrete aspects
of reconciliation. As Jean-Luc Nancy says, "one could say that to be just,
once everything is said and done, once the minimum of what is owed to
everybody is recognized, is to understand that everyone has the right to be
recognized."[53] The claim that recognition and symbolic concessions are at
the heart of reconciliation maps nicely on to Kearney's hermeneutic work
on reconciliation in the Northern Ireland peace process:

> Only when the Irish and British communities inhabiting Ulster
> learned to retell their stories (greatly helped by writers and his-
> torians), and to acknowledge that they could be 'British or Irish
> or both,' could they be reconciled. Not as a unitary national
> identity, of course, but as a multiple post-national one where a
> thousand stories could be told. British and Irish, Unionist and
> Nationalist, Loyalist and Republican, eventually came to realise
> that there were no essential identities carved from opposing
> cliffs, only 'imagined communities' that could be reimagined in
> alternative ways.[54]

Each of us—individuals and groups—must come to appreciate that identity is not fixed, at least not in the practical and relevant sense of *ipse-*

identity. Identity, even in the most homogenous society, is inevitably made up of multiple narrative threads; it is "contingent and relational . . . and is best understood as an interaction between several different histories and stories."[55]

Ethical Formation: Application and Cultivation

But how are we to make the leap from narrative to life? We cannot become better people by reading if reading is all that we do. A person won't achieve virtue in the dusty stacks of a library or archive, but in the choices, affects, habits, and dispositions of her actual life. I've claimed that narrative throws a bridge—the bridge of "as-if" experience—between abstract, faceless, life-less theory and concrete, particular, lived experience. But how firm is this bridge? How closely can it bring us to the lived reality of actual experience, which seems essential for virtuous habituation?

On one hand, we've seen that narratives do give us a kind of experience, and that this experience can be much more powerful and much more useful than is commonly supposed. Narratives add to our experience, because "as-if" experience is one kind. Adding to our experience, they broaden our perspectives and expand our horizons. In so doing, they contribute to the development of practical wisdom (*phronesis*) and, presumably, to the development of virtue. For these reasons I believe that the idea that narrative can actually make us better, or worse, people is one that is well-established.

However, on the other hand, we must remember that the "as-if" experience of narrative is different from the actual experience of things; it cannot, on its own, fully accomplish the work of habituation so central to virtue ethics, environmental or otherwise. If the interplay of proximity and distance brings us closer to experience than mere theory, it also keeps us at one remove from actual experience. The "as-if" experience of narrative bridges the gap between theory and experience, but does so incompletely. And if narrative's particular power can reveal, project, and amplify aspects of experience, its characteristic limitations insure that it can never fully replace actual experience. Reading *Walden* is qualitatively different from experimenting with simplicity, experiencing solitude, or embracing wild-ness in one's own life, and no matter how many narratives one absorbs, no matter how varied, no matter how responsibly coduced, a gap remains between the narrative experience and the actual experience.

However, while reading cannot replace living without loss, we've seen that reading and living can complement each other in many ways—reading well can help us to live well, if we consciously and intelligently put it to that use.

All Habituation Employs Narrative

We should begin by noting that, absolutely speaking, no experience is unmediated.[56] There is no bare fact, raw experience, view from nowhere, or innocent eye. All our experience—whether "actual" or "as if"—is filtered and framed by our worldview, and the contours of that worldview are shaped by narratives. If all our experience is, in varying degrees, shot through with narrative, then the habituation of virtue is more complicated than generally supposed. So let's reconsider the role of experience in habituation.

A person attempting to develop virtue is, obviously, not yet virtuous. To get started, she needs some way of identifying the goal or *telos* toward which she should aim and beginning the process of developing virtues that will help to achieve it. If one is going to start living in a manner that will, hopefully, lead to virtuous habits, one needs to know what a virtuous agent looks like, how she conducts herself, and so forth. This might happen in one of several ways. One might have the good fortune to be "brought up in good habits" that engender the desire to be good and offer some rough sense of what goodness looks like.[57] Alternatively, one might have good friends who stimulate one to "noble actions" and with whom it is easier to become and be virtuous.[58] Finally, even if one does not have the good fortune of fine friends or quality upbringing, it is always possible to turn to the community to find those identified as virtuous—those we credit with *phronesis*—and hear what is said about them.[59] Each of these instances represents a way of giving a person a model of what virtue looks like (not just in theory but also in practice), an archetype she can emulate in developing her own, as yet unformed, virtuous habits.

But how well will this actually work?

Take, for example, the situation of someone who, happily, finds herself in close association with a *phronimos*. She has an ideal role model, but how does such a person become virtuous herself? Aristotle makes it very clear that moral virtues cannot be taught by conveying some formulaic or programmatic method. Habituating oneself to virtue is unlike memorizing and applying the Pythagorean Theorem, Avogadro's Number, or Planck's Constant. One might think that the process is more akin to copying the *phronimos*. This, however, is also impossible with respect to moral virtues. The student cannot literally *copy* the master, at least not for long, for the master is a different person, with different skills and abilities, in a different situation—and all virtues are relative to the agent. The master's courageous action may well be rash and foolhardy if undertaken by the student. So neither simple instruction committed to memory nor faithful mimicry, if it is mere mimicry, will work for the cultivation of virtue. The aspirant in virtue cannot simply study at the foot of the *phronimos* as a student who memorizes formulae or as an apprentice who unreflectively copies the work of a master.

The *phronimos*—actual or narrative—is not someone to be copied, but someone who inspires those who are not yet virtuous to attempt to act virtuously themselves and who serves as a guide in doing so. The proper question for the ethical aspirant is not "what would the *phronimos* do?" The *phronimos* is a different person, with different skills, a different background, different relationships, and so forth; therefore, much of the relevant context is different. The proper question is, "what would I do if I were *like* the *phronimos*, that is, if I had the virtue in question, as the *phronimos* does?"[60] Asking this latter question is more akin to the "as-if" experience of hearing a story and imaginatively projecting oneself into the narrative than it is to copying or blind imitation. So, even when the cultivation of a given virtue does take place under the guidance of a figure like the *phronimos*, the experience is much more like narrative refiguration (*mimesis₃*) than is generally supposed. Not only does narrative help us to identify and understand virtues by exposing us to more nuance and variety than we could ever experience in actual life, it is also involved in the actual cultivation of any virtue.

When narrative opens up an imaginative "as-if" world or ethical laboratory, it not only allows us to imagine what it would be like to be *another person*, it also allows us to imagine what it would be like to be *another version of ourselves*. The former allows us to cultivate the sympathy necessary for good judgment, as Nussbaum correctly points out, to gain "as-if" experience that develops the habit of and skill in ethical discernment, and to deepen our understanding of ethically relevant details. The latter, however, is actually a critical component in the cultivation of any virtue, whether the model is actual or narrative. Cultivating a virtue is like the experience of reading a good story (good in both the sense of well-crafted and in the sense of edifying) in which a person imagines a different version of herself (a more virtuous self, for example) in the context and horizon of the world of the text (with its relevant particularities and potentialities). All successful habituation to virtue requires some use of the imagination characteristic of narrative, so exercising those imaginative skills and expanding our imaginative repertoire will ultimately help in the cultivation of virtue.

Or, put another way, cultivating a virtue is quite like apprenticeship in a craft, as long as we have an appreciation for how genuine apprenticeship works. The mindless and robotic mimicry criticized above is a caricature, or at best a half-truth, of the actual process. The goal of apprenticeship, at least in the era before mechanization and mass production, was not to produce something that would be identical to or indistinguishable from that one produced by one's master. Rather, the goal of apprenticeship was to learn the craft so that one could produce one's own original work with the excellence characteristic of one's master, school, or tradition. This process incorporates imitation, but it does not stop there. The apprentice starts with imitation in order to lay a sound foundation; but imitation is not the goal. The goal is full ownership of the skill in question and, eventually, the mastery necessary to develop one's own innovations: imitation leading to innovation. In this vein Ralph Waldo Emerson claimed good books should be used for inspiration rather than imitation; they inspire us to better ourselves.[61] Neither narrative nor the *phronimos* can provide us with formulaic or programmatic step-by-step instructions for virtue. Both should inspire emulation of a certain trait or archetype rather than mindless imitation. Developing virtue requires that we be inspired to thoughtfully emulate a certain model or archetype—whether physical or textual matters little since we employ narrative techniques in either case—and that we gain experience with the virtue in question in our own lives, all with the hope of ultimately expressing the relevant virtuous trait.

Or, to make one final analogy, the "as-if" experience of narrative can be thought of in terms of "practice" or "rehearsal," with which it shares some family resemblance. Neither practice nor rehearsal is a full replacement for the actual event, but both are useful and both make the final product better. Just as athletes are told to visualize success—to imagine themselves executing a technique or play flawlessly, responding to obstacles and so forth—the "as-if" experience of narrative emplotment allows a person to visualize herself acting successfully, that is in ways that will be conducive to her well-being or flourishing (*eudaimonia*). There is a huge body of literature that documents the beneficial effects of visualization for athletic endeavors, and there is no reason to think that the same technique would not apply to virtue ethics.[62] Indeed, the revelatory and amplitive power of narrative makes it likely that narrative visualization would be uncommonly effective. Narrative not only helps us to apply the knowledge gained from our own past experience to the present and future, it allows us to apply knowledge gained from the experience of others.

Narratives Shape Belief, and Belief Shapes Action

Aristotle argues that virtue—at least moral virtue, which includes the sorts of "environmental" virtues with which we are primarily concerned—"comes about as the result of habit."[63] We practice something virtuous until we become someone virtuous. But for virtue ethics *hexis* is something deeper and more complex than a mere automatic or compulsive response, and has been rendered as "disposition," "state," "having," "possession," and "active condition" in addition to the more common "habit." A *hexis* is a stable condition that comes about as the result of long practice or habituation, and in the case of virtue it requires feeling a certain way during the commission of the act, taking the right things into consideration, being motivated by the right things, and so forth. The relationship between habit and action is perhaps the most significant of the various factors in the cultivation of virtue—if we do not actively practice a virtue we cannot fully develop that virtue.

So, in order to develop a habit (*hexis*), we must engage in repeated actions that will nurture, develop, and ultimately fix the disposition in question. But our actions are driven by beliefs as often as not, because believing and desiring are not so different.[64] Choice (*prohairesis*) "belongs to both the cognitive and the conative faculties and is not to be broken down into two bits, a belief and a desire."[65] Beliefs—which may be conscious or unconscious—shape our desire, choice, and action more often than "objective" reason, deduction, syllogistic argument, or bare facts. Such beliefs, in turn, are often grounded firmly in narratives. So habits are the results of actions, actions are driven by belief, and belief is deeply connected to narrative—making narrative influential in the development of habits.

I noted in Chapter 6 the way that the "backfire" effect seems to indicate that facts, logical argumentation, and the like often fail to change our beliefs. Because facts often fail to change our beliefs, they often fail to change our behavior. This is true whether we are talking about voting behavior and political partisanship or about environmental virtues and the behaviors that nourish them.

Bare facts do not have normative force. That gravity accelerates objects on the surface of the Earth at about 9.8 m/sec^2 is a fact. But, even for a physicist, it's not that fact that structures behavior. Rather, it is experience—both personal and narrativial—that shapes our fear of falling and its consequences. That "carbon saturation in the atmosphere has increased from a pre-industrial level of about 280 parts per million to a current level of about 395 parts per million" is also a fact, but again it has no normative force. This is true even when it is presented together with other significant facts having to do with the radiative forcing of carbon and its effect on the Earth's temperature, the disruptions to climate and weather this will cause, and the overwhelming human contribution to carbon levels in the atmosphere from the burning of fossil fuels and deforestation. These facts fail to move people for complex reasons: our tendency to focus on the immediate rather than the long term; the relative complexity of the relationship of cause-and-effect in this case; lingering uncertainties as to the form of the effect; the absence of a responsible agent to blame; and the difficulty in crafting an easy solution to the problem all play a part in our resistance to the facts.

However, one of the major obstacles to facts altering our behavior with respect to climate change is the widespread attitude or belief that human behavior cannot possibly fundamentally reshape or alter something as big and resilient as the Earth itself. As the backfire effect, motivated reasoning, and confirmation bias predict, when confronted with facts that fly in the face of these beliefs we engage in all manner of cognitive tricks to dismiss or otherwise minimize the "inconvenient truth." Facts are absolutely indispensable component parts of ethical decision making, including the cultivation of environmental virtue; but facts alone are inadequate to the tasks of knowledge, understanding, ethical discernment, ethical motivation, and the habituation of virtue.

If facts tend not to have sufficient normative force to change belief and behavior, what does? Narrative.

Recent research in psychology supports the claim that narrative plays a central role in identity and action. In contrast to postmodern literary theorists who suggest the end of the story, psychology is beginning to recognize that life narratives, which have always been constitutive of identity, are growing in importance and driving our actions in increasingly significant ways. It appears that the heralds of the death of the story jumped the gun. The "narrative processing" of a life includes the construction of "storied accounts of past events that range from brief anecdotes to fully developed autobiographies. These accounts rely on vivid imagery, familiar plot structures, and archetypal characters and are often linked to predominant cultural themes or conflicts."[66] This psychological account supports the extension of narrative analysis beyond "thick" narratives such as fully developed autobiographies to include "thin" quasi-narratives like brief anecdotes. It also suggests that we are acting from "scripts" based on familiar plots and archetypes much more often than we suspect. Indeed one camp among the personality psychologists suggests that "the central structural elements of human personality are internalized scenes and scripts."[67] These scripts tell us how to act appropriately in a wide variety of different circumstances.[68] We might have scripts that tell us how to act when we encounter the sublime in nature, when we are heartbroken, when we forgive, when we are victorious, when we grieve, and so on. But scripts tell us more than how we should act; they also tell us how we should feel. Mary Gergen describes how lovers throughout history have shaped their relationships based on existing myths and literature.[69] Any given agent understands her actions in light of a library of scripts drawn from myth, fables, oral history, non-fiction, biographies, literature, popular entertainment, and the like.

Thus, we use narrative not only to understand life retrospectively, but also to motivate and shape our actions prospectively. "Once we have filtered life experiences through the narrative lens, we can *make use* of the narratives we have created [to] . . . *guide our actions*. . . ."[70] We base our future actions on our understanding of our own identities, which is itself related to a number of social, cultural, and traditional narratives. Every time we act, and every time we encounter a new narrative, there is an opportunity to assess whether the action or narrative brings us closer to our goals, whether those goals are proximate (the accomplishing of a given task) or remote (achieving *eudaimonia*). But the point is that our actions depend, at least in part, on the narratives that inform our identity, our sense of the human *telos*, what we take to be good or bad, noble or base, worthy of pursuit or disdain.

These insights from psychology are not, we should note, novel. Umberto Eco argues that we actually experience love, fear, hope, and similar states through the filter of images we have already seen, and while he leaves it to "moralists" to argue whether or not this state of affairs should be deplored, "we must bear in mind that mankind has never done anything else."[71] Wayne Booth makes a similar point:

> . . . anyone who conducts honest introspection knows that "real life" is lived *in* images derived in part from stories. Although usually our imitations are not highly dramatic, especially once we pass adolescence, everyone who reads knows that whether or not we should imitate narrative heroes and heroines, we in fact do. Indeed, our imitations of narrative "imitations of life" are so spontaneous and plentiful that we cannot draw a clear line between what we are, in some conception of a "natural," unstoried self, and what we have become as we have first enjoyed, then imitated, and then, perhaps, criticized both the stories and our responses to them.[72]

Real life is lived in images derived in part from stories. If this sounds dramatic, consider a curious phenomenon that has developed over the past two decades. In 1993 the Hughes brothers released the film *Menace II Society*, in which a character used his handgun held sideways, horizontal to the ground.[73] Although the Hughes brothers claim to have seen this unorthodox grip in action during a 1987 robbery, there are very few reports of it prior to the release of their movie in 1993. After the release of the movie this "horizontal" technique of holding a handgun became more frequent, even commonplace, both in movies and in the real world (to the benefit, no doubt, of a number of potential victims who were spared because the absurd technique is both impractical and inaccurate). Actual gangsters adopted the technique to pose and project the cool arrogance of characters using the technique in movies, television, and music videos. It is not at all improbable to imagine similar narrative transfers happening as books, theater, movies, and television subtly alter the way we speak, move, and interact with the world.

Consciously or unconsciously, we act out narrative roles. Paul Hunter wonders how much of modern history "has gone the way it has because people at crucial moments have said or done a certain thing in imitation of some character in a novel."[74] How, we might imagine, would history have been different if major figures had been raised on and committed to different narratives? How did the narrative plots, characters, themes, scripts, and archetypes in the personal backgrounds of JFK and Khrushchev affect their conduct during the Cuban Missile Crisis? How did narrative affect the possibilities for reconciliation in Northern Ireland, South Africa, Rwanda, Germany, and elsewhere? On a more personal level, how many loves have been won or lost on the basis of actions undertaken in the light of different narrative archetypes, scripts, and themes? How many victories have been achieved as the result of discipline, effort, and sacrifice in imitation of stories lauding these very virtues? How many tragedies or defeats have been borne defiantly, nobly, or stoically because of narratives that have show us how do to so?

Eco may well be correct in suggesting that we have always experienced the world and lived our lives through the screens or filters provided by narrative; however, the narrative aspect of life is arguably becoming more important in our postmodern, multicultural, and global world, in which traditional narratives are breaking down and loosening up, as it were, narrative roles. Psychologist Dan McAdams argues that "cultural modernity"—by which he means the contemporary context in which we find ourselves at the start of the third millennium—presents us with distinctive problems that require us to become adept at assimilating our actions and lives into intelligible stories:

> In the modern world, the self is a reflexive project that a person
> is expected to "work on," to develop, to expand, and strive to
> perfect. Modern people see the self as complex and multifaceted,

as containing many layers and depth, and as changing relent-
lessly over time. At the same time, they feel a strong urge to
find some coherence in the self, to fashion a self that is more
or less unified and purposeful within the discordant cultural
parameters that situate their lives.[75]

And where do we look for ethical models?

From the media to everyday discourse, modern life is filled with
models and examples of how to live a meaningful life and how
not to. Yet, virtually every positive model has its drawbacks,
nothing close to a consensus exists, and even if some modest
level of cultural consensus could be reached, modern people are
socialized to find their own way, to craft a self that is true to
who one "really" is. As a consequence, people pick and chose
and plagiarize selectively from the many stories and images they
find in culture to formulate a narrative identity.[76]

If this is the case, when we are talking about environmental virtues—indeed,
when we are talking about virtue in any context—we should be at least as
concerned with the narrative aspects of our understanding and motivation
as we are with more traditional philosophical analysis, logical argumentation, and the presentation of facts. We can't simply overwhelm people
with facts or bombard them with arguments, no matter how convincing;
we must tell stories that both illustrate the reality of environmental harm
and illuminate the environmental, social, and personal benefits of virtue.

Narratives shape a person's worldview. That worldview dictates in
large measure what a person thinks is good or valuable and what she takes
to be the goal or purpose of human life. Those beliefs, in turn, circumscribe what sorts of actions, habits, dispositions, beliefs, and emotions a
person cultivates. Thus, our actions, which we frequently try to ground with
"objective" reasons, often spring from a much more hermeneutic and narrative soil. The stories we tell ourselves—individually and collectively—about
who we ought to be are an absolutely determinative factor in shaping the
persons we do in fact become.

Epilogue

The "Narrative Goodness" Approach

Stories have actually neither beginning or end. Every story is like a river: it began flowing with the beginning of the world, and will not cease 'til the world comes to an end.

> —H. L. Davis, in a review of Robinson Jeffers's
> *The Women at Point Sur*

Life is painting a picture, not doing a sum.

> —Oliver Wendell Holmes, Address to the
> Harvard Alumni Association Class of '61

That you are here—that life exists, and identity; / That the powerful play goes on, and you will contribute a verse.

> —Walt Whitman, *Leaves of Grass*

We are what we pretend to be, so we must be careful about what we pretend to be.

> —Kurt Vonnegut, *Mother Night*

The Need for Virtue Ethics and the Need for Narrative

By the middle of the summer when I was seventeen I had yet to see myself become part of a story. I had as yet no notion that life every now and then becomes literature—not for long, of course, but long enough to be what we best remember, and often enough so that what we eventually come to mean by life are those moments when life, instead of going sideways, backwards, forward, or nowhere at all, lines out straight, tense and inevitable, with a complication, climax, and, given some luck, a purgation, as if life had been made and not happened.[1]

Narrative and life fit hand-in-glove. We cannot avoid using narrative when we attempt to understand human actions. Narrative *mimesis*, the imitation of human action, is the means by which we make sense of our conduct in the world and by which we, ultimately, give the diverse actions and happenings in our lives meaning as events in our lives' stories. Actions, in turn, are manifestations of various sorts of dispositions, whether they are virtuous, vicious, or somewhere in between. They are mirrors of one's constantly evolving character. Since virtues are tied to actions and understanding action is tied to narrative, a full understanding of virtue will, necessarily, be narrative in nature. This insight opens up a whole field of possibilities for the use of narrative in the formation and reformation of character.

One area of critical importance in the contemporary milieu is the formation of *environmentally* virtuous characters. Although there are human commonalities that stretch across time and culture, resulting in widely shared accounts of certain aspects of "the good life," it is also true that each situation is unique and that certain eras or contexts call for an emphasis on certain virtues. While courage is a virtue that is widely agreed to be essential to full human flourishing, certain generations are called to courage in particularly striking ways. Think here of the sacrifices of the "greatest generation" on the beaches of Normandy, or those of civil rights activists facing beatings, fire hoses, and police dogs on the streets of Birmingham, or the nonviolent members of *Khudai Khidmatgar* facing down British machine guns in Peshawar during the struggle for independence on the Indian subcontinent.

In a similar way, those of us alive at the dawn of the twenty-first century are called in a special way to exhibit, foster, and promote environmental virtue. Without abandoning other more "traditional" virtues—which retain their importance for a fully *eudaimon* life—we must place a particular emphasis on those characteristics and dispositions that will help us to act wisely and virtuously in the face of numerous, looming, serious environmental crises. Dispositions like simplicity, care, humility, adaptability, and creativity have always been virtues, but they will become increasingly prominent themes in the story of what it means to live well in an age of climate change, overpopulation, species extinctions, and the like.

The field of environmental ethics has been growing, but it will remain incomplete without a robust virtue ethics component. There are difficulties with this approach to be sure, chief among them the difficulty of virtue language expressing itself in ways that lend themselves to political, economic, and legislative debate, which will be a necessary part of any attempt to act collectively on global problems like climate change. Nevertheless, we've seen that the virtue ethics approach offers substantial benefits when it comes to understanding the ethical and moral choices we encounter in our day-to-day lives.

However, it turns out that virtue ethics, whether or not it is attuned to environmental issues, is shot through with narrative. "I can only answer the question 'What am I to do?' if I can answer the prior question 'Of what story or stories do I find myself a part?' "[2] Moreover, we understand, articulate, and debate the importance of different character traits and dispositions in the context of narrative examples in which those traits or dispositions contribute to or frustrate the achievement of a good human life.

Thus, what we need is a "narrative, environmental virtue ethics," an awkward but hopefully temporary turn of phrase that indicates the significance of both narrative and environmental virtue in a complete understanding of what it means to live, act, and fare well in the twenty-first century. Once these lacunae are fully appreciated and addressed, we will be able to dispense with the clumsy pleonasm of modifying "virtue ethics" with either "narrative" or "environmental," recognizing that any complete virtue ethics will include both so-called "environmental" virtues and a deep appreciation for the role played by narrative in the cultivation of virtuous character.

This approach to virtue ethics has a great deal to recommend it. Virtue ethics is capable of addressing a broad array of phenomena that narrower, moral approaches tend to overlook, which makes it particularly adept at engaging environmentally significant issues that fall outside discussions of rights, duties, and obligations. This broad scope is possible, in part, through a nuanced sensitivity to context and to the relevance of particulars in ethical life that narrative is concerned with expressing and developing. The use of narrative develops in us a responsiveness to the multiplicity and non-commensurability of ethical goods, reminding us that there are often genuine trade-offs in the quest to live well. The narrative approach is also superior to alternatives in terms of motivational force, since narratives are often better than facts and deductive reasoning at inducing people to change their lives. Once the hard work of self-cultivation is underway, the narrative approach allows us to "live more" by providing us with additional "as-if" experience that helps us to develop the skill of ethical discernment and, along with our own firsthand experience, sharpen *phronesis*. Although "as-if" experience can never fully replace firsthand experience or complete the work of habituation on its own—narratives supplement direct experience rather than replacing it—artistic license allows literature to emphasize and amplify certain truths or insights, and the subtle interplay of proximity and distance in "as-if" experience allows narrative to connect us with experiences we cannot, or would not want to, have ourselves.

How to Story Well: Principles for the Good Use of Narrative

We cannot escape narration or interpretation—nor should we want to—so it is important to try to narrate and interpret well. What, then, does it mean to narrate well in the context of virtue ethics?

Certainly we ought be more conscious and deliberate in employing narrative as a tool in shaping our moral and ethical selves. We must disabuse ourselves of the notion that the instructive use of narrative is just a poor substitute for comprehensive objectivity, detached and disinterested reason, utilitarian calculation, or analytical logic. At this point it should be abundantly clear that narrative contributes something distinctive to ethical discernment, something that enriches traditional philosophical analysis without claiming to displace or supplant it. This is not to say that all reading of literature should be undertaken only with the conscious and practical goal of self-improvement. Literature is valuable for many reasons other than its potentially edifying nature. Nevertheless, we ought to take seriously Mallory's introduction to *Le Morte d'Arthur*, in which, anticipating the challenge of morally complex characters like Lancelot, he entreats the reader to "do after the good, and leave the evil."[3] In adopting the narrative approach to virtue we should also keep in mind that the ultimate goal is not to *read* well, but to *live* well; and while some form of good narration is a necessary condition for good living, no form of good narration is a sufficient cause for good living.

In addition to this general appeal to the deliberate use of narrative for self-cultivation, we can, on the basis of the preceding chapters, identify a number of principles that circumscribe the responsible and virtuous use of narrative. There are no hard and fast rules here, only yardsticks that admit of varying degrees of rigidity and specificity; but we can nevertheless discern certain guidelines that will help us in employing narration in the service of living well.

First, we have to navigate the tension between selectivity and censorship. Selectivity is inevitable because there are only so many narratives one can engage in one's life, only twenty-four hours in the day. We must choose which narratives we will engage from a field of options so large we can scarcely imagine its edges.[4] However, we want to avoid the perils associated with self-censorship; therefore, we should consciously engage otherness in our reading, seeking out foreign, unfamiliar, or challenging narratives that will force us to reevaluate our beliefs and think clearly about why we hold them. It is all too easy to allow one's narrative habits to erect walls against new ideas or opinions. The result is an echo chamber in which one's existing position—along with its existing biases, prejudices, blind spots, constraints, and limitations—becomes entrenched to such a degree that one can no longer grow or develop. Such a person's horizons of interpretation stagnate or atrophy rather than grow, mature, and blossom. No single narrative is likely to cause us irreparable damage; but narrative parochialism can, over time, do significant harm.[5] Thus, for example, the dominance of anthropocentric voices in the narratives of our culture suggests that responsible readership would entail seeking out narratives that call into question that default perspective by giving attention to biocentric or ecocentric perspectives. Conscious engagement with diverse literary genres, diverse literary perspectives, and diverse ethical worldviews will go a long way toward guarding against unjustified bias.

Second, when reading, we should compare our "as-if" experience with our actual lived experience, evaluating and appraising our narrative insights in light of what we have come to know, understand, and believe about life as the result of our personal experience with it. In this way we test our narrative insights against our lived insights and vice versa. The ready availability of diverse "as-if" experiences helps to correct against the narrowness of many lives and the fact that "we have never lived enough." In turn, the practical understanding that comes with lived experience tempers the possibility of certain narrative excesses.

Third, when engaging any narrative we should reference our background library of "as-if" experience, drawn from other narratives—literary, folkloric, cinematic, poetic, oral, and otherwise—that we have encountered. As with drawing on lived experience, when we juxtapose a narrative claim with other "as-if" experiences, we get multiple perspectives on which we can draw for insight. Whether the claim in question is about the aim or *telos* of the good life, or what sorts of actions and emotions are laudable or deplorable, or how one should react to certain sorts of situations, or what goals one should aspire to, or what temptations one should avoid, or the consequences of various actions for oneself, one's community, or the environment, the more experience we can bring to bear—either lived or "as if"—the better.

Fourth, in addition to bringing our emplotment of narratives into conversation with lived experience and with other narratives we have encountered, we should engage in coduction with other readers. The process of coduction emphasizes the social nature of narrative and of virtue. As with selecting narratives, we should take care when choosing partners in coduction, lest we end up, again, in an echo chamber. Coduction works best when it challenges us, revealing relevant details our own reading overlooked, forcing us to consider other plausible interpretations of actions and events, and obliging us to justify and defend our own interpretations. This simultaneous deepening of one's understanding and sharpening of one's arguments is important, since one is simultaneously, if paradoxically, searching for both the best life *for oneself* and searching for universal aspects of living well to which any other reasonable person would assent. Thus, when we coduce we should engage a variety of other readers representing a range of perspectives. Undertaken responsibly, coduction—along with consciously and openly engaging a diversity of narrative accounts—is one important way to combat troubling psychological phenomena like confirmation bias and motivated reasoning. By forcing us to more clearly assess the plausibility of various interpretations, coduction helps us to develop a habit of and skill in ethical discernment. This process should never stop. Coduction, and interpretation more broadly, is, or should be, an open-ended project. Since we modify our hermeneutic understanding on the basis of each new experience—lived or "as if"—the process only ends when we do. It is no doubt for this reason that André Gide wrote, "believe those who *seek* the truth, doubt those who *find* it."[6]

Nevertheless, the suspicion with which we should meet strong claims about truth should not turn us toward a dogmatic skepticism, relativism, or nihilism. Thus, a fifth guideline for responsible use of narrative is to balance the hermeneutics of suspicion with a hermeneutics of affirmation. Critical readings, hermeneutic readings, deconstructive readings and the like are all well and good; but such readings should take place in the context of an aspiration for greater understanding and virtuous living. Of course, neither greater understanding nor ethical progress is assured. The process of going out to engage the other and returning to understand anew is one that entails significant risk, and it is not clear until the end of our individual stories whether and to what extent things work out for the good. Ricoeur wagers and hopes that the hermeneutic spiral will be a virtuous one, leading us heavenward. But like Jacob's ladder hermeneutics can take us in one of two directions, toward either virtue or vice. Despite this danger, coduction chooses the risk of critique, jeopardizing any easy or uncritical relationship to truth and tradition. It does so not with the goal of destroying the possibility of any narrative foundation, burning truth to the ground and plowing its fields with salt. Rather, the goal of critique is to come to new conviction, abandoning conviction in the face of critique in order to return to a new, more mature, wiser conviction—an open-ended process of challenging conviction with critique, arriving at a new conviction that is itself challenged by critique, and so on. In running the gauntlet of suspicion, we lose our innocence and naïveté, but with the goal of returning to a second belief, a second naïveté. Recalling William James's trope regarding the battle for understanding, responsible coduction dares to seek truth (and virtue), risking the engagement with otherness rather than seeking safety by foregoing the thrust and parry of dialogue and discussion for fear of making an error during the fray.

Finally, when we employ narrative in our ethical lives, we must be certain to engage in other ways of knowing that will complement the narrative approach. The narrative approach to environmental virtue ethics does not claim that narrative is all that matters, or that all we need to do is to tell the right story and all will be right with the world and with ourselves. Narrative accounts of flourishing, virtue, and the like should be checked not only against alternative readings and against other narratives, but also against insights from ecology, biology, psychology, anthropology, and any other spheres of inquiry relevant to the question at hand. There are diverse ways of understanding ourselves, our relationship to others, and our place in the world; insight and genuine wisdom are more likely to come from drawing from multiple ways of knowing, circumventing the biases inherent in any one.

Three Important Clarifications

There are at least three potential misunderstandings that should be addressed by way of sketching out just what narrative virtue ethics implies or claims to accomplish, one related to each of the main fields of philosophical inquiry broadly conceived: ethics, epistemology, and metaphysics. More specifically, there are clarifications to be made regarding what narrative virtue ethics has to say about what we ought to value, how we know, and what is real or true.

The Valued and the Valuable

The final principle for the good use of narrative in virtue ethics—the need to engage other ways of knowing—constitutes an essential part of the response to Katie McShane's justifiable concern that while narrative can help us to identify the valued, it does not really help us to identify the valuable.[7] The worry, in other words, that while an analysis of narrative can reveal what we do in fact value, it has no reliable way of showing us what is actually valuable, that which we ought to value. Indeed, narratives can, and often have, led us astray in moral and ethical deliberations—minimizing the consequences of climate change, leading to inaction; misleading people about how food, particularly meat, is grown and harvested in the United States, leading to silence and apathy with respect to CAFOs; and narratives about growth and progress that lead people to embrace unfulfilling consumerist lifestyles. So McShane's worry is certainly apposite to the concerns of ethics and we should remain on guard as we engage in narrative virtue ethics. However, the full and responsible use of narrative in virtue ethics that was sketched out above is actually well-equipped to help us discern the valuable and to differentiate it from the merely valued.

Even before engaging alternative ways of knowing, narratives themselves give us a sort of argument not just about how something is valued, but also about why it is valued. In doing so they make implicit or explicit claims about what we actually ought to value, what is in fact valuable. Narratives do this by showing us the consequences of valuing certain things or valuing in certain ways; they show us what it looks like to live a life valuing some specific thing or set of things. Each tradition, expressed in its narratives, is a "historically extended, socially embodied argument" about the good life and the virtues that constitute it.[8] Is this an unerring way to discern the valuable? Certainly not. Narratives make arguments about the valuable, but they can do so well or poorly, foolishly or wisely, virtuously or viciously. This, however, is true of any other possible approach. Philosophical argumentation, for example, can also be used to induce people to do "very stupid things."[9]

A narrative approach to virtue is, for good reason, fundamentally at odds with the premise that a cold, utilitarian, non-narrative, rational choice model for decision making will accurately get us to the valuable. Reason devoid of emotion and perspectival bias is, practically speaking, impossible. However, even if it were possible for us, such thinking would be *less* equipped to get to the right ethical answers, not more. Pure rationality, if by that we mean "rationality devoid of and at odds with emotional connection, attention to particulars, sensitivity to place, and so on," is both impossible and undesirable. Narrative seems no less likely to lead us astray when thinking about the valuable than many other options, and when it is done well, following the criteria outlined above, it is actually far more likely to lead us aright in our quest for virtue than other methods. Nevertheless, narrative alone is certain to run into problems of its own: misinterpretations, blinds spots, omissions, unjustified prejudice and bias, anthropocentric reasoning, and so on. Thus, at the danger of repetition, narrative must engage and make use of other ways of knowing in its search to distinguish the valuable from the merely valued.

Reason

The hermeneutic commitments central to a narrative virtue ethics also tend to provoke charges of irrationality—claims that emphasizing interpretation, perspective, construction, emotion, and the like undermine or even vilify the traditional role of reason in philosophy. When we judge and choose it is reason and reason alone that should be our guide, reason freed from the "prison houses" of materiality, history, and the bonds of affection.[10]

However, while hermeneutics does challenge a specific conception of reason used a certain way, it does not reject reason outright; and it should be clear that the application of hermeneutics to narrative and virtue as developed in previous chapters does not repudiate or forsake rationality. Reason and philosophical argumentation have significant roles to play in a narrative virtue ethics. What I am after is a more reasonable reason, a humbler reason that recognizes both its strengths and its limitations. Post-modernity generally and hermeneutics specifically undermine reason only insofar as it claims to be something it is not, when it claims to be capable of stepping out of history and materiality in order to view the world from nowhere, when it claims to have secured a God's-eye perspective on things. Such over-confident claims about the power of reason are too optimistic in general, but they are especially troubling in ethics, which deals not with the purportedly unchangeable world of pure forms, but with quite change-able and practical issues here in the dirt of the world.

Our rationality is a wonderful thing, something to be valued, culti-vated, praised, and put to use in the world—but ours is a *human* rational-ity, with both the powers and the limitations that implies. No doubt we have accomplished a great deal with reason, and we have the potential to accomplish a great deal more. But reason is not omnipotent; it is not our only faculty, nor is it the faculty best suited to all questions or applica-tions, trumping or excluding all others. Think here of Nussbaum's very convincing argument—using both literary and philosophical sources—that ethical judgment is actually enhanced by the sensible use of narrative and emotion, and that "purely rational" judgment, if such a thing were pos-sible, would actually judge more poorly. We are humans, not computers, and we err when we aspire to the cold, heartless, programmable judgment of computers. However, once we realize that reason works in concert with other faculties and that doing so can actually enhance rather than degrade reason, hermeneutics and reason become allies in the search for truth, to which we now turn.

Truth, Reality, and Fact

As we saw in Chapter 6, no perspective, including the scientific perspective, is without its biases. There is no objective view from nowhere, no innocent eye, no escaping the hermeneutic circle. What, then, becomes of truth, reality, and fact? Must we abandon these ideas? In Chapter 5 I indicated that anthropogenic climate change would shape the context of human flourishing in ways that suggest the virtue of simplicity should be a significant part of contemporary expressions of flourishing, especially in affluent countries. Can we say that anthropogenic climate change is "true," or "real," or that it is a "fact"? If not, must we resign ourselves to relativistic anarchy, caught, as Yeats feared, in a moral and ethical maelstrom that may yet fashion us into "rough beasts"?

> Turning and turning in the widening gyre
> The falcon cannot hear the falconer;
> Things fall apart; the centre cannot hold;
> Mere anarchy loosed upon the world,
> The blood-dimmed tide is loosed, and everywhere
> The ceremony of innocence drowned;
> The best lack all conviction, while the worst
> Are full of passionate intensity.[11]

Does hermeneutics leave us in a world of opinion in which "the centre cannot hold," unable to adjudicate between competing claims to truth by means other than combat between incommensurable, passionate convictions?

Fortunately, no. A full-length account of the ways in which the constructed nature of reality implied by hermeneutics is not, ultimately, at odds with the autonomous nature of facts and reality would take a book-length treatise, such as that undertaken by Bruno Latour in *Pandora's Hope*.[12] However, we are not engaged in an attempt to prove reality in science studies, but rather in the question of truth as it pertains to virtue in general and environmental virtue in particular. Here we can make do with addressing a more focused issue: what does it mean to speak of truth, reality, and fact in environmental ethics? This is a radically different question, for as we have seen the most plausible accounts of flourishing and virtue are shaped not only by nature, the supposed domain of facts, but also by culture, where reality is widely acknowledged to be significantly more malleable. Living well must take into account both facts about the world in which we live and facts about the cultures in which we live, and the "facts" about living well are, as Aristotle suggests, substantially less precise, fixed, and certain than their mathematical counterparts. One way to think of the multivocal account of reality relevant to environmental ethics, virtue ethics, and narrative ethics—which includes truth and opinion, facts and interpretations, reality and narrative—is in terms of a palimpsest in which we find written various accounts of the same phenomena from the diverse perspectives of science, philosophy, psychology, theology, history, and so forth.[13]

The preceding chapters make abundantly clear that narrative virtue ethics, whether focused on the environment or not, is allergic to relativistic accounts of truth, based on the claims of narrative itself and on the responsible way in which narrative virtue ethics engages both narrative and other ways of knowing. Thus, narrative virtue ethics should be comfortable using the language of truth, reality, and fact as they are used in everyday common conversations, and environmentalists everywhere can heave a sigh of relief on hearing that a hermeneutic account of ethics need not dismiss the notion that climate change is a fact. However, hermeneutics is also allergic to absolute or closed accounts of truth, reality, or fact. So any use of those terms in narrative virtue ethics must come with the hermeneutic caveat that we are talking about truth, reality, or fact from the perspective of our best current understanding—a claim no scientist should deny—an understanding that is structurally, and therefore inevitably, partial, incomplete, and revisable. Sometimes it is appropriate to emphasize the fact-nature of reality, at other times it is appropriate to emphasize the constructed nature of reality, and at most times it is appropriate to stress some combination of the two residing in the spectrum between these poles.

These claims preserve and hold in tension (1) the common sense meaning of "fact" as something that is true or which corresponds in some way to the actual state of affairs, alongside (2) the scientific sense of "fact" which both seeks to confirm truth claims empirically and, as a result, recognizes that facts are revisable on the basis of new insights and (3) the hermeneutic sense of "fact" which points out that our partial and perspectival view of things ensures there will always be new insights that can come to light and reshape our current understanding of truth, fact, and reality. It is no more contradictory to say that there is no escaping the hermeneutic circle but there are nevertheless facts regarding how we ought to live in the world we are in, than it is to say evolution and gravity are theories, and they describe real facts about the way the world works. The idea of one, closed, complete Grand Narrative is inimical to both narrative ethics and virtue ethics. However, the idea of an open, dialogical, revisable narrative (perhaps even a grand one), a narrative that is a work-in-progress, one with multiple regional and local translations and interpretations, is just what we need.

The Literature of Life:
A Life Worth Living, a Story Worth Telling

Ricoeur suggests that a life worth living is a life worth recounting in story. This resonates with the claim that virtues are distinguished by their *kalon*— good, noble, beautiful—nature. Each person seeks to craft her life into a story she would be pleased to recount or to have recounted, and when she fails to do so she generally hopes that those failures will not become major episodes in the story of her life. A good life makes a good story and a bad life makes a bad story—or perhaps a good cautionary tale. This, however, raises one final and significant concern having to do with authorial control. I've spoken often about a person's life story in the context of virtue and self-cultivation, but can a person really write her own story?

It's clear enough that I am the protagonist of my life's story—and, when I am my best self, its hero—but the identity of my story's author is less clear. Our lives are such an intractable web of freedom and necessity, contingency and inevitability, novelty and tradition. Ricoeur himself seems to suggest different things at different times with respect to this difficult question. For example, in the third volume of *Time and Narrative*, he claims that the subject "appears both as a reader *and writer* of its own life."[14] However, in the essay "Life in Quest of Narrative" he is significantly more circumspect, asserting, "we learn to become the narrator and the hero of our own story, *without actually becoming the author* of our own life."[15] The difference between these two statements highlights a critical issue for narrative virtue ethics: to what extent can a person *actively* shape the story of her life? If she finds herself in a ruinous or unhealthy story—one that is vicious or otherwise at odds with flourishing—can she "narrate her way out" so to speak? What degree of authorial control can we exercise over our life stories?

Just as our reason is a human reason, our creativity is human creativity. When we choose and act, we simultaneously write the story of our lives; however, narrating a life differs substantially from narrating a story. In fiction, there are no limits to what we can create, but the story of a life is limited in various ways by truth, facts, and reality, even if these are themselves hermeneutically construed. In the case of narrative identity, hermeneutic entanglement with fact leads to a situation in which it's often impossible to fully disentangle truth and fiction, reality and interpretation.[16] For example, when we are dealing with narrative self-cultivation, should our stories focus on being as factual as possible, or as efficacious as possible?

On the one hand, self-development requires a clear and honest assessment of oneself, one as unclouded as possible by delusions or self-congratulatory images. While I can of course say anything I want about my actions, my relationships, my choices, my virtues and vices, my well-being, and my life, not everything I say is necessarily true. On the other hand, there is a certain value to the creative use of narrative as an aspirational tool. In striving to be better than we are, there is something useful in acting out the roles we hope to play and characters we hope to be. "What is forgotten in our universal condemnation of hypocrisy is that a kind of play-acting with characters, or characteristics, a kind of *faking* of characters, is one of the main ways that we build what becomes *our* character."[17] This sort of "productive" or "aspirational" hypocrisy is not vicious unless we deceive ourselves by thinking (or others by implying) we have actually acquired a virtue that we are, as yet, only aping. However, if we remain aware that we are aspiring to be better than we actually are, that our performance is part of the hard work of becoming a better self, and that such acting cannot be divorced from difficult philosophical questioning of whether we are playing the role properly, such simulation can be an ethically valuable tool. Fake it until you make it, so to speak.

Nevertheless, I cannot create my life's story out of whole cloth to suit some particular image I have of myself, but must work creatively within certain limits. Our life stories contain elements we have not chosen, things imposed upon without our consent; they are also something we write with the free choices that we make in life. For this reason we should say that we both discover and create our life's narrative. We discover insofar as we come to know, understand, and appropriate the narratives into which we find ourselves thrown, the narratives of our personal history, culture, tradition, family, religion, and so forth. We create insofar as we are autonomous agents who both act to reinterpret those discovered narratives in light of our own experiences, and make free choices that modify and continue those stories, writing subsequent chapters.

Therefore, the most accurate model for narrative figuration and refiguration, the best we can aspire to in writing the stories of our lives, is actually one of co-authorship—creative freedom in which we take the material we have been given, make it our own, and attempt to author the sort of life we hope to live. Co-authorship is genuine authorship—it is distinct from being a mere reader or interpreter of a story authored by another—but it is authorship under constraint: "It is always both the case that there are constraints on how the story can continue *and* that within those constraints there are indefinitely many ways that it can continue."[18]

> What the agent is able to do and say intelligibly as an actor is deeply affected by the fact that we are never more (and sometimes less) than the co-authors of our own narratives. Only in fantasy do we live what story we please. In life, as both Aristotle and Engels note, we are always under certain constraints. We enter a stage which we did not design and we found our selves part of an action that was not of our making. Each of us being a main character in his own drama plays subordinate parts in the dramas of others, and each drama constrains others.[19]

Narrative self-cultivation, therefore, must take into account both the free-doms and the constraints associated with refiguration, with an eye toward telling the "best" possible story in whatever sense is relevant to the matter at issue: truest, most just, most effective, most virtuous, and so forth. Doing so will entail a degree of Stoic acceptance of things we cannot change—even, perhaps, Nietzschean endorsement of those things—but, in addition, it entails the free exercise of imagination and choice. If a person's life story can be read as an extended response to Mary Oliver's question, "tell me, what will you do / with your one wild and precious life?" we each aspire to be able to say, as did Henry David Thoreau, "my life has been the poem I would have writ."[20]

Notes

Chapter 1

1. The letter that became knows as "The Wilderness Letter" appears as "To: David Pesonen, December 3, 1960" in *The Selected Letters of Wallace Stegner*, ed. Page Stegner (Shoemaker and Hoard, 2007), 352–357.

2. Ibid., 353–352. For a variety of reasons, I've chosen to leave the gender-neutral use of the masculine pronoun in all direct quotations, although I will use the feminine pronoun as gender-neutral in much of my own prose.

3. See, among a large variety of examples, J. Baird Callicott and Michael P. Nelson eds., *The Great New Wilderness Debate* (Athens, GA: University of Georgia Press, 1998).

4. John Muir, *John of the Mountains: The Unpublished Journals of John Muir*, ed. Linnie Marsh Wolfe (Madison, WI: University of Wisconsin Press, 1938), 439.

5. Stegner, "The Wilderness Letter," 354–355.

6. Ibid., 356.

7. Although many people seem to use "ethics" and "morality" more or less interchangeably, given the nature of this work it makes sense to attempt, where possible, to adhere to the convention followed by Bernard Williams and others whereby "morality" designates work like Kant's, which is focused more narrowly on duty and obligation, and "ethics" designates a wider scope of concern that resonates with the tradition of virtue ethics. See, for example, Bernard Williams, *Ethics and the Limits of Philosophy* (Cambridge, MA: Harvard University Press, 1985).

8. In what follows, we'll look at deontology and utilitarianism in their most classic formulations. It is true that later philosophical work—for example, the development of act utilitarianism or preference utilitarianism—attempts to address some of the objections raised here. It's also true that some work in deontology and virtue ethics attempts to bring these two traditions closer together. However, the number and variety of objections to these two most common moral-ethical frameworks still leaves us in a situation in which deontology and utilitarianism have significant liabilities for a full, rich environmental ethics.

9. Immanuel Kant, *Groundwork of the Metaphysics of Morals* in *Immanuel Kant: Practical Philosophy*, trans. and ed. Mary J. Gregor (Cambridge: Cambridge University Press, 1996), 45.

10. Ibid., 47.

11. Ibid., 57.

12. Immanuel Kant, "On a Supposed Right to Lie From Philanthropy" in *Immanuel Kant: Practical Philosophy*, trans. and ed. Mary J. Gregor (Cambridge: Cambridge University Press, 1996), 612.

13. Ibid., 611–615.

14. Kant, *Groundwork of the Metaphysics of Morals*, 80.

15. Ibid., 79.

16. John Stuart Mill, *Utilitarianism* (Indianapolis, IN: Hackett Publishing, 1979), 7. The ubiquity of utilitarian thinking today is no doubt the consequence of its adoption by economists, the de facto high priests of social and political policy.

17. Ibid., 10.

18. See, among others, Peter Singer "A Utilitarian Defense of Animal Liberation" in *Environmental Ethics: Readings in Theory and Application*, 5th Edition, eds. Louis P. Pojman and Paul Pojman (Belmont, CA: Thompson Wadsworth, 2008), 76.

19. See Singer, "A Utilitarian Defense of Animal Liberation," 77.

20. Tom Regan, "The Radical Egalitarian Case for Animal Rights" in *Environmental Ethics: Readings in Theory and Application*, 5th Edition, eds. Louis P. Pojman and Paul Pojman (Belmont, CA: Thompson Wadsworth, 2008), 88 and 87. Italics in original.

21. True, some virtue ethicists have addressed animal rights, among them Rosalind Hursthouse, "Virtue Ethics and the Treatment of Animals" in *The Oxford Handbook of Animal Ethics*, eds. Tom L. Beau Champ and R. G. Frey (New York: Oxford University Press, 2011), 119–143 and Nathan Nobis, "Vegetarianism and Virtue: Does Consequentialism Demand Too Little?" in *Social Theory and Practice*, vol. 28, no. 1 (January 2002) 135–156. However, while these essays go some way toward filling a gap in the scholarship on animal ethics, they remain isolated efforts and neither argument appears in the popular textbooks alongside the ubiquitous arguments of Singer and Regan.

22. Kant, *Groundwork of the Metaphysics of Morals*, 45.

23. Immanuel Kant, *The Metaphysical Elements of Justice: Part I of the Metaphysics of Morals*, trans. J. Ladd (Indianapolis: Hackett, 1965), 25. For a conflicting view, see Martha Nussbaum, *The Fragility of Goodness: Luck and Ethics in Greek Tragedy and Philosophy* (Cambridge: Cambridge University Press, 2001) as well as many other essays in *Love's Knowledge: Essays on Philosophy and Literature* (Oxford: Oxford University Press, 1990), which emphasize the possibility of irresolvable tragic situations, including those in which duties come into conflict. For some particularly sharp criticisms of Kant's practical philosophy, see *The Phenomenology of Spirit*, trans. A. V. Miller (Oxford: Oxford University Press, 1977), 365 ff. (on "the moral view of the world"). My thanks to Donald Boyce for his insight on this, and other matters.

24. Martha Nussbaum, *Poetic Justice* (Boston: Beacon Press, 1995), 14 ff. Also see *Love's Knowledge*.

25. Note that I don't intend to dismiss entirely either utilitarianism or deontology. I merely point out certain problematic aspects of their general approach to ethics. Indeed, there is good reason to think that a virtue ethics approach to ethics is fruitfully supplemented by recourse to deontological thinking. See, for example, Rosalind Hursthouse, *On Virtue Ethics* (Oxford: Oxford University Press, 1999).

26. A virtue ethic approach to rules might use "v-rules" as cognitive shortcuts to express things that are "for the most part true" (Aristotle, *Nicomachean Ethics*, trans. David Ross [Oxford: Oxford University Press, 1925], 3). However, we should not put the cart before the horse. Rules don't excuse us from thinking and we can be led into error if we follow them blindly, as if there are not occasions when the rule should be bent or even broken. Ethical rules are useful but limited expressions that attempt to concisely capture a much more complicated and nuanced account of how a good human would act. See chapter seven below. On v-rules, see Rosalind Hursthouse, *On Virtue Ethics*, 36–39.

27. See Nussbaum, *Love's Knowledge*, 13.

28. Kant, *Groundwork of the Metaphysics of Morals*, 45.

29. Ronald Sandler, *Character and Environment: A Virtue-Oriented Approach to Environmental Ethics* (New York: Columbia University Press, 2007), 3. These designations taking their inspiration, clearly, from the first, second, and third "waves" of feminist thought.

30. Philip Cafaro, "Virtue Ethics (Not Too) Simplified" in *Auslegung: A Journal of Philosophy* 22: 49–67. Emphasis mine.

31. Philip Cafaro, "Thoreau, Leopold, and Carson: Toward and Environmental Virtue Ethics" in *Environmental Virtue Ethics*, eds. Ronald Sandler and Philip Cafaro (New York: Rowan and Littlefield, 2005), 31–44.

32. For this, and the following three points, see Nussbaum, *Poetic Justice*, 14ff.

33. Nussbaum, *Poetic Justice*, 14.

34. Thomas Hill, "Ideals of Human Excellence and Preserving Natural Environments" in *Environmental Ethics* 5 (1983): 211–224.

35. Thomas Hill, "Ideals of Human Excellence and Preserving Natural Environments" in *Environmental Virtue Ethics*, eds. Ronald Sandler and Philip Cafaro (New York: Rowman and Littlefield Publishers, Inc., 2005), 47.

36. See Louke van Wensveen, *Dirty Virtues: The Emergence of Ecological Virtue Language* (New York: Humanities Books, 2000), 3.

37. "Americans' Outlook for Morality Remains Bleak," Gallup Politics, accessed April 25, 2012, <http://www.gallup.com/poll/128042/americans-outlook-morality-remains-bleak.aspx>.

38. Madeline Bunting, "Fanning the Flames of a Vital Debate" in *Citizen Ethics in a Time of Crisis* an online publication of the Citizen Ethics Network (2010), 4, accessed April 25, 2012, <http://www.citizenethics.org.uk/docs/Ethics-TemplateDoc.pdf>.

39. Transcript of President Obama's Press Conference on October 6, 2011, Chicago Sun-Times, accessed May 8, 2012, <http://www.marketwatch.com/story/transcript-ofOobamas-press-conference-2011-10-06>.

40. Kurt Eichenwald, *Conspiracy of Fools: A True Story* (New York: Random House, 2005).

41. See, for example, Naomi Oreskes and Erik M. Conway, *Merchants of Doubt* (New York: Bloomsbury Press, 2010) and David Michaels, *Doubt is Their Product: How Industry's Assault on Science Threatens Your Health* (Oxford: Oxford University Press, 2008).

42. Madeline Bunting, "Fanning the Flames of a Vital Debate" in *Citizen Ethics in a Time of Crisis* an online publication of the Citizen Ethics Network (2010), 5, accessed April 15, 2012, <http://www.citizenethics.org.uk/docs/Ethics-TemplateDoc.pdf>.

43. See, for example, Kurt Hahn, "Outward Bound: Address to the Annual Meeting of the Outward Bound Trust on 20th July, 1960," accessed March 5, 2012, <http://www.kurthahn.org/writings/obt1960.pdf>. For James's essay see, William James, "The Moral Equivalent of War" in *William James: Writings 1902–1910* (New York: The Library of America, 1987), 1281–1293.

44. *Citizen Ethics in a Time of Crisis* an online publication of the Citizen Ethics Network (2010), accessed April 25, 2012, <http://www.citizenethics.org.uk/docs/EthicsTemplateDoc.pdf>.

45. Rowan Williams, "How to Live as if We Were Human" in *Citizen Ethics in a Time of Crisis* and online publication of the Citizen Ethics Network (2010), 10, accessed April 15, 2012, <http://www.citizenethics.org.uk/docs/EthicsTemplateDoc.pdf>.

46. Ibid.

47. See, for example, Bill McKibben, *Deep Economy: The Wealth of Communities and the Durable Future* (New York: Hold and Company, 2007), 127 and 210. Wendell Berry is also brilliant on these topics. Among myriad examples of poetry and prose, see *The Art of the Commonplace: The Agrarian Essays of Wendell Berry*, ed. Norman Wirzba (Washington, DC: Counterpoint, 2002), Wendell Berry, *The Gift of Good Land: Further Essays Cultural and Agricultural* (San Francisco: North Point, 1981), and Wendell Berry, *The Unsettling of America: Culture and Agriculture* (San Francisco: Sierra Club, 1977).

48. See my "Environmentalism and Public Virtue" in *Virtue Ethics and the Environment*, eds. Philip Cafaro and Ronald Sandler (Springer, 2010), 9–28.

49. Sandler, *Character and Environment*, 1.

50. Dick Cheney made this claim in a speech in Toronto, Canada on April 30, 2001.

51. "For those of us raised on North American environmentalism in particular, it is tempting to contemplate our environmental heroes as walkers in the woods or hikers of the mountains. The image is of an individual with personal excellence flourishing in harmony with and appreciation of the wild (or near wild) environments" (Sandler, *Character and Environment*, 49). When we view environmentalism as a purely individual choice, we risk falling into the error that we can,

as individuals, save ourselves. However, many of the most pressing environmental crises are very large in scope, often dealing with some form of a "commons," and there are no individual solutions to problems in a commons. Individuals cannot opt out or extract themselves from a commons problem, as if they could row away from a sinking ship to save themselves. In a commons problem, either we are all saved or no one is saved.

52. Aristotle, *Nicomachean Ethics*, 3.

53. And, as Phil Cafaro has pointed out to me, "plot" taken as a verb would suggest the *plan* by which we cultivate virtue.

54. Aristotle, *Nicomachean Ethics*, 30. Emphasis mine. Surely these two goals are intertwined; nevertheless academic philosophy too often distinguishes between theoretical and practical, or applied, ethics as if the two were independent and unrelated discourses.

Chapter 2

1. When I claim that Aristotle is the preeminent virtue ethicist, I'm speaking here of virtue theory in the Western tradition. It's true that Confucius was writing around 500 BC and that his work stands in the tradition of virtue ethics. It's also true that Plato, to say nothing of epic poets like Homer, also addressed the virtues. Nevertheless, it's safe to say that Aristotle remains a giant, perhaps *the* giant, in any philosophical discussion of virtue.

2. J. O. Urmson, *Aristotle's Ethics* (Oxford: Blackwell, 1988), 71. Playing, of course, on the well-known anecdote about a woman who, returning from a production of *Hamlet*, commented that while she thought it was a lovely play, she was a bit disappointed that it was so full of quotations.

3. Alasdair MacIntyre, *After Virtue* (Notre Dame, IN: University of Notre Dame Press, 1984).

4. Aristotle, *Nicomachean Ethics*, 1. Aristotle is aware that sometimes the good at which an activity aims is intrinsic to the activity itself. For example, a person may dance for no other reason than to dance. It is true that other people may dance to win competitions or as part of a social obligation or in the process of seduction, but there are presumably people who dance only in order to dance. A similar point could be made with many other activities: surfing, hiking, playing music, and so forth. However, whether the good of an activity is intrinsic or extrinsic to the activity, all human actions aim at some good.

5. Note that the fact that some people, unfortunately, eat because they are bored or depressed does not change the fact that the activity of eating is directed at some end; it merely illustrates that one activity can be motivated by more than one *telos* and that some of these goals are beneficial (alleviating hunger, socializing as a family, or building community) while others are not (compensating for boredom or depression).

6. Richard Layard, *Happiness: Lessons from a New Science* (New York: Penguin, 2005), 29.

7. This useful image comes from Bill McKibben's *Deep Economy: The Wealth of Economies and the Durable Future* (New York: Holt Paperbacks, 2007), 1–2. Though numbers vary in different studies, economist Richard Layard suggests that "more" and "better" part ways after about $20,000 per capita GNP (Layard, *Happiness*, 35).

8. Aristotle, *Nicomachean Ethics*, 28. That is to say that, while a person may have a disposition conducive to the development of courage, she cannot possess that virtue just on the basis of her bold, rather than timorous, personality. Virtue requires more than this "natural inclination"; it requires rational choice, understanding, and entrenched habit, among other things. So, while a bold child may have a leg up on a timorous child in terms of eventually acquiring the virtue of courage, neither one is born courageous and both children have the capability to develop the virtue of courage. In this sense, "habit" is perhaps a poor translation, since Aristotle has in mind something more like a settled disposition or character trait rather than a behavioral tic.

9. Note as well that the term "moral" virtues is a standard translation for the non-intellectual virtues and does not imply the narrower sense of moral addressed above in Chapter 1, note 7. Aristotle does distinguish between moral virtues, which will be our primary concern in this book, and intellectual virtues. While the former are brought about through a process of habituation, the latter can be taught. Moreover, the translation of *hexis* as habit is not unproblematic. *Hexis* is a kind of disposition (*diathesis*) that is acquired by habituation, is relatively stable, and which arranges things well (that is, contributes to excellence).

10. See Aristotle, *Nicomachean Ethics*, 5–6. Indeed, the vast majority of people concern themselves with not being bad rather than with being good. But these are very different things. It is relatively easy to avoid being bad or evil; it is substantially more difficult to be good.

11. See Aristotle, *Nicomachean Ethics*, 89–95 and St. Thomas Aquinas, *Summa Contra Gent.*, bk. IV, ch. lv.

12. Aristotle, *Nicomachean Ethics*, 2–3.

13. Ibid., 3.

14. The point being that the engineer does not care what the 1000th or even the 10th digit of π is; she merely wants to know that her bridge or building will not fall down, that is, that *it will work*. Nevertheless, we don't berate the engineer for her lack of precision vis-à-vis the mathematician. Indeed, in this case I'd venture to guess that many people, for better or worse, value the work of the less precise field (engineering) over the work of the more precise field (mathematics). The arrangement of this note as number 14 in this chapter, and the consequent appearance of "three.14" was a humorous and, I trust, not too confusing coincidence!

15. Aristotle, *Nicomachean Ethics*, 30–31.

16. Ibid., 36–40.

17. Ibid., 37. Emphasis mine. That is to say, for example, that the mean amount of food is not a property of the food, as if 6 oz. of food is always better than 2 oz. or 10 oz. Rather, the mean or proper amount of food is relative to the

person eating the food, relative to her size, metabolism, activity level, relative state of hunger, and so forth.

18. Oscar Wilde, *A Women of No Importance* (London: Methuen and Co., 1908), 127.

19. Ibid., 39. Similarly, one might argue that love is good per se, and that it is impossible to love too much, though there are objections to be made to such a claim.

20. On top of this, the role of the emotions seems to suggest that it is difficult to *know* that we have achieved a virtue; rather, there is a degree to which we simply *feel* that we have done so: "But up to what point and to what extent a man must deviate before be becomes blameworthy is not easy to determine by reason, any more than anything else that is perceived by the senses; such things depend on particular facts, and the decision [or 'discernment'] rests with perception" (Aristotle, *Nicomachean Ethics*, 47).

21. Aristotle, *Nicomachean Ethics*, 39.

22. We will see in what follows that there are all sorts of legitimate ways of developing experience—both literal (personal experience) and figurative (narrative experience).

23. Aristotle, *The Nicomachean Ethics*, 142.

24. Arthur C. Clarke, *2001: A Space Odyssey* (New York: Penguin, 1993). The film adaptation is Stanley Kubrick's *2001: A Space Odyssey* (1968).

25. Ronald Sandler, *Character and Environment: A Virtue Oriented Approach to Environmental Ethics* (New York: Columbia University Press, 2007), see especially Chapter 4.

26. Aristotle, *Nicomachean Ethics*, 38. "Again, the case of the arts and that of the virtues are not similar; for the products of the arts have their goodness in themselves, so that it is enough that they should have a certain character, but if those acts that are in accordance with the virtues have themselves a certain character, it does not follow that they are done justly or temperately. The agent also must be in a certain condition when he does them; in the first place he must have knowledge, secondly he must choose the acts and choose them for their own sakes, and thirdly his action must proceed from a firm and unchangeable character . . . Actions, then, are called just and temperate when they are such as the just or the temperate man would do; but it is not the man who does these that is just and temperate, but the man who also does them *as* just and temperate men would do" (Ibid., 34–35).

27. See, for example, Urmson's *Aristotle's Ethics* on this distinction. However, for a compelling complication of the ethical status of those who struggle with virtue, see Rosalind Hursthouse, *On Virtue Ethics* (Oxford: Oxford University Press, 1999), 94 ff.

28. Aristotle, *Nicomachean Ethics*, 31–32.

29. Aristotle goes so far as to suggest that some people can become so deeply habituated to vice that they are beyond redemption or become so thoroughly habituated to virtue as to be beyond temptation. I'll leave it to the reader to come

to a conclusion regarding whether or not self-perfection is actually possible and, if it is, whether it can be accomplished by human efforts alone.

30. Aristotle, *Nicomachean Ethics*, 3.

31. Ibid., 45.

32. G. E. M. Anscombe, "Modern Moral Philosophy," *Philosophy*, 33 (1958), 1–19. Of course, there had always been philosophers interested in virtue ethics in the Aristotelian tradition. However, Anscombe is frequently credited with the contemporary *resurgence* of interest in virtue theory.

33. See Sandler, *Character and Environment*, 14ff.; Hursthouse, *On Virtue Ethics*, chapter 9 passim; Foot, *Natural Goodness*, chapter 2 passim.

34. Louke van Wensveen, *Dirty Virtues: The Emergence of Ecological Virtue Ethics* (New York: Humanity Books, 2000); Geoffrey Franz, "Environmental Virtue Ethics: Toward a New Direction for Environmental Ethics" in *Environmental Ethics* 15 (1993): 259–274; and Thomas Hill, "Ideals of Human Excellence and Preserving Natural Environments" in *Environmental Ethics* 5 (1983): 211–224. Earlier essays by a number of other thinkers could be cited as somewhat more isolated examples of a way of thinking that would eventually come to be called environmental virtue ethics.

35. Wensveen, *Dirty Virtues*, 5.

36. Ibid.

37. Ibid.

38. Ronald Sandler, "Introduction" in *Environmental Virtue Ethics*, eds. Ronald Sandler and Philip Cafaro, (New York: Rowman and Littlefield, 2005), 4–6. Also see Sandler, *Character and Environment*, 9–13.

39. Ibid., 4.

40. Ibid., 5.

41. Sandler, *Character and Environment*, 10.

42. Regarding the necessity of a wider view of environmental concern see, in addition to the literature on environmental virtue ethics, Shellenberger and Nordhaus, *The Death of Environmentalism: Global Warming Politics in a Post-Environmental World* (2004), accessed June 15, 2011, <www.thebreakthrough.org/images/ Death_of_Environmentalism.pdf>.

43. C. S. Lewis, *Mere Christianity* (New York: MacMillan, 1952), 72.

44. Borrowing from James here, who wrote: "It is only in the lonely emergencies of life that our creed is tested: then routine maxims fail, and we fall back on our gods" (William James, *The Will to Believe* [New York: Dover, 1987], 105).

45. See *The Environmental Politics of Sacrifice*, eds. Michael Maniates and John M. Meyer (Cambridge, MA: MIT Press, 2010).

Chapter 3

1. Aristotle, *Nicomachean Ethics*, trans. David Ross (Oxford: Oxford University Press, 1980), 30.

2. Alasdair MacIntyre, *After Virtue: A Study in Moral Theory* (Notre Dame, IN: University of Notre Dame Press, 1984), 2. Here again, MacIntyre uses "morality" in a manner somewhat different from that suggested in chapter one, note 7. Rather than littering direct quotations with "sic," I've chosen to leave his words as they appear in the text.

3. Joshua Colt Gambrel and Philip Cafaro, "The Virtue of Simplicity" in *The Journal of Agricultural and Environmental Ethics*, vol. 23, no. 1–2 (2010), 85–108.

4. "Equipped" to succeed rather than "successful at" because, as Martha Nussbaum, Rosalind Hursthouse, and others point out, possessing the virtues does not ensure happiness or flourishing. Virtuous people are still subject to the vagaries of fate, luck, circumstance, and tragic dilemmas. See Martha Nussbaum, *The Fragility of Goodness* (Cambridge: Cambridge University Press, 2001) and Rosalind Hursthouse, *On Virtue Ethics* (Oxford: Oxford University Press, 1999).

5. See Alasdair MacIntyre, *After Virtue*, 52–58, 148ff. Note that, in their article, Cafaro and Gambrel are silent regarding the idea of a *telos*, though their emphasis on a coherent idea of a "good human life" provides a very similar goal. Nevertheless, in line with the tradition I think the explicit addition of the idea of a *telos* is useful here, at the "ground floor" of their typology.

6. Thus, on one account, "men need virtues as bees need stings. An individual bee may perish by stinging, all the same bees need stings; an individual man may perish by being brave or just, all the same men need courage and justice" (Peter Geach, *The Virtues* [Cambridge: Cambridge University Press, 1977], 17).

7. Aristotle, *Nicomachean Ethics*, 1–2 and 269–276.

8. John Muir, "Hetch Hetchy Valley" in *Muir: Nature Writings*, ed. William Cronon (New York: The Library of America, 1997), 814.

9. John Muir, *Our National Parks* (New York: Houghton, Mifflin, and Co., 1901), 4.

10. Gambrel and Cafaro, "The Virtue of Simplicity," 2. Also see Rosalind Hursthouse, *On Virtue Ethics* (Oxford: Oxford University Press, 1999), 192ff., and Philippa Foot, *Natural Goodness* (Oxford: Clarendon Press, 2001), 5–25.

11. Foot, *Natural Goodness*, 26. For a helpful explanation, see Rosalind Hursthouse, *On Virtue Ethics* (Oxford: Oxford University Press, 1999), 195–205.

12. Ibid., 26–27.

13. See Rosalind Hursthouse, *On Virtue Ethics*, chapters 9 and 10 passim, especially 202.

14. Note that Foot and Hursthouse both acknowledge that rationality makes humans a special sort of case. Sandler's very clear account of the natural goodness approach, as well as his development of it in working out his pluralistic teleological account, is very helpful here. See Ronald Sandler, *Character and Environment: A Virtue-Oriented Approach to Environmental Ethics* (New York: Columbia University Press, 2007), 14–30.

15. Sandler, *Character and Environment*, 13.

16. Ibid., 14.

17. It will become obvious in what follows that I agree scientific natural-ism is incomplete by itself; however, exactly what Sandler means by this claim is not entirely clear. In discussing the ends at which virtues aim, he writes: "Not all realizations of ends are equally endorsable . . . accounts of the meaningfulness of life that are *inconsistent* with ethical naturalism are not endorsable, since they are *contrary to the best information* about ourselves and the world" (*Character and Environment*, 34, italics mine). So on Sandler's account these ends must be consis-tent with, but not necessarily fully justified by, naturalism. They cannot *contradict* naturalistic evidence. Indeed, Sandler goes so far as to suggest that naturalism gives us the best information about ourselves (Ibid.). "Only" naturalism? It's not exactly clear. However, he does say that, "on the pluralistic teleological account, character traits are not *merely* biological appraisals. The account is not *fully* justi-fied by scientific naturalism. The ends constitutive of human flourishing are not *fixed* by the biological facts about us. Human goodness (virtue) is not *reducible* to biological functioning" (35, italics mine). This suggests that virtues are more than simply biological, so biological science or ethology does not *fully* justify a *complete* account of virtue. He continues, "the pluralistic teleological account is *consistent* with scientific naturalism and the naturalistic premise. Its justification, content, and application *do not involve non-natural properties or supernatural phenomena*" (36, italics mine). So the full position seems to be that the pluralistic teleological account is grounded in naturalism, including scientific naturalism and biological naturalism; but that, insofar as it is ethical, it goes beyond the scientific and bio-logical in describing "ethical naturalism," which seems to be a "natural" account of ethics absent "non-natural" or "supernatural" phenomena. Those familiar with debates in environmental philosophy will note a contentious point here. What counts as "natural"? As "supernatural"? Is "culture" natural? Sandler seems to sug-gest so, but without any further discussion. However, we seem to make meaningful distinctions between nature and culture, and not all of these are explainable by an unjustifiable nature/culture dualism. Sandler also mentions genetic engineering and nanotechnology as new frontiers for ethics. Are these technologies, and the transformations they are capable of working on the world and on us, natural? If we use these new technologies to modify human nature, at some point, arguably, we become post-human. Of course, such an outcome is entirely consistent with a certain reading of naturalism, but it might suggest that such manipulations are not part of *human* flourishing and virtue.

18. Sandler, *Character and Environment*, 22.

19. Ibid., 26–28.

20. Ibid., 28.

21. "Primary" in several senses: as "originally," as "most commonly," and, perhaps, as "most importantly."

22. Martha Nussbaum develops a similar claim with respect to the moral achievement of certain literary images: "it is relevant that his image [itself a 'moral accomplishment' for Nussbaum] was not a flat thing but a fine work of art; the 'tone' and 'color' of the language and image matter and are in fact inseparable from the image and, thus, from the moral accomplishment" (Martha Nussbaum, "Finely

Aware and Richly Responsible: Literature and the Moral Imagination" in *Love's Knowledge* [Oxford: Oxford University Press, 1990], 150–155).

23. Aristotle, *Nicomachean Ethics*, 24.

24. Ibid., 16.

25. Engaging environmental virtue ethics, and environmental ethics more broadly, this account has been and will continue to focus on naturalism as an important constraint on the sorts of things we can say about living well as the types of beings that we are. However, this is not to discount "non-naturalistic," "trans-naturalistic," "hyper-naturalistic," or "hypo-naturalistic" constraints—that is to say, constraints not reducible to pure biology, material causality, and so on—regarding what would count as living well as the type of beings that we are. Indeed, the narrative approach to virtue ethics strongly suggests that a narrowly naturalistic approach to flourishing or virtue will miss, by a wide margin, what it aims at explaining. Thus, for the present I am leaving open the possibility of, for example, spiritual, religious, or other components of teleology.

26. MacIntyre, *After Virtue*, 52.

27. Jean Paul Sartre, *Existentialism and Human Emotions*, trans. Bernard Frechtman (New York: Citadel Books, 1985), 13. Also see, MacIntyre, *After Virtue*, 1–61.

28. MacIntyre, *After Virtue*, 55.

29. Ibid., 57–59.

30. Charles Taylor, "Responsibility for the Self" in *The Identities of Persons*, ed. Amelie Oksenberg Rorty (Berkeley, CA: University of California Press, 1976), 281.

31. MacIntyre, *After Virtue*, 58–59.

32. Alasdair MacIntyre, *Dependent Rational Animals: Why Human Beings Need the Virtues* (Chicago: Open Court, 1999), x.

33. At this stage, we need not specify the distinctively human function or functions, but merely point out that it makes sense to speak of it or them. My concern here is not to give an account of the human *telos*, or to argue whether or not it is structured by our biology, our rationality, transcendent concerns, or other specific criteria. However, I do maintain that a full accounting of the human *telos* cannot be fully captured by a strictly scientific approach.

34. Thus, this section offers "a" typology of virtue rather than "the" typology of virtue. For example, it would be appropriate, and illuminating, to differentiate virtues and analyze them on the basis of whether they are eudaimonistic or non-eudaimonistic. On such an alternative typology my "individual" virtues would all be eudaimonistic, but my "social" and "environmental" virtues would fall partly into eudaimonistic and partly into non-eudaimonistic categories.

35. See Gambrel and Cafaro: "It is necessary to distinguish individual, social, and ecological flourishing for analytic purposes. But in our opinion, all three are so supremely valuable and intimately related that no human character trait that undermines any one of these counts as a genuine virtue." (Gambrel and Cafaro, "The Virtue of Simplicity," 87). Also see my "Environmentalism and Public Virtue" on the necessary but limited usefulness of distinguishing between different types of virtue ("Environmentalism and Public Virtue" in the *Journal of Agricultural and Environmental Ethics*, vol. 23, no. 1, [2010]).

36. Of course, in a broader, more general sense, all virtues "benefit" the individual insofar as virtues help us to live a good life and living a good life is what we ought to do. Thus, the virtues we might classify as "social" or "environmental" also benefit the individual to some degree. However, the "individual" virtues are characterized by their self-reflexive aim; the intention of these virtues is to benefit the individual. Frugality, for example, may benefit society and may benefit the environment, but its aim is to benefit the frugal agent.

37. Technically speaking, the temperate person (who is virtuous) no longer requires much self-control, though self-control is critical for those who aspire to virtue. If one is virtuous one has, presumably, already made a habit of right desire and right action. In the case of temperance, a virtuous person will have already developed the habit of healthy and moderate eating and will no longer be seriously tempted—and may be actually repulsed—by the thought of, for example, fast "food." See book VII of the *Nicomachean Ethics*.

38. See, for example, the FAO statistical division's global map, which puts North American Average calorie consumption at above 3,700 calories per day for years 2005–2007, accessed May 26, 2011. <http://www.fao.org/fileadmin/templates/ess/ess_test_folder/Publications/yearbook_2010/maps/map07.pdf>. Note, however, that some other estimates of American consumption are lower. Also see the second chapter of The United States Department of Agriculture: Center for Nutrition Policy and Promotion, *The Dietary Guidelines for Americans, 2010* (Policy Document, Released 1/31/11) accessed on May 26, 2011, <http://www.cnpp.usda.gov/DGAs2010-PolicyDocument.htm>.

39. MMWR Weekly, February 6, 2004 / 53(04), 80–82, accessed April 25, 2012, <http://www.cdc.gov/mmwr/preview/mmwrhtml/mm5304a3.htm>. In addition see: (1) The United States Department of Agriculture: Center for Nutrition Policy and Promotion, *The Dietary Guidelines for Americans, 2010* (Policy Document, Released 1/31/11), 10, accessed on May 26, 2011, <http://www.cnpp.usda.gov/DGAs2010-PolicyDocument.htm>; and (2) the Center for Disease Control *Overweight and Obesity Data and Statistics*, accessed May 25, 2012, <http://www.cdc.gov/obesity/data/index.html>.

40. True, some people might be motivated to specific kinds of temperance for social or environmental reasons. One might, of course, become a vegetarian for environmental reasons. Take, for example, the temperance evident in Doris Janzen Longacre's *More-with-Less Cookbook* (Scottdale, PA: Herald Press, 1976) and its sequel, *Living More with Less* (Scottdale, PA: Herald Press, 1980) which is clearly motivated by religious, social, environmental, and individual reasons. Nevertheless, temperance writ large—as opposed to temperance focused on food resources—still seems to *emphasize* the individual. After all, it's hard to imagine what social or environmental harms might result from an intemperate and excessive obsession with sex—assuming for the moment that there is no abuse, no children result from the activity, and so on.

41. Sandler helpfully points out that virtues may qualify as environmental by being environmentally responsive (responding to some environmental entity), environmentally justified (justified by environmental considerations), or environmen-

tally productive (promoting an environmental good or value (Sandler, *Character and Environment*, 42). For an interesting argument against the notion that ecosystems are proper objects of ethical concern, see Sandler, *Character and Environment*, 78.

42. Louke van Wensveen, *Dirty Virtues*, 163. This list is certainly not exhaustive, as *Dirty Virtues* was written over a decade ago.

43. See Jacques Derrida, *The Animal That Therefore I Am*, trans. David Willis (New York: Fordham University Press, 2008), Leonard Lawlor, *This is Not Sufficient* (New York: Columbia University Press, 2007); Jean-Christophe Bailly's *The Animal Side*, trans. Catherine Porter (New York: Fordham University Press, 2011); Kelly Oliver's *Animal Lessons* (New York: Columbia University Press, 2009); and Donna Haraway's *When Species Meet (Posthumanities)* (Minneapolis, MN: University of Minnesota Press, 2007).

Chapter 4

1. Gambrel and Cafaro, for example, treat simplicity in material terms (Joshua Colt Gambrel and Philip Cafaro, "The Virtue of Simplicity" in *The Journal of Agricultural and Environmental Ethics*, vol. 23, no. 1–2 [2010]). In the case of Cafaro and Gambrel this is certainly a concession to the limits of space, as Cafaro is an authority on Henry David Thoreau and knows, as well as anyone, that simplicity has non-material manifestations. See Cafaro's excellent *Thoreau's Living Ethics: Walden and the Pursuit of Virtue* (University of Georgia Press, 2006).

2. Phil Cafaro makes the best and most comprehensive argument that Thoreau was in fact a sort of virtue ethicist. This is not to say that Thoreau's own account of simplicity is the one we should take as a model of virtue—though we could surely do worse—but to point out that the virtue of simplicity is much wider in scope than is suggested by rather narrow application it receives in the popular imagination.

3. Phil Cafaro, *Thoreau's Living Ethics: Walden and the Pursuit of Virtue* (University of Georgia Press, 2006).

4. Henry David Thoreau, *Walden* (Princeton, NJ: Princeton University Press, 2004), 291. There are many other passages that suggest a tendency toward something like a virtue ethics. For example, Thoreau suggests that one of the benefits of reading the classics well is that we are bid to "emulate [our] heroes" (Ibid., 100), which can become a noble or moral exercise.

5. Thoreau, *Walden*, 291.

6. Ibid., 315.

7. Henry David Thoreau, "Life Without Principle" in *The Higher Law*, ed. Wendell Glick (Princeton: Princeton University Press, 1973), 156. Emphasis mine.

8. Joseph Wood Krutch, "Introduction to Life Without Principle" *Walden and Other Writings*, ed. Joseph Wood Krutch (New York: Bantam Books, 1981), 353.

9. Thoreau, *Walden*, 31.

10. Ibid., 5.

11. Thoreau, "Life Without Principle," 156.

12. Ibid., 160. Though Thoreau does not use the term "vocation," this is clearly what he has in mind.

13. Thoreau, "Life Without Principle," 158.

14. Thoreau, *Walden*, 90–91.

15. Ibid., 157.

16. Ibid., 160.

17. There are many excellent examples of this in recent literature. For example, James Gleick, *Faster* (New York: Vintage, 2000) and Madeline Bunting, *Willing Slaves* (New York: HarperCollins, 2005).

18. Thoreau, "Life Without Principle," 156.

19. Thoreau, *Walden*, 8. The very word "pastime" is indicative of the folly such activities represent. We do not need to "pass time," or worse, to "kill time." *Tempus fugit.* Time will pass and die quickly enough on its own and we should cherish the time we have rather than rushing through every moment, unable or unwilling to slow down.

20. Thoreau, "Life Without Principle," 160.

21. "I went to the woods because I wished to live deliberately, to front only the essential facts of life, and see if I could not learn what it had to teach, and not, when I came to die, discover that I had not lived" (Thoreau, *Walden*, 90).

22. Thoreau, *Walden*, 6.

23. Ibid., 10.

24. Ibid., 15.

25. For a complete version of this argument, see my "The Virtue of Simplicity: Reading Thoreau with Aristotle" in *The Concord Saunterer*, vol. 15, 2007.

26. Thoreau, "Life Without Principle," 171.

27. Ibid., 173.

28. Ibid., 171–173. This is only one of several places where Thoreau seems to stress the importance of habituation, a central theme in most versions of virtue ethics.

29. Thoreau, *Walden*, 52.

30. Ibid. Of course, there are genuine advantages to remaining abreast of news that actually matters, that actually concerns one's well-being, and this could perhaps include news of the world; however, while there are virtues to a certain kind of cosmopolitanism, it can't be denied that the vast majority of information that passes for news has little or no bearing on those virtues and merely caters to a sort of globalized pool of gossip and trivia.

31. Ibid., 173.

32. Ibid., 92.

33. See Bill McKibben, *Deep Economy: The Wealth of Communities and the Durable Future* (New York: Holt, 2007), 10. And Benjamin Friedman, *The Moral Consequences of Economic Growth* (New York: Vintage, 2005), 12.

34. Ibid. Also see John McMillan, *Reinventing the Bazaar* (New York: W. W. Norton and Company, 2002), 7–8.

35. John Arlidge, "I'm Doing God's Work: Meet Mr. Goldman Sachs" in *The Sunday Times*, November 8, 2009.

36. Eric Lipton and Stephen Labaton, "Deregulator Looks Back, Unswayed" in the *New York Times*, November 16, 2008.

37. Robert Putnam, *Bowling Alone* (New York: Simon and Schuster, 2000); John De Graff, et al., *Affluenza: The All-Consuming Epidemic* (San Francisco, CA: Berrett-Koehler Publishers, Inc., 2005), 114–124; Richard Layard, *Happiness: Lessons from a New Science* (New York: Penguin Books, 2006); Robert H. Frank, *Luxury Fever: Money and Happiness in an Era of Excess* (Princeton, NJ: Princeton University Press, 1999); and Barry Schwartz, *The Paradox of Choice: Why More is Less* (New York: Harper Perennial, 2005).

38. McKibben, *Deep Economy*, 1.

39. Layard's *Happiness* suggests that more and better no longer come together after about $20,000 per person (34). McKibben's *Deep Economy* pegs it closer to $10,000 per person (41). Other studies do suggest a higher amount, and clearly the amount at which more not longer nets better will vary depending on a number of factors having to do with costs of living. Again, however, research shows that speaking in terms of absolute wealth, the main point is having sufficient resources to secure the *basic* goods of life: food, clothing, shelter, security, modest luxuries, and so on.

40. This sentiment has, I am sure, been expressed earlier, elsewhere, and better; however, having recalled and paraphrased it from the depths of memory, I cannot say where or by whom. We should also note that there are still many people in the world for whom the problem of basic resources has not been answered, for whom the birds of More and Better still share a roost. Nevertheless, for most, perhaps all, readers of this book, the case is otherwise.

41. Layard, *Happiness*, 41.

42. De Graff, et al., *Affluenza*, 29.

43. Layard, *Happiness*, 53.

44. Pete Engardio, "Nice Dream If You Can Live It," *Business Week*, September 13, 2004.

45. Layard, *Happiness*, 48 ff.

46. Ibid., 48–53.

47. Organization for Economic Co-operation and Development statistics, accessed May 26, 2012, <http://stats.oecd.org/Index.aspx?DatasetCode=ANHRS>.

48. Layard, *Happiness*, 29; McKibben, *Deep Economy*, 32.

49. "Video Consumer Mapping Study" undertaken by Ball State University, accessed on April 25, 2012, <http://www.researchexcellence.com/vcmstudy.php>.

50. Bill McKibben, *The Age of Missing Information* (New York: Random House, 1992).

51. Thanks are due to the students of my environmental philosophy class for alerting me to a number of these cultural "treasures."

52. McKibben, *The Age of Missing Information*, 75.

53. Ibid., 159.

54. De Graff, et al., *Affluenza*, 14 and The Nielsen Company blog (the data are from 2009): <http://blog.nielsen.com/nielsenwire/online_mobile/americans-watching-more-tv-than-ever/>.

55. Ibid., 55.

56. Ibid., 14.

57. Ibid., 61 (and elsewhere).

58. Ibid., 20.

59. Ibid.

60. Mary Oliver, "The Summer Day" in *The Truro Bear and Other Adventures: Poems and Essays* (Boston: Beacon Press, 2008).

61. Jacob S. Hacker and Paul Pierson, *Winner Take All Politics: How Washington Made the Rich Richer—And Turned Its Back on the Middle Class* (New York: Simon and Schuster, 2010), 4. Also see Chapter 3.

62. In an interview in *Women's Own* magazine, October 31, 1987, which was widely reported and cited thereafter.

63. McKibben, *Deep Economy*, 98. See also Edward N. Luttwak, et al., *Turbo-Capitalism: Winners and Losers in the Global Economy* (New York: Harper, 2000).

64. De Graff, et al., *Affluenza*, 52.

65. Adam Smith, *The Theory of Moral Sentiments* (Greensborough, NC: Empire, 2011), IV.I.10. Also see Adam Smith, *The Wealth of Nations* (New York: Penguin, 2000). See, alongside Smith, Garrett Hardin's influential "The Tragedy of the Commons," *Science* 162 (3859): 1243–1248. As I note to students when covering these issues, the tragedy of the commons suggests that, while there may well be an invisible hand at work, it could be that it is making a rude gesture at us.

66. McKibben, *Deep Economy*, 103.

67. Ibid., 11. And Heather Boushey and Christian E. Weller, "What the Numbers Tell Us" in *Inequality Matters*, eds. James Lardner and David A. Smith, (New York: New Press, 2005), 36; and David Cay Johnston, "The Great Tax Shift," in *Inequality Matters*, eds. James Lardner and David A. Smith, (New York: New Press, 2005), 167.

68. De Graff, et al., *Affluenza*, 42.

69. Bertrand Russell, *In Praise of Idleness* (London: Routledge, 1935).

70. De Graff, et al., *Affluenza*, 41.

71. Ibid., 144.

72. Ibid.

73. McKibben, *Deep Economy*, 115–116.

74. De Graff, et al., *Affluenza*, 144–145.

75. Robert Putnam, *Bowling Alone* (New York: Simon and Schuster, 2000).

76. Dr. Seuss's *The Lorax* (New York: Random House Books for Young Readers, 1971), which has now been turned into a movie (*The Lorax* 2012) that seems strangely, if not surprisingly, antithetical to the book, insofar as it distinguishes itself primarily though its appalling number of product tie-ins and sales pitches.

77. Carlo Petrini, *Slow Food Nation: Why Our Food Should be Good, Clean, and Fair*, trans. Clara Furlan and Jonathan Hunt (New York: Random House), 8–9.

78. McKibben, *Deep Economy*, 65.

79. Ibid., 64–65.

80. Ibid., 100.

81. See, for example, Mathis Wackernagel and William Rees, *Our Ecological Footprint: Reducing Human Impact on Earth* (New Society Press, 1996).

82. The Center for Sustainable Economy Ecological Footprint, accessed April 30, 2012, <www.myfootprint.org/en/about_the_quiz/what_it_measures/>.

83. Canadian Living Planet Report 2007, a publication of the World Wildlife Fund, accessed April 30, 2012, <http://assets.wwf.ca/downloads/canadianlivingplanetreport2007.pdf>.

84. Gay Daly, "Bad Chemistry" in *On Earth Magazine*, published by the National Resources Defense Council, accessed April 30, 2012, <http://www.nrdc.org/onearth/06win/chem1.asp>. While specific numbers do vary, concerns similar to those raised in this paragraph are documented by the State of California (<http://www.dtsc.ca.gov/assessingrisk/emergingcontaminants.cfm>) and the Environmental Working Group (<http://www.ewg.org/about>), among many others.

85. Ann Misch, "Assessing Environmental Health Risks" in *Environmental Ethics: Concepts, Policy, Theory*, ed. Joseph DesJardins, (London: Mayfield Publishing Co., 1999), 262–278. See also De Graff, et al., *Affluenza*, 102, and Sandra Steingraber, *Living Downstream: An Ecologist Looks at Cancer and the Environment* (Reading, MA: Addison-Wesley, 1997).

86. Edward A. G. Schuur, et al., *"Vulnerability of Permafrost Carbon to Climate Change: Implications for the Global Carbon Cycle"* in *BioScience* 58(8): 701–714.

87. Megan C. Guilford, et al. "A New Long Term Assessment of Energy Return on Investment (EROI) for U.S. Oil and Gas Discovery and Production" in *Sustainability* (2011), vol. 3, accessed on April 26, 2012, <http://www.mdpi.com/2071-1050/3/10/1866/pdf>.

88. David J. Murphy and Charles A. S. Hall, "Year in review—EROI or energy return on (energy) invested" in *Annals of the New York Academy of Sciences*, vol. 1185, Ecological Economics Reviews, 102–118 (January 2010). Note that nuclear, often offered as a sort of saving grace with respect to energy and climate change, only offers an EROI of 5–15:1. Coal is 80:1 and therefore outcompetes many renewables, though where hydropower is available it can exceed 100:1. Of course, there are other environmental and social consequences to nuclear, coal, hydropower, and most any other energy source. EROI is only one very specific sort of measure: efficiency at converting energy to more energy.

89. Cafaro, *Thoreau's Living Ethics*, 10.

90. Ibid., 11.

91. Ibid., 12.

92. Thoreau, *Walden*, 99–110.

93. Ibid., 51–52.

94. Ibid., 101.

95. Ibid., 102.

96. Ibid., 51.

97. Ralph Waldo Emerson, "The American Scholar" in *Ralph Waldo Emerson: Essays and Lectures* (New York: The Library of America, 1983), 57. He continues, "books are the best things, well used; abused, among the worst" (Ibid.).

98. Thoreau, *Walden*, 108. Or, as Franz Kafka wrote in a letter to Oskar Pollak dated January 27, 1904: "We need the books that affect us like disaster, that grieve us deeply, like the death of someone we loved more than ourselves, like being banished into forests far from everyone, like a suicide. A book must be the axe for the frozen sea inside us" (Languagehat.com, accessed on April 30, 2012, <http://www.langaugehat.com/archives/001062.php>).

99. Ibid., 100. For more on emulation as mimicry versus emulation as inspiration, see Chapter 7 below.

Chapter 5

1. Aristotle, *Nicomachean Ethics*, trans. David Ross (Oxford: Oxford University Press, 1980), 3.

2. "But up to what point and to what extent a man must deviate before he becomes blameworthy is not easy to determine by reason, any more than anything else that is perceived by the senses; such things depend on particular facts, and the decision rests with perception" (Aristotle, *Nicomachean Ethics*, 47).

3. Aristotle, *Nicomachean Ethics*, 37.

4. There are other components to Aristotle's rejoinder to relativism, including his teleological and metaphysical biology. While the contemporary understanding of evolution, biology, and ecology dismisses the idea of a purposive teleology to nature, Aristotle's position has something in common with contemporary naturalistic approaches to virtue ethics insofar as they both limit the scope of possible accounts by insisting that they conform to facts about the type of natural creatures that we are.

5. Aristotle, *Nicomachean Ethics*, 5 and 15, respectively.

6. Ibid., 15–16. He also asserts the importance of having been brought up well, which certainly includes, among other things, being a free citizen of Athens (Ibid., 5).

7. Ibid., 142. Nussbaum points out that, in other places, Aristotle seems more circumspect with respect to the evolution of culture and ethics.

8. One might object to the current government in China, or express a distaste for Chinese food, or concern with population growth and resource use in China; however, none of these objections or opinions are tied—outside of the rubric of relatively uncommon racist discourse—to something fundamentally deficient in the difference.

9. It's true that a reasonable critique can be made of an idealistic caricature of Japanese virtue in the wake of the disaster, insofar as there were in fact instances of people *in extremis* taking things without paying and salvaging things that were not theirs. It's also true that it's fairly easy to document similar behaviors being labeled as "looting" when conducted by African-American people and "foraging" or "surviving" when conducted by others in the wake of, for example, hurricane Katrina. However, in spite of these legitimate critiques, it's also reasonable and

appropriate to point out the admirable community resilience of Japanese culture and the relative absence of vicious opportunism seen in the wake of other disasters.

10. *The Los Angeles Almanac*, accessed April 30, 2012, <http://www.laalmanac.com/LA/la10b.htm>.

11. "Of the world's 100 largest economic entities, 51 are now corporations and 49 are countries," compiled by Sarah Anderson and John Cavanagh of the *Institute for Policy Studies*, accessed May 1, 2012, <http://www.corporations.org/system/top100.html>.

12. McDonald's Canada, accessed March 20, 2011, <http://www.mcdonalds.ca/en/aboutus/faq.aspx>. The main site for McDonald's has slightly different information. See McDonald's, accessed March 20, 2011, <http://www.aboutmcdonalds.com/mcd/our_company.html>.

13. Jean-Francois Lyotard, *The Postmodern Condition: A Report on Knowledge*, trans. Geoff Bennington and Brian Massumi (Minneapolis, MN: The University of Minnesota Press, 1984), xxiv–xxv.

14. John D. Caputo, *More Radical Hermeneutics* (Bloomington and Indianapolis, IN: Indiana University Press, 2000), 182.

15. Ibid.

16. See Martin Heidegger, *Being and Time*, trans. John Macquarrie and Edward Robinson (New York: Harper and Row, 1962); Hans-Georg Gadamer, *Truth and Method*, trans. Joel Weinsheimer and Donald G. Marshall (London: Continuum, 2003); and Paul Ricoeur, *Oneself as Another*, trans. Kathleen Blamey (Chicago: University of Chicago, 1992).

17. Caputo, *More Radical Hermeneutics*, 1. Note, however, that one can maintain that the hermeneutic circle is inescapable with asserting that there is no absolute Truth or System. See, among other examples, the work of Merold Westphal. In an interview with B. Keith Putt, Westphal is asked, if there "*is* a metanarrative." He responds, "Yes. There is truth with a capital 'T,' but our truth is truth with a small 't.'" For Westphal, this is because "the world is a system for God, but not for us" ("Talking to Balaam's Ass: A Concluding Conversation" in *Gazing Through a Prism Darkly: Reflections on Merold Westphal's Hermeneutical Epistemology*, ed. B. Keith Putt [New York: Fordham University Press, 2009], 184).

18. Ibid.

19. Alasdair MacIntyre, *After Virtue* (Notre Dame, IN: University of Notre Dame Press, 1984), 190.

20. I won't, here, try to pin this position to any particular thinker. I've addressed at length the degree to which philosophical postmodernity, in the form of deconstruction, at least flirts with this sort of relativism. Though my position on this matter has evolved somewhat, see my *Aspects of Alterity* (New York: Fordham University Press, 2006). However, whether or not deconstruction is itself guilty of relativism, and of what stripe, it remains the case that a large number of people flirt with this possibility.

21. MacIntyre, *After Virtue*, 11–12.

22. William James, *The Will to Believe* (New York: Dover, 1987), 18–19.

23. Ibid., 18. Of course, James also suggests that the tendency to seek truth or avoid error is a fundamentally dispositional one. Thus, just as some people are "tough minded" and others are "tender minded," some people fear error and others desire truth. In either case, the point is not to choose one of the extremes, as if being tough-minded or desiring the truth are entirely unproblematic. The soundest approach is no doubt a blend of these positions.

24. Richard Kearney, *The God Who May Be: A Hermeneutics of Religion* (Bloomington, IN: Indiana University Press, 2001), 48. See also my "Blessed are Those Who Have Not Seen and Yet Believe" in *Analecta Hermeneutica*, vol. 2, 2010, and "The Anatheistic Wager: faith after Faith" in *Religion and the Arts* vol. 14 (2010).

25. Richard Kearney, *On Stories* (London and New York: Routledge, 2002), 149 (citing Julian Barnes's *History of the World in 10 and a Half Chapters*).

26. For example: Martha Nussbaum, "Non-Relative Virtues: An Aristotelian Approach" in *The Quality of Life*, eds. Martha Nussbaum and Amartya Sen (Oxford: Clarendon Press, 1993), 242–269.

27. Ibid., 243.

28. Ibid. Emphasis mine.

29. Ibid., 246. Note that "objective" here is to be taken in the manner in which she uses the term in her essay "Non-Relative Virtues."

30. See, for example, *The Quality of Life*, eds. Martha Nussbaum and Amartya Sen (Oxford: Oxford University Press, 1993); Martha Nussbaum, *Creating Capabilities: The Human Development Approach* (Cambridge, MA: The Belknap Press, 2011); and Amartya Sen, *Development as Freedom* (New York: Anchor, 2000).

31. Martha Nussbaum, *Women and Human Development: The Capabilities Approach* (Cambridge: Cambridge University Press, 2001), 5.

32. Ibid., 78–80 and Martha Nussbaum, *Creating Capabilities*, 33–34. Also see *The Quality of Life*, eds. Martha Nussbaum and Amartya Sen (Oxford: Clarendon Press, 1993).

33. Nussbaum, "Non-Relative Virtues," 251.

34. Ibid., 260.

35. Ibid., 261.

36. Ronald Sandler, *Character and Environment: A Virtue-Oriented Approach to Environmental Ethics* (New York: Columbia University Press, 2007), 32.

37. Ibid.

38. Ibid.

39. Ibid., 109.

40. Ibid., 14. Emphasis mine. Note that this qualification neatly sidesteps any clumsy implication of the naturalistic fallacy. On Sandler's account—and certainly on mine—a trait is not good simply because it seems to be natural. We don't want to fall into the trap of suggesting that, because humans have some natural tendency toward violence, or xenophobia, or gluttony, or polygamy, that these are traits that should be encouraged or which contribute to flourishing in our contemporary lives. Just because virtues are related to an understanding of the "type of being" that we are does not mean that we should just accept the type of being that we are, as

should be evident from MacIntyre's distinction between "humans as they are" and "humans as they ought to be."

41. MacIntyre, *After Virtue*, 258. Emphasis mine.

42. Alasdair MacIntyre, *Whose Justice? Which Rationality?* (Notre Dame, IN: The University of Notre Dame Press, 1988); and "Moral Relativism, Truth and Justification" in *The MacIntyre Reader*, ed. Kelvin Knight (Notre Dame, IN: The University of Notre Dame Press, 1998), 202–220.

43. MacIntyre, "Moral Justice, Truth and Justification," 202.

44. Ibid., 207. See also, "The concept of warranted assertibility always has application only at some particular time and place in respect of standards then prevailing at some particular stage in the development of a tradition of inquiry, and a claim that such and such is warrantedly assertible always, therefore, has to make implicit or explicit references to such times and places. The concept of truth, however, is timeless" (MacIntyre, *Whose Justice? Which Rationality?*, 363).

45. MacIntyre, "Moral Justice, Truth and Justification," 208.

46. MacIntyre, *Whose Justice? Which Rationality?*, 166.

47. Ibid., 166–167.

48. MacIntyre, "Moral Justice, Truth and Justification," 219.

49. MacIntyre, *Whose Justice? Which Rationality?*, 167.

50. MacIntyre, "Moral Justice, Truth and Justification," 219.

Chapter 6

1. One place we can find a long-standing association between narrative and ethics is in various religious traditions, where didactic stories, metaphors, parables, and the like are very common indeed.

2. Plato, *Phaedrus* in *The Collected Dialogues of Plato*, eds. Edith Hamilton and Huntington Cairns (Princeton, NJ: Princeton University Press, 1989), 478 (230a).

3. Paul Ricoeur, *Oneself as Another*, trans. Kathleen Blamey (Chicago: The University of Chicago Press, 1992); *Time and Narrative* vol. 1, trans. Kathleen McLaughlin and David Pellauer (Chicago: The University of Chicago Press, 1984); *Time and Narrative* vol. 2, trans. Kathleen McLaughlin and David Pellauer (Chicago: The University of Chicago Press, 1985); and *Time and Narrative* vol. 3, trans. Kathleen Blamey and David Pellauer (Chicago: The University of Chicago Press, 1988).

4. Ricoeur, *Oneself as Another*, 115–116.

5. Paul Ricoeur, *Time and Narrative*, vol. 3, 246. Richard Kearney, Ricoeur's student and friend, puts it this way: "Telling stories is as basic to human beings as eating. More so, in fact, for while food makes us live, stories are what make our lives worth living. They are what make our condition *human*" (Richard Kearney, *On Stories* [London: Routledge, 2002], 3). Kearney goes on to point out that stories make reality shareable—implying that they are therefore essentially ethically loaded, dealing as they do with intersubjective discourse—and that they humanize time, making it memorable on the most basic level.

6. Ricoeur, *Oneself as Another*, 2–3.

7. Ibid., 118ff.

8. Ibid., 121. However, character is never fixed absolutely for Ricoeur, who suggests the key to forgiveness is the assertion that "you [the one being forgiven] are more than your actions." Also see below on the ability of narration to "redeploy" what character has sedimented.

9. Ibid., 122.

10. Ibid. On this point I believe Ricoeur is indebted to his friend Gabriel Marcel. See Gabriel Marcel, *Creative Fidelity*, trans. Robert Rosthal (New York: Farrar, Strauss, and Company, 1964).

11. Paul Ricoeur, "Narrative Identity," in David Wood, *On Paul Ricoeur: Narrative and Interpretation* (London and New York: Routledge, 1991), 188. It is for this reason that Ricoeur suggests that the essence of forgiveness is to treat someone as if she is "more than her actions," freeing her to shape her narrative in a way that, if it remains constrained by prior acts, is not fully determined by them.

12. Ricoeur, *Oneself as Another*, 122.

13. Ricoeur, *Time and Narrative*, vol. 3, 246.

14. Rainer Maria Rilke, "Archaic Torso of Apollo" in *The Selected Poetry of Rainer Maria Rilke*, trans. and ed. Stephen Mitchell (New York: Vintage, 1989), 61.

15. Ricoeur, *Oneself as Another*, 170.

16. Ibid., 114–115.

17. Paul Ricoeur, *Time and Narrative*, vol. 1, 55.

18. Ibid., 58.

19. Ibid., 59.

20. Ibid., 65–66.

21. Ibid., 77. *Finnegan's Wake* would be an even more apt example.

22. Ibid., 71. See Nussbaum *Poetic Justice*, 7 on the distinction between the world of the novel, the world of the authorial voice, and the world of the reader. The first distinction between the world of the novel and the world of the author could help to explain why we sometimes think it important to understand the context in which the text was written, not just the context in which it is read. It enriches a reading of *Ulysses* to know something of Dublin, the Catholic Church, Joyce himself, and so on.

23. Wayne Booth, *The Company We Keep: An Ethics of Fiction* (Berkeley, CA: University of California Press, 1988), 231.

24. Among many possible examples, see Plato, *The Republic* in *The Collected Dialogues of Plato*, eds. Edith Hamilton and Huntington Cairns (Princeton, NJ: Princeton University Press, 1989). Though, of course, Plato employs many myths himself in the course of his dialogues: the Allegory of the Cave and the myth of Er in the *Republic*, the hollow world in the *Phaedo*, and the like).

25. Jack Turner, *The Abstract Wild* (Tucson: The University of Arizona Press, 1996), 36. People flocked to the Sierras and other natural sites in the wake of Muir's writing, but they did not "hear the trees speak," that is to say they did not

experience the same reverence for the natural world that Muir did. Moreover, in popularizing Yosemite Muir arguably merely altered the method of its degradation—that is, from conscious exploitation by logging to unconscious exploitation and degradation from overuse.

26. Ibid., 33.

27. Paul Ricoeur, "Life in Quest of Narrative" in *On Paul Ricoeur: Narrative and Interpretation*, ed. David Wood (London: Routledge, 1992), 20.

28. Kearney, *On Stories*, 134.

29. Turner, *The Abstract Wild*, 25. Though, drawing on Augustine, Caputo reverses this relationship: "We usually think that we first have to get to know something or someone in order subsequently to get to love them. But one of the great lessons of St. Augustine's writings is that it is love that drives our search to know" (John D. Caputo, *On Religion* [London: Routledge, 2001], 30).

30. Turner seems to be in good company here, insofar as there are common-sense reasons to suppose that those without personal experience of a phenomenon cannot really understand or appreciate it. Hence, the arguments that only survivors, if anyone, can really speak of the Holocaust. See some of the positions considered in Richard Kearney, "Narrative and the Ethics of Remembrance" in *Questioning Ethics: Contemporary Debates in Philosophy*, eds. Richard Kearney and Mark Dooley (London: Routledge, 1999), 18–32. For problems related to "the spirit of abstraction," see my "Constellations: Gabriel Marcel's Philosophy of Relative Otherness." *American Catholic Philosophical Quarterly*, vol. 80, no. 3, 2006.

31. Henry David Thoreau, *Walden* (Princeton: Princeton University Press, 1971), 3.

32. Thoreau, *Walden*, 300–301. Ultimately, such experience is thoroughly individual. Thus, when Thoreau meets John Field and seeks to help him "with [Thoreau's] experience," the help is ineffectual (Ibid., 451–452).

33. See Richard Louv, *Last Child in the Woods: Saving Our Children from Nature Deficit Disorder* (New York: Algonquin Books, 2008).

34. Clearly, another aspect of the response to this problem is to simply limit population growth, which would simultaneously help to preserve wilderness, allow a greater percentage of the population to experience it (and so cultivate the virtues associated with it), and address myriad other environmental issues caused or exacerbated by population growth.

35. Wallace Stegner, "Crossing into Eden" in *Where the Bluebird Sings to the Lemonade Springs* (New York: The Modern Library, 2002), 40.

36. Aristotle, *Nicomachean Ethics*, trans. David Ross (Oxford: Oxford University Press, 1980), 87.

37. One might argue whether *magnificence* and *liberality* are really two different virtues or if, rather, they are the exact same virtue applied in slightly different spheres. The liberal person is virtuously generous with her wealth, whether that wealth is great or small. The magnificent person seems to be practicing the very same virtue, with the exception that her spending of money takes place on a grand scale. But is there really a significant difference in *the character trait* of the person

who gives ten percent of her $25,000 salary to improve her community and the person who gives ten percent of her $250,000 salary? There is certainly a difference in benefit to the community; but that there is a philosophically significant difference in the virtue of these two givers is less clear.

38. "Nature" here being used to mean nature as it is often traditionally construed in the United States—wilderness, National Parks, Big Sky country, and so on. Of course, without collapsing the distinctions between the wild, the rural, the suburban, and the urban, "nature" exists in suburban and urban environments as well, allowing for the cultivation of certain environmental virtues in those places. See my "Environmental Virtue and Public Virtue" in *Journal of Agricultural and Environmental Ethics*, vol. 23, no. 1, (2010).

39. Aristotle, *Nicomachean Ethics*, 3.

40. Ibid., 159–191. The rule could just as well be provided by a tradition, which has identified certain virtuous ways of being based on a long history of trial and error.

41. Ibid., 29.

42. On the nature of this particular chicken/egg problem, see Aristotle, *Nicomachean Ethics*, 28–29 and 34–35.

43. Ricoeur, *Time and Narrative*, vol. 1, 59.

44. Ibid. Strictly speaking, Ricoeur says this of action; but his definition of narrative is based in *mimesis* as an imitation of action. Also see Nussbaum, *Poetic Justice* (Boston: Beacon Press, 1995), 1–2. All novels are normative.

45. Richard Kearney, *Paul Ricoeur: The Owl of Minerva* (London: Ashgate, 2004), 114. Achilles, Socrates, and St. Francis are Kearney's examples. Thoreau and Leopold are offered as exemplars of their respective virtues by Phil Cafaro in "Thoreau, Leopold, and Carson: Toward an Environmental Virtue Ethics" in *Environmental Virtue Ethics*, eds. Ronald Sandler and Philip Cafaro (New York: Rowman and Littlefield, 2005), 31–44. I offer Muir as a further example. See my *"Phronesis* Without a *Phronimos*: Narrative Environmental Virtue Ethics" in *Environmental Ethics*, vol. 30, no. 4, 2008.

46. Kearney, *Paul Ricoeur: The Owl of Minerva*, 114. See also Paul Ricoeur, "Life in Quest of Narrative" in *On Paul Ricoeur: Narrative and Interpretation*, ed. David Wood (London: Routledge, 1994). Virtue ethics recommends itself, in part, because of its sensitivity to particular contexts, while deontology and utilitarianism both, to some extent, remain caught up in the attempt to generate and clarify universal rules. However, insofar as this is a strength of virtue ethics, it is a strength that is utterly dependent on narrative, for it is precisely through narratives—the thin narratives of examples or the thick narratives of literature—that virtue ethics does connect with the context of concrete and particular reality.

47. Kearney, *On Stories*, 25. He is referring here to the use of narrative as part of the "talking cure" of psychoanalysis.

48. Dermot Healy, *The Bend for Home* (London: The Harvill Press, 1996), 57. Cited in Kearney, *On Stories*, 25–26.

49. Jeffrey Meyers, *Hemingway: A Biography* (Cambridge, MA: DeCapo Press, 1999), 138.

50. Said in conversation with Frank Budgen, Zurich, 1918, as told by Budgen in *James Joyce and the Making of "Ulysses"* (Oxford: Oxford University Press, 1989).

51. Marilynne Robinson, *Gilead* (New York: Picador, 2004), 91.

52. Kearney, *On Stories*, 19.

53. Emily Brady, "Imagination and Aesthetic Appreciation of Nature" in *The Journal of Aesthetics and Art Criticism*, vol. 56, no. 2 (Spring 1998): 143ff.

54. Ernest Hemingway, *A Farewell to Arms* (New York: Scribner Classics, 1997), 117.

55. John Updike, *Self-Consciousness: Memoirs* (Fawcett, 1989).

56. Mary Oliver, "Last Night the Rain Spoke to Me," in *What Do We Know: Poems and Prose Poems* (Cambridge, MA: Da Capo Press, 2002), 36–37.

57. Martha Nussbaum, *Love's Knowledge: Essays on Philosophy and Literature* (Oxford: Oxford University Press, 1990). See especially "Form and Content: Philosophy and Literature," 3–53.

58. Nussbaum, "Form and Content: Philosophy and Literature" in *Love's Knowledge: Essays on Philosophy and Literature* (Oxford: Oxford University Press, 1990), 5.

59. Ibid., 8. See here Kearney's criticism of Nussbaum's inattentiveness to the hermeneutics of suspicion, as well as my own concerns with her too-narrow emphasis on novels, and indeed a certain class of novels (on the latter, Ibid., 45ff.). Nussbaum argues against the "correct, scientific, abstract, hygienically pallid," form of much "analytic" philosophy, which is regarded as a kind of "all-purpose solvent" in which philosophical issues of any kind can be efficiently disentangled (Ibid., 19). She also dismisses deconstruction rather quickly (Ibid., 21).

60. Ibid., 14 and 26. Also see, among other examples, Plato's *Republic*, Sophocles's *Antigone*, etcetera.

61. Ibid., 45.

62. Ibid., 46.

63. See Martha Nussbaum, "Reading for Life" in *Love's Knowledge: Essays on Philosophy and Literature* (Oxford: Oxford University Press, 1990), 237–238.

64. Nussbaum, "Form and Content," 9.

65. Ibid.

66. A charge he also levels against Alasdair MacIntyre and Wayne Booth. See Kearney, *On Stories*, 83.

67. Friedrich Wilhelm Nietzsche, *Daybreak: Thoughts on the Prejudice of Morality*, trans. R. J. Hollingdale (Cambridge: Cambridge University Press, 1997), 5.

68. From Thoreau: "Nature and human life are as various as our several constitutions. Who shall say what prospect life offers to another?" (Thoreau, *Walden*, 10). Here I again hear the ruminations of John Ames in *Gilead*: "I have often thought about that very often—how the times change, and the same words that carry a good many people into the wilderness in one generation are irksome or meaningless to the next" (Marilynne Robinson, *Gilead* [New York: Picador, 2004], 176).

69. Nussbaum, "Form and Content," 47.

70. Ibid.

71. Ibid., 47–48.

72. Others have criticized the effect of her sustained focus on Greek tragedy and the fiction of Henry James on her conclusions. See Pamela M. Hall, "Limits of the Story: Tragedy in Recent Virtue Ethics" in *Studies in Christian Ethics* 17:1 (2004).

73. Martha Nussbaum, "Form and Content: Philosophy and Literature," especially 35–44. Also see "The Discernment of Perception: An Aristotelian Conception of Private and Public Rationality" in *Love's Knowledge* (Oxford: Oxford University Press, 1990), 54–105, as well as *The Fragility of Goodness* (Cambridge: Cambridge University Press, 1986), 290–317.

74. Nussbaum, "The Discernment of Perception," 63.

75. Aristotle, *Nicomachean Ethics*, 192.

76. Nussbaum, "Form and Content," 36.

77. Ibid. Emphasis mine.

78. For myself, I can say that I've harbored this suspicion on many occasions.

79. Nussbaum, "Form and Content," 37. When I lived in Japan, the *sensei* under whom I studied often suggested that the goal was to imitate in order to attain basic competence (what others may well have called mastery), after which it was finally permissible to innovate and make the practice one's own. Imitation was indeed a start, but the goal was assimilation and, then, cultivation and innovation. In a similar vein, my student James Costello pointed out to me that Clark Terry, one of Miles Davis's mentors, said "One must imitate, then assimilate, and this will ultimately lead to being able to innovate" (Scotty Barnhart, *The World of Jazz Trumpet: A Comprehensive History and Practical Philosophy* [Milwaukee: Hal Leonard Corporation 2005], 164).

80. Ibid., 38.

81. Ibid., 43–44 as well as *The Fragility of Goodness*, (Cambridge: Cambridge University Press, 1986).

82. Marcus Aurelius, *Meditations*, trans. Maxwell Staniforth (London: Penguin, 1964), 48.

83. See Gabriel Marcel, *Tragic Wisdom and Beyond*, trans. Stephen Jolin and Peter McCormick (Evanston, IL: Northwestern University Press, 1973). Or again, in "On the Ontological Mystery" he writes dismissively of thinking that "ignores the tragic" (*The Philosophy of Existentialism*, trans. Manya Harari [New York: Carol Publishing, 1995], 15). Finally, in *Creative Fidelity*: "Personally, I am inclined to deny that any work is philosophical if we cannot discern in it what may be called the sting of reality" (Gabriel Marcel, *Creative Fidelity*, 64). The recognition of the tragic aspects of life does not, for Marcel, preclude hope, and does not go so far as Iris Murdoch's famous, "Almost everything that consoles is a fake" (Iris Murdoch, *The Sovereignty of the Good* [London: Routledge, 1970], 59).

84. Nussbaum, "Form and Content," 40. Also see, more generally, *Poetic Justice*.

85. Nussbaum, *Poetic Justice*, 36.

86. Ibid., 5.

87. Ibid., 72 ff. Also see Adam Smith, *The Theory of Moral Sentiments* (New York: Empire Books, 2011).

88. Ibid., 73.

89. Ibid. Emphasis mine.

90. A similar balance between the objective, general, or disinterested and the particular, unique, and engaged is, arguably, at work in *phronesis*. So there is an important affinity between poetic catharsis, narrative imagination, and *phronesis*

91. Nussbaum, *Poetic Justice*, 27–28. Nussbaum also claims that the judicious spectator must go "beyond identification" to ask what is to be done, what is the most appropriate reaction (Ibid., 92). This, again, places her very close to Kearney, for whom the question of interpretation is always followed by the question of what is to be done. For Kearney and Ricoeur hermeneutics is deeply connection to action.

92. Kearney, *On Stories*, 138.

93. Nussbaum, *Poetic Justice*, 60 and 67.

94. On programmability, among many possible sources, see John D. Caputo, *The Prayers and Tears of Jacques Derrida: Religion without Religion* (Bloomington, IN: Indiana University Press, 1997).

95. Nussbaum, *Poetic Justice*, 8.

96. Ibid.

97. In Nussbaum, *Poetic Justice*, see: the delicate balance of detachment and involvement-by-fancy (73), the need to be sensitive to the facts of the case (74), the importance of precedent (118), the dimensions of the judge's history and perspective that might distort judicious spectatorship (74), the need for critical judgment (76), technical knowledge and a knowledge of history (121), and the importance of philosophical argumentation (12).

98. Booth, *The Company We Keep*, 25.

99. Ibid., 43.

100. Ibid., 27–37.

101. David Hume, *A Treatise on Human Nature* (Oxford: Clarendon Press, 1978), 455–470.

102. René Descartes, *Meditations on First Philosophy*, trans. John Cottingham (Cambridge: Cambridge University Press, 1986).

103. Among a great many examples documenting this perception, see *Thaddeus Hoffmeister's article for CNN*: "Programs such as 'CSI: Crime Scene Investigation,' in which forensics play a key role in solving crimes in 60 minutes or less, are thought by many prosecutors and legal analysts to create unreasonable expectations for jurors deciding fates in the real world," accessed July 6, 2011, <http://www.cnn.com/2011/OPINION/07/06/hoffmeister.anthony.jury/index.html?hpt=hp_t2>.

104. Booth, *The Company We Keep*, 36.

105. Indeed, in this example, the word choice itself—phlegmatic, stoic, and so forth—suggests a certain ethical evaluation of his characters. For myself, I think no single adjective really captures Ishiguro's carefully crafted characters. Perhaps, as others have suggested, the mood of this work is best captured by the Latin phrase *lacrimae rerum* ("tears of [or 'for'] things"), or the parallel Japanese notion of *mono no aware* (roughly, "the poignancy of things").

106. Booth, *The Company We Keep*, passim (for example, 26).

107. Ibid., 27.

108. Ibid., 51.

109. Nussbaum, *Poetic Justice*, xvii. See also Richard Kearney: "The power of empathy with living things other than ourselves—the stranger the better—is a major test not just of poetic imagination but of ethical sensitivity. And in this regard we might go so far as to say that genocides and atrocities presuppose a radical failure of narrative imagination" (Richard Kearney, *On Stories*, 139). Note, however, that it's not immediately clear that "unequal sympathies" are a defect. Surely, for example, one's sympathies for one's family should exert a special force. This is not to say that a judge—to keep the example close to Nussbaum's—should find in favor of her child when doing so flies in the face of justice. Rather, it simply suggests that not all examples of unequal sympathy or concern are vicious. Indeed, some are virtuous.

110. Booth, *The Company We Keep*, 71.

111. Ibid., 76. Booth, like all the other hermeneutic thinkers discussed, maintains a pluralistic position with respect to hermeneutic truth (Ibid., 58–59). On my reading, hermeneutics should reject both the idea of a single, absolute, immutable interpretation of things—at least one we can grasp completely and accurately—and the idea that any interpretation is as good as any other.

112. Think here of Briony's catastrophic misinterpretation of her sister's relationship with Robbie Turner in Ian McEwan's tragic *Atonement* (New York: Random House, 2003).

113. Nussbaum, *Poetic Justice*, 84.

114. Booth, *The Company We Keep*, 73.

115. Nussbaum *Poetic Justice*, 84. Most people do not require "proof" for the vast majority of things they believe, from the love of their children and spouses to the working of the Internet. However, for environmental philosophers, facts, proof, and truth remain an important standard when considering issues like climate change, a point to which we will return in Chapter 8.

116. *The Republic* in *The Collected Dialogues of Plato*, eds. Edith Hamilton and Huntington Cairns (Princeton, NJ: Princeton University Press, 1989), 740–751. Because narrative and art are merely imitative, Socrates and his friends refuse "to admit at all so much of it as is imitative, for that is certainly not to be received" (820, 595a). Imitation captures "the appearance of [things], but not the reality and the truth" (821, 596e).

117. Ricoeur, "Life in Quest of Narrative," 20. Of course, I've argued here that life is lived *and* recounted.

118. Turner, *The Abstract Wild*, 88. Turner's claim does not appear to go as far as Hume, who claims: "Reason is, and ought only to be the slave of the passions, and can never pretend to any other office than to serve and obey them" (David Hume, *A Treatise on Human Nature* [Oxford: The Clarendon Press, 1978], 415).

119. Ibid., 89. In a similar vein, Christian Beckwith, speculating on the long-standing enigma of why people climb, gave one of the more honest and eloquent answers to this question—one that certainly resonates with my own experience—when he wrote that "frequently, alpinists don't start in the mountains, but come to them from a distance, lured as often as not by something they'll spend the rest

of their lives trying to understand" (Christian Beckwith, the "Editors Note" in *Alpinist* 12 [Autumn 2005], 8).

120. See Arturo Perez-Reverte, *Capitan Alatriste: Purity of Blood* (New York: Plume, 2006). A sentiment drawn, no doubt, from Alatriste's nonfictional compatriot, Miguel de Unamuno, who once said, "the more books one reads, the less harm they do."

121. Also see the work of Joseph Campbell, *The Hero with a Thousand Faces* (San Francisco, CA: New World Library, 2008)

122. *Analects of Confucius*, trans. Roger Ames (New York: Bellantine Books, 1998), 189.

123. Nussbaum, *Poetic Justice*, 59.

124. Ibid.

125. Here we should think of the philosophy done in the wake of Emmanuel Levinas's account of the *face*. See Emmanuel Levinas, *Totality and Infinity: An Essay on Exteriority*, trans. Alphonso Lingis (Pittsburg, PA: Duquesne University Press, 1969). My addition of *place* connects narrative to knowledge along the lines of Stegner's comment that "no place is a place until it has had a poet" (Wallace Stegner, "The Sense of Place" in *Where the Bluebird Sings to the Lemonade Springs: Living and Writing in the West* [New York: The Modern Library, 2002], 265). Place, unlike space, has a position in some constellation of meaning; place is meaningful space. Interestingly, contemporary research in psychology supports a fairly robust link between ethical thinking and concrete particulars, details, and vivid imagery akin to that provided by narrative. See Elinor Amit and Joshua D. Greene, "You See, the Ends Don't Justify the Means: Visual Imagery and Moral Judgment" in *Psychological Science* August 2012, vol. 23, no. 8, 861–868.

126. "Once upon a time, in some out of the way corner of that universe which is dispersed into numberless twinkling solar systems, there was a star upon which clever beasts invented knowing. That was the most arrogant and mendacious minute of 'world history,' but nevertheless it was only a minute. After nature had drawn a few breaths, the star cooled and congealed, and the clever beasts had to die" (*Philosophy and Truth: Selections from Nietzsche's Notebooks of the Early 1870's*, ed. and trans. Daniel Breazeale [Atlantic Highlands: Humanities Press, 1979], 79). John D. Caputo claims to have "never recovered" from reading this challenging passage (Caputo, *Against Ethics*, 16–17), itself, perhaps, a good example of a life and career refigured by what we might call a "thin" philosophical narrative.

127. Joel and Ethan Coen, *The Big Lebowski* (1998).

128. A narrative approach to virtue suggests that the metaethical debate about the existence of absolute truth and/or our access to it will remain an abstract and theoretical debate because no one behaves, at the end of the day, as a relativist. Thus, even those who are inclined toward relativism of some stripe *act* as if there are some things that are universally true and that there are criteria for determining which account (of flourishing, virtue, or whatever) is preferable to another. Truth might be pluralistic—perhaps because of (1) the fact that we never have unmediated access to truth and (2) epistemic fallibilism—but it is not relativistic in the strong or exaggerated sense. As Charles Sanders Pierce put it: "Do you call

it doubting to write down on a piece of paper that you doubt? If so, doubt has nothing to do with any serious business" (Charles Sanders Peirce, *The Essential Writings*, ed. Edward C. Moore [New York: Prometheus Books, 1998]). Nevertheless, while relatively few serious thinkers seek to embrace the "hard" relativism of subjectivism, other forms of "soft" relativism can be almost as pernicious.

129. See Nussbaum, "Reading for Life," 242. Nussbaum goes on to suggest that while literary pluralism can also account for "plural world versions" that are not in contradiction, she draws the line at including plural world versions that include irresolvable contradictions. The latter exclusion is, I take it, an insistence that the plurality of goods and interpretations cannot extend indefinitely or include simply any (contradictory) account, which is to say that pluralism does not extend to relativism.

130. Katie McShane, "Some Challenges for Narrative Accounts of Value" in *Ethics and the Environment*, vol. 17, no. 1 (Spring 2012), 45–69. Many thanks to Professor McShane for her very helpful comments and questions regarding my own position on narrative and nature.

131. Nussbaum, *Poetic Justice*, 76.

132. See, for example, Descartes's rules for thinking in the *Discourse on Method*, among them: "never to accept anything as true if I did not have evident knowledge of its truth . . . to include nothing more in my judgments than what presented itself to my mind so clearly and distinctly that I had not occasion to call it into doubt" and "to make enumerations so complete, and reviews so comprehensive, that I could be sure of leaving nothing out" (Rene Descartes, *Discourse on Method* in *Descartes: Selected Philosophical Writings*, trans. John Cottingham, Robert Stoothoff, and Dugald Murdoch (Cambridge: Cambridge University Press, 1988), 29.

133. Marcia Muelder Eaton, "Fact and Fiction in the Aesthetic Appreciation of Nature" in *The Journal of Aesthetics and Art Criticism*, vol. 56, no. 2 (Spring 1998), 153.

134. Ibid., 152.

135. Ibid.

136. Indeed, as the father of two avid young readers, I can report that a cottage industry of sorts has sprung up around books about anthropomorphized animals. See, among many possible examples, the *Warriors* and *Seekers* series by Erin Hunter.

137. See Jacques Perrin, *Winged Migration* (2001), Luc Jacquet, *March of the Penguins* (2005), and Michael Gunton, *One Life* (2011) A review of *One Life* from *The Guardian*, objects to the "anthropomorphic sentimentality" of the film. The reviewer castigates the film for claiming the animals it shows are "just the same as us." In the film, "animals not only share our virtues, but surpass us in their pursuit." However, "a self-sacrificial octopus is . . . no more worthy of applause than a cat who tortures mice is worthy of blame" because animals are not moral agents. See "One Life Peddles One Big Lie" in *The Guardian*, accessed May 1, 2012, <http://www. guardian.co.uk/film/filmblog/2011/jul/25/one-life-animal-wildlife-documentaries>.

138. Eaton, "Fact and Fiction in the Aesthetic Appreciation of Nature," 153.

139. Kearney, *On Stories*, 139.

140. Rachel Carson, "Memo to Mrs. Eales on *Under the Sea-Wind*" in *Lost Woods: The Discovered Writing of Rachel Carson*, ed. Linda Lear (Boston: Beacon Press, 1998), 55–56. Also see Rachel Carson, *Under the Sea-Wind* (New York: Penguin, 2007). I thank Phil Cafaro for alerting me to this particularly apt example.

141. This is not to suggest the two examples are identical. In the case of Holocaust testimony, the narrative is told by a human survivor of the Holocaust. However, in the case of narratives about nature or wild animals, the narrative is told by another human rather than by nature or the animal itself. Nevertheless, there is no reason to assume that narratives about animals are any less capable of eliciting empathy or love or respect than actual experience with animals, for in the case of actual experience the animals also remain mute (unable to communicate with language) and foreign (other, strange, alien). Obviously we can relate to some narratives more easily than others; however, our understanding is not limited to those narratives to which we can easily relate. Also, on the extent to which nature can "speak" or to which we can "read" nature, see Scott Cameron, "Socrates Outside Athens: Plato, the Phaedrus, and the Possibility of 'Dialogue' with Nature" in *Phenomenology 2010, vol. 5: Selected Essays from North America. Part 2: Phenomenology beyond Philosophy*, eds. Lester Embree, Michael Barber, and Thomans J. Nenon (Bucharest: Zeta Books/Paris: Arghos-Diffusion, 2010), 43–68, and Forrest Clingerman, "Reading the Book of Nature: A Hermeneutical Account of Nature for Philosophical Theology" in *Worldviews* 13 (2009): 72–91. Also Steve Vogel, "The Silence of Nature" in *Environmental Values*, vol. 15, no. 2 (May 2006), 145–171.

142. As I've argued at length in other settings, the claim that we can come to know something of an other need not bleed into the claim that we can comprehend the other, know it objectively or exhaustively. See my *Aspects of Alterity: Levinas, Marcel and the Contemporary Debate* (New York: Fordham University Press, 2006); "Constellations: Gabriel Marcel's Philosophy of Relative Otherness," *American Catholic Philosophical Quarterly*, vol. 80, no. 3, 2006; and "Judging the Other: Beyond Toleration" in *Interpretando la experiencia de la tolerancia* (Interpreting the Experience of Tolerance), ed. Rosemary Rizo-Patrón de Lerner (Lima, Peru: Pontificia Universidad Católica del Perú/Fondo Editorial, 2006). See also Alasdair MacIntyre, *Dependent Rational Animals* (Chicago: Open Court, 1999), 14–15: "Knowledge of others . . . is a matter of responsive sympathy and empathy elicited through action and interaction and without these we could not, as we often do, impute to those others the kind of reasons for actions that, by making their actions intelligible to us, enable us to respond to them in ways that they too can find intelligible . . . In the case of the relationship of human beings to human beings none of this is, or should be, controversial. But I want to suggest, there is no significant difference in the case of the relationship of human beings to members of certain other animal species." The "responsive activity" between humans and certain non-human animals gives us a certain "interpretive knowledge" of their thoughts and feelings (Ibid., 17). While it is true that such interpretation can overreach and become a kind of misleading ascription, the practical experience of many people suggests

that this need not always be the case, as MacIntyre suggests in his analysis of dogs and dolphins. Turner agrees: "In our effort to go beyond anthropocentric defenses of nature, to emphasize its intrinsic value and right to exist independently of us, we forget the reciprocity between the wild in nature and the wild in us, between knowledge of the wild and knowledge of the self that was central to all primitive cultures." (Turner, *The Abstract Wild*, 26).

143. Turner, *The Abstract Wild*, 78.

144. Ibid., 79. Turner concludes his reflections on the song of the White Pelicans thus: "When I see white pelicans riding mountain thermals, I feel their exaltation, their love of open sky and big clouds. Their fear of lightning is my fear, and I extend to them the sadness of descent. I believe the reasons they are soaring over the Grand Teton are not so different from the reasons we climb mountains, sail gliders into great storms, and stand in rivers with tiny pieces of feathers from a French duck's butt attached to a barbless hook at the end of sixty feet of a sixty-dollar string thrown by a thousand-dollar wand. Indeed, in love and ecstasy we are closest to the Other, for passion is at the root of all life and shared by all life. In passion, all beings are at their wildest; in passion, we—like pelicans—make strange noises that defy scientific explanation" (Ibid., 79–80). Cafaro goes so far as to make the further connection to virtue ethics: "Human and nonhuman beings may share some virtues because we are in some respects similar" (Phil Cafaro, "Thoreau, Leopold, and Carson: Toward an Environmental Virtue Ethics," in *Environmental Virtue Ethics*, eds. Ronald Sandler and Phil Cafaro [New York: Rowman and Littlefield, 2005], 34).

145. Doug Peacock, *Grizzly Years: In Search of the American Wilderness* (New York: Holt Paperbacks, 1996), 143.

146. See Ricoeur, *On Translation*, trans. Eileen Brennan (London: Routledge, 2006).

147. See, for example, "In Science We Trust," an article by the editors of *Scientific American*, accessed September 26, 2010: <http://www.scientificamerican.com/article.cfm?id=in-science-we-trust-poll>.

148. Holmes Rolston III, "Does Aesthetic Appreciation of Landscapes Need to be Science-Based?" in *Environmental Ethics: Concepts, Policy, Theory*, ed. Joseph DesJardins (London: Mayfield, 1999), 164 and 166. To be fair—I don't want to over-state the case—Rolston does argue that it is important to both understand and to "stand-under," that is to grasp scientifically and to experience personally. However, it is clear that science remains *primus inter pares*. And, in any case, the acknowledgement of "standing under" is a concession to lived experience, not narrative "as-if" experience (Rolston, "Does Aesthetic Appreciation of Landscapes Need to be Science-Based?" 166.)

149. Thomas S. Kuhn, *The Structure of Scientific Revolutions* (Chicago: University of Chicago Press, 1996). See also William Whewell, *Theory of Scientific Method* (Cambridge: Hackett, 1989), and Karl Popper, *The Logic of Scientific Discovery* (London: Routledge, 2002).

150. Ibid., 170 passim.

151. Ibid., 4. One of the remarkable consequences of this arbitrariness is the "decline effect" and its problematic implications for consistency and, indeed, the idea of "proof." See Jonah Lehrer, "The Truth Wears Off" in *The New Yorker*, accessed May 1, 2012, <http://www.newyorker.com/reporting/2010/12/13/101213fa_fact_lehrer>.

152. Ibid., 89–90. Emphasis mine. In some sense a paradigm shift results in scientists seeing a 'different world.' (Ibid., 111–112).

153. Ibid., 151. Emphasis mine.

154. Ibid. Though arguments are, nevertheless, potentially effective.

155. Ibid., 155 and 156. Emphasis mine.

156. Ibid., 126 and 192.

157. Ibid., 147.

158. Gabriel Marcel, *Man Against Mass Society*, trans. G. S. Fraser (Chicago: Henry Regnery Company, 1967), 155ff.

159. Michael Pollan, *In Defense of Food: An Eater's Manifesto* (New York: Penguin, 2008).

160. Ibid., 28. Emphasis mine.

161. "How Facts Backfire" by Joe Keohane in *The Boston Globe*, accessed October 7, 2010, <http://www.boston.com/bostonglobe/ideas/articles/2010/07/11/how_facts_backfire/>. Regarding some of the original research about which this article reports, see Brendan Nyhan and Jason Reifler, "When Corrections Fail: The Persistence of Political Misperceptions" in *Political Behavior* (2010) 32: 303–330.

162. David Brower, "Conservation and National Security," accessed May 1, 2012, <http://www.wildnesswithin.com/security.html>.

163. Rosalind Hursthouse, *On Virtue Ethics* (Oxford: Oxford University Press, 1999), 114.

164. Keohane, "How Facts Backfire."

165. Brendan Nyhan and Jason Reifler, "When Corrections Fail: The Persistence of Political Misperceptions" in *Political Behavior* (2010) 32: 303–330. Also see Brendan Nyhan and Jason Reifler, "Opening the Political Mind? The effects of self-affirmation and graphical information on factual misperceptions," accessed May 1, 2012, <http://www.dartmouth.edu/~nyhan/opening-political-mind.pdf>.

166. Aristotle, *Nicomachean Ethics*, 270.

167. James, *Pragmatism* (New York: Dover, 1995), 64.

168. "How Do Conservatives and Liberals View the World?," interview and transcript on *Moyers and Company*, February 3, 2012, accessed April 15, 2012, <http://billmoyers.com/episode/how-do-conservatives-and-liberals-see-the-world/>. Also see Jonathan Haidt, *The Righteous Mind: Why Good People are Divided by Politics and Religion* (Pantheon, 2012).

169. "How Do Conservatives and Liberals View the World?," interview and transcript on *Moyers and Company*, February 3, 2012, accessed April 15, 2012, <http://billmoyers.com/episode/how-do-conservatives-and-liberals-see-the-world/>.

170. "How Do Conservatives and Liberals View the World?," interview and transcript on *Moyers and Company*, February 3, 2012, accessed April 15, 2012, <http://billmoyers.com/episode/how-do-conservatives-and-liberals-see-the-world/>.

171. Nyhan and Reifler, "When Corrections Fail," 308.

172. Jack Turner, *The Abstract Wild*, 66.

173. Henry David Thoreau, *The Heart of Thoreau's Journals*, ed. Odell Shepard (New York: Dover, 1961), 213–214.

Chapter 7

1. Rosalind Hursthouse, *On Virtue Ethics* (Oxford: Oxford University Press, 1999), 14.

2. John Stuart Mill, *Utilitarianism* (Cambridge: Hackett Publishing, 1979), 7 and 11, and Immanuel Kant, "Groundwork of the Metaphysic of Morals" in *The Cambridge Edition of the Works of Immanuel Kant: Practical Philosophy*, trans. Mary J. Gregor (Cambridge: Cambridge University Press, 1999), 57.

3. C. S. Lewis, *Mere Christianity* (New York: MacMillan, 1952), 73.

4. Aristotle, *Nicomachean Ethics*, 133. Also see Nussbaum, "An Aristotelian Conception of Rationality" in *Love's Knowledge: Essays on Philosophy and Literature* (Oxford: Oxford University Press, 1990), 70.

5. Hursthouse, *On Virtue Ethics*, 35

6. Ibid., 35–39.

7. Ibid., 36.

8. Ibid., 37.

9. Paul Ricoeur, *Oneself as Another*, trans. Kathleen Blamey (Chicago: University of Chicago Press, 1992). See studies 7–9.

10. Ibid., 170.

11. Nussbaum, "An Aristotelian Concept of Rationality," 74.

12. Thoreau, *Walden*, 107.

13. Miguel de Cervantes Saavedra, *The Adventures of Don Quixote*, trans. J. M. Cohen (New York: Penguin Books, 1950), 935.

14. Cervantes, *Don Quixote*, 54.

15. See John Krakauer, *Into the Wild* (New York: Anchor Books, 1997).

16. Ibid., 184.

17. Ibid., 22. Perhaps McCandless was too much the Romantic or the idealist. Friends say he "thought too much" (Ibid., 18). The same charge leveled against Somerset Maugham's semi-fictional Larry Darrell (Somerset Maugham, *The Razor's Edge* [New York: Penguin, 1995]).

18. Augustine, *Confessions*, trans. Henry Chadwick (Oxford University Press, 1991), 139. Emphasis mine.

19. Rosalind Hursthouse, *Ethics, Humans and Other Animals* (London: Routledge, 2000), 165.

20. Ibid.

21. Aristotle, *Nicomachean Ethics*, 5.

22. Rowan Williams, "How to Live as if We Were Human," p. 9, in *Citizen Ethics in a Time of Crisis* and online publication of the Citizen Ethics Network

(2010), accessed March 15, 2012, <http://www.citizenethics.org.uk/docs/EthicsTemplateDoc.pdf>. Critically, the Archbishop goes on to point out that this imaginative play goes on in the lives of adults to some degree, and that we should nurture this aspect of ourselves.

23. Arthur W. Ryder, trans., *The Panchatantra* (Chicago: University of Chicago Press, 1956), 3–7.

24. See, for example, Plato, *Republic*, ed. Edith Hamilton and Huntington Cairns (Princeton: Princeton University Press, 1989), 658ff.

25. Grimm's Fairy Tales have frequently been criticized as inappropriate for children—because of violence or sexuality for example—suggesting perhaps that these tales are not just, or even primarily, for children. A. S. Byatt points out that "the Allied occupying forces in Germany after the Second World War briefly tried to ban the Grimms because it was felt that their bloodthirstiness, gleeful violence, heartlessness, and brutality had helped form the violent nature of the Third Reich" (A. S. Byatt, "Introduction" to *The Grimm Reader*, trans. and ed. Maria Tartar [New York: W. W. Norton and Company, 2010], xv). The unexpurgated versions of the Grimm's tales include stories of "murder, mutilation, cannibalism, infanticide, and incest" (Maria Tartar, *The Hard Facts of the Grimms' Fairy Tales* [Princeton: Princeton University Press, 2003], 3).

26. J. R. R. Tolkien, "On Fairy Stories" in *The Tolkien Reader* (New York: Ballantine Books, 1996), 49. Interestingly, Tolkien excludes "beast tales" of the sort found in Lang's Fairy Books or, one presumes, Aesop or the *Panchatantra* (Ibid., 42–44).

27. Ibid., 43.

28. Ibid., 67.

29. Ibid., 55.

30. Ibid., 56.

31. There are currently around 7 billion people on Earth. Estimates of Christian adherents (2.1 billion) and Hindu adherents (900 million) were taken from adherents.com, accessed April 12, 2012, which was last updated in late 2007. The data is culled from various sources, with varying dates of origin, and so is at best a rough estimate. Note that the estimated adherents of Judaism (14 million), Islam (1.5 billion), traditional Chinese devotions (394 million), and other traditional indigenous practices (300 million)—all of which have a significant narrative component—make up another 2.2 billion people hailing from religious traditions deeply influenced by narrative. Most other subgroups of religious adherents also represent and communicate their beliefs in narrative form to one degree or another.

32. *Great Speeches by Native Americans*, ed. Bob Blaisdell (Mineola, NY: Dover Publications Inc., 2000), iv.

33. John G. Neihardt and Nicholas Black Elk, *Black Elk Speaks: Being the Life and Story of a Holy Man of the Oglala Sioux* (Albany, NY: SUNY Press, 2008), 298.

34. Ibid., 290.

35. Ibid., 39 and 61.

36. Ibid., xvii and xxv.

37. Thomas King, *The Truth About Stories: A Native Narrative* (Minneapolis, MN: University of Minnesota Press, 2003), 153 (citing Ben Okri, *A Way of Being Free* [London: Phoenix House, 1997], 46).

38. Philip Pullman, "Introduction" to *Citizen Ethics in a Time of Crisis* and online publication of the Citizen Ethics Network (2010), p. 1, accessed March 15, 2012, <http://www.citizenethics.org.uk/docs/EthicsTemplateDoc.pdf>.

39. Hursthouse, *On Virtue Ethics*, 36.

40. Aristotle, *Nicomachean Ethics* 3, 146, and 148, respectively.

41. Paul Ricoeur, "Life in Quest of Narrative" in *On Paul Ricoeur: Narrative and Interpretation*, ed. David Wood (London: Routledge, 1994), 27.

42. Paul Ricoeur, *Time and Narrative* vol. 1, trans. Kathleen McLaughlin and David Pellauer (Chicago: The University of Chicago Press, 1984), 59.

43. Richard Kearney, "Ethics of the Narrative Self" in *Between Philosophy and Poetry: Writing, Rhythm, History* (London: Continuum, 2002), 94. See also Paul Ricoeur, "Life in Quest of Narrative" in *On Paul Ricoeur* (London: Routledge, 1991).

44. Ricoeur, "Life in Quest of Narrative," 23.

45. Nussbaum, "Form and Content, Philosophy and Literature" in *Love's Knowledge* (Oxford: Oxford University Press, 1990), 17. For an extended argument about the role of tragedy in ethics see Martha Nussbaum, *The Fragility of Goodness* (Cambridge: Cambridge University Press, 2001).

46. Ibid., 47.

47. Ibid.

48. Indeed, in some sense it is difficult to distinguish narrative from life, or at least difficult to make the distinction as clearly as we commonly think we can. This seems to be part of the lesson of *Don Quixote*. The Second part of the novel—written years after the First and, in part, a response to a fraudulent sequel written by a rival—is deeply self-referential, interweaving events and characters from Cervantes's First Part, the fraudulent sequel by Cervantes's rival, and Cervantes's Second Part. In so doing it confuses the distinction between fact and fiction, history and fantasy. Complicating matters, Cervantes claims his own story is translated from an original historical work by one "Cide Hamete Benengeli." Thus the reader is confronted with at least three or four authorial authorities: the supposed original story by Benengeli; Cervantes's "translation" of that tale in two parts; the sequel written by Cervantes's rival and published before Cervantes's Part Two; and, interestingly, Don Quixote's attempt to wrest authorial control for himself in Cervantes's Part Two. This tangled web of fact and fiction calls into question the truth or objectivity of any history and suggests that there is "poetic license" of a sort in all truth telling. The character Don Quixote encounters people who have read the First Part and people who have read the fraudulent sequel, and acts consciously in such a way as to affirm the aspects of his own tale he wants to affirm and to deny, *even rewrite*, the parts of his tale with which he takes issue. Not unlike the protagonist of the 2006 movie *Stranger than Fiction*, Quixote seeks to consciously alter his own narrative or fate, as when he defiantly chooses to go to Barcelona rather than Saragossa after being told that "history" (as related in the sequel by

Cervantes's rival) has recorded that he has traveled/will travel to Saragossa. At several stages in Part Two, the "real" world begins to reflect Quixote's "fantasy" world, and Cervantes suggests that the delusional Quixote and gullible Panza are, in fact, more virtuous and noble than the "normal" people they encounter.

49. See Robert Sapolsky, "This Is Your Brain on Metaphors" in the *New York Times*, Opinionator/The Stone, accessed May 1, 2012, <http://opinionator.blogs. nytimes.com/2010/11/14/this-is-your-brain-on-metaphors/>.

50. Sapolsky, "This Is Your Brain on Metaphors." For example, subjects who evaluated potential job candidates judged resumes attached to a heavier clipboard to be more serious, but the weight of the clipboard had no effect on the evaluation of candidates' congeniality. Physical weightiness and personal weightiness or gravitas seem, at least to our brains, similar enough to be connected.

51. Annie Murphy Paul, "Your Brain on Fiction" in the *New York Times Sunday Review*, accessed May 25, 2012, <https://www.nytimes.com/2012/03/18/opinion/sunday/the-neuroscience-of-your-brain-on-fiction.html?_r=1&pagewanted=all>.

52. See Scott Atran, Robert Axelrod, and Richard Davis, "Sacred Barriers to Conflict Resolution," in *Science* vol. 317, no. 5841 (August 2007): 1039–1040.

53. Jean-Luc Nancy, *God, Justice, Love, Beauty: Four Little Dialogues*, trans. Sarah Clift (New York: Fordham University Press, 2011), 47–48.

54. Kearney, *On Stories* (London: Routledge, 2002), 96.

55. Ibid., 97.

56. This is true for all hermeneutic philosophers; however, we might also refer here to Kant's categories, Marion's treatment of anamorphosis, and other similar accounts of the way in which our perception and perspective "filter" the world at the most fundamental level. Take Turner's argument for wild understanding and virtue. Though he comes out very strongly for the power of gross contact and the loss experienced when we settle for abstraction, in other passages he expresses a guarded admiration for the power of narrative. Therefore, I think it is worthwhile to engage in a charitable—and, I think, more accurate—reading of Turner's critique of "abstract" experience. His preference for gross contact need not suggest that we can actually have a *completely* raw experience, unfiltered by any concept or narrative. Rather, we can frame the preference for gross contact in terms of privileging direct experience as undiluted *as possible* by concepts, categories, and narrative structures, especially those that are foreign to the environment of the experience. Another way of putting this is that we should try to balance our inescapably perspectival engagement of the world with a genuine attempt to be open to the otherness of the other—human or non-human—that allows the other to be other.

57. Aristotle, *Nicomachean Ethics*, 5.

58. Ibid., 192.

59. Ibid., 15, 142, and elsewhere.

60. No one cultivating virtue would seriously say something like, "I want to *become* X," where X is the *phronimos*, the unique individual who serves as a model for the trait in question. Anyone seriously thinking about self-cultivation thinks, "I want to *become like* X" in respect to the trait in question. The goal is not copying, but imitation insofar as imitation is an attempt to develop some specific trait in

oneself, to "own" or "possess" that trait. And, of course, the trait in question will be different in different people, so it's not a question of simple copying or duplication.

61. See, for example, Ralph Waldo Emerson, "The American Scholar" in *Ralph Waldo Emerson: Essays and Lectures* (New York: The Library of America, 1983), 57.

62. Among scores of possible examples and many decades of research, see the classic by Chungliang Al Huang and Jerry Lang, *Thinking Body, Dancing Mind* (New York: Bantam, 1994).

63. Aristotle, *Nicomachean Ethics*, 28.

64. This is not to say that actions are strictly determined by beliefs. The causality is more complex than that.

65. Hursthouse, *On Virtue Ethics*, 16.

66. Jefferson A. Singer, "Narrative Identity and Meaning Making Across the Adult Lifespan: An Introduction" in *Journal of Personality* 72:3 (June 2004), 442. Singer is here citing J. A. Singer and S. Bluck, "New perspectives on autobiographical memory: The integration of narrative processing and autobiographical reasoning" in *Review of General Psychology* 5, 92.

67. Dan P. McAdams, "The Psychology of Life Stories" in the *Review of General Psychology*, vol. 5 no. 2 (2001), 111.

68. Singer, "Narrative Identity and Meaning Making Across the Adult Lifespan: An Introduction," 441.

69. M. M. Gergen and K. J. Gergen, "What is this thing called love? Emotional scenarios in historical perspective" in *Journal of Narrative and Life History* 5, 221–237.

70. Singer, "Narrative Identity and Meaning Making Across the Adult Lifespan: An Introduction," 442. Second instance of italicized emphasis mine.

71. Umberto Eco, *Travels in Hyperreality* (New York: Harvest, 1986), 214.

72. Wayne Booth, *The Company We Keep: An Ethics of Fiction* (Berkeley, CA: University of California Press, 1988), 228–229.

73. *Menace II Society*, Allen and Albert Hughes (1993). See Brian Palmer, "Why Do Rappers Hold Their Guns Sideways? Because it looks so Hollywood" in *Slate*, Monday, Dec. 14, 2009, accessed March 10, 2012, http://www.slate.com/articles/news_and_politics/explainer/2009/12/why_do_rappers_hold_their_guns_sideways.html; and Edward Lewine, "Ready, Aim. No, Wait a Second. Hold That Gun Sideways" in the New York Times, November 5, 1995, accessed March 10, 2012, <http://www.nytimes.com/1995/11/05/movies/ready-aim-no-wait-a-second-hold-that-gun-sideways.html>.

74. Paul Hunter, "The Young, the Ignorant, and the Idle: Some Notes on Readers and the Beginnings of the English Novel" in *Anticipations of the Enlightenment in England, France, and Germany*, eds. Alan Charles Kors and Paul J. Korshin (Philadelphia, PA: University of Pennsylvania Press, 1987), 269.

75. Dan P. McAdams, "The Psychology of Life Stories" in the *Review of General Psychology*, vol. 5 no. 2 (2001), 115.

76. McAdams, "The Psychology of Life Stories," 115.

Chapter 8

1. Norman Maclean, "USFS 1919: the Ranger, the Cook, and a Hole in the Sky" in *A River Runs Through It and Other Stories* (Chicago: University of Chicago Press, 1976), 127.

2. Alasdair MacIntyre, *After Virtue* (Notre Dame, IN: University of Notre Dame Press, 1984), 216.

3. Sir Thomas Mallory, *Le Morte Darthur* (Wadsworth, 1997), xvii.

4. Indeed, given this fact the issue of censorship recedes in significance, at least in terms of making individual ethical choices. I need not justify the extreme claim that a book should not be read by anyone, only the claim that given my own limited time I will choose any number of other books before the book in question. It seems likely that there are few if any narratives so evil or harmful that they cannot be put to some good use, however limited, in some situations, however rare. Emplotment, you will recall, happens at the intersection of the world of the text and the world of the reader; though emplotment is limited and shaped by a variety of constraints, including what the text has to offer, it does not come pre-formed or pre-digested in the leaves of a book. Therefore, we cannot foreclose in advance the possibility that some reader in some circumstance will derive some benefit from reading a book that might look, to an external observer, like a waste of time or even a source of ethical harm. Nevertheless, we ought to attempt to choose well and spend our limited time with worthwhile narratives that will contribute, in some way, to our well-being. However, precisely because it is difficult to tell in advance of reading which narratives will teach us something ethically useful, we also need to read well.

5. "No single work is likely to do us much good or harm, except when we are very young. But a steady immersion at any age in any one author's norms is likely to be stultifying" (Wayne Booth, *The Company We Keep: An Ethics of Fiction* [Berkeley, CA: University of California Press, 1988], 282).

6. "*Croyez ceux qui cherchent la vérité, doutez de ceux qui la trouvent*" (André Gide, *Ainsi soit-il; ou, Les Jeux sont faits* [Paris: Gallimard, 1952], 174). Emphases mine.

7. Katie McShane, "Some Challenges for Narrative Accounts of Value" in *Ethics and the Environment*, vol. 17, no. 1 (Spring 2012), 45–69.

8. MacIntyre, *After Virtue*, 222.

9. Katie McShane, "Some Challenges for Narrative Accounts of Value" in *Ethics and the Environment*, vol. 17, no. 1 (Spring 2012), 45–69.

10. See the arguments made by Socrates in Plato's *Phaedo* and elsewhere (Plato, *Phaedo* in *The Collected Dialogues of Plato*, eds. Edith Hamilton and Huntington Cairns [Princeton, NJ: Princeton University Press, 1994]).

11. William Butler Yeats, "The Second Coming" *Later Poems* (Charleston, SC: Forgotten Books, 1922), 289.

12. Bruno Latour, *Pandora's Hope: Essays on the Reality of Science Studies* (Cambridge, MA: Harvard University Press, 1999).

13. While others have used the metaphor of a palimpsest in nature, here I am indebted to the work of Martin Drenthen, who to my knowledge spearheaded

its use in environmental ethics and introduced me to using the trope in this way. See, for example, Martin Drenthen, "Ecological Restoration and Place Attachment; Emplacing nonplace?," *Environmental Values*, vol. 18, no. 3 (August 2009): 285–312.

14. Paul Ricoeur, *Time and Narrative*, vol. 3, trans. Kathleen Blamey and David Pellauer (Chicago and London: The University of Chicago Press, 1988), 246–247. Emphasis mine.

15. Paul Ricoeur, "Life in Quest of Narrative" in *On Paul Ricoeur: Narrative and Interpretation*, ed. David Wood (London and New York: Routledge, 1991), 32. Emphasis mine.

16. Richard Kearney, *On Stories* (London: Routledge, 2002), 33.

17. Booth, *The Company We Keep*, 252. Second instance of italicized emphasis mine.

18. MacIntyre, *After Virtue*, 216.

19. Ibid., 213.

20. Mary Oliver, "The Summer Day" in *The House of Light* (Boston: Beacon Press, 1992), and Henry David Thoreau, "My Life Has Been the Poem" in *Collected Poems of Henry Thoreau*, ed. Carl Bode (Baltimore, MD: John's Hopkins Press, 1965).

Index

Index